"What the photographer Weegee
did for New York sixty years ago
with his camera, Toni Schlesinger has done
for twenty-first-century New York
with her words. These portraits of Gotham's
people caught in their habitats
limn the city's spirit and essence
as nothing else written in a long, long time.
They are hypnotic reading."

—NICHOLAS VON HOFFMAN

"Toni Schlesinger's book describes the relationship
of the accidental to the profound, the domestic
to the totally weird; she visits, draws out, and celebrates
this permanent impermanence better than anyone ever has.
The book is so funny, so rich, so full of wonderful surprises—
the people you know and the people you wish you knew
and the people you never want to know,
each one in her/his box, and all jumbled together,
like New York City itself."

—TONY KUSHNER

"You just can't get this stuff over the phone.
You have to ride the train, climb the stairs,
ring the doorbell, and charm your way inside.
And then the hard work begins:
convincing the people to open their homes,
their hearts, and their lives.
Toni Schlesinger crosses the threshold
with her own deep curiosity about the
fascinating lives that all of us secretly live at home.
She gets an eyeful, and so do we!"

—ELLIS HENICAN, *NEWSDAY*

"Toni Schlesinger's 'Shelter' columns are
like playscripts, revealing the theatricality of New York life
through her animated relationship with her subjects.
Part reporter and part poet,
Schlesinger has written a unique and beautiful book
that is a delight to read."

—CLAUDIA GONSON, THE MAGNETIC FIELDS

"The most three-dimensional portrait of New York I know!
Toni Schlesinger's book is composed of hundreds of
magnificent dots of the lives and apartments of real New Yorkers.
Taken together, her book forms a literary DPI
that conveys real life in New York with unsurpassed clarity."

—ALEKSANDR MELAMID, ARTIST

"Toni Schlesinger, with her no-holds-barred viewpoint
on New York lifestyles, interviews her subjects
with associative questions that can often sound like rap poetry,
exposing the idiosyncratic layers of domestic life
caught in the cracks of the mad, mad world of the city."

—WID CHAPMAN, PARSONS SCHOOL OF DESIGN

FIVE FLIGHTS UP

AND OTHER
NEW YORK APARTMENT STORIES

TONI SCHLESINGER

PRINCETON ARCHITECTURAL PRESS, NEW YORK

PUBLISHED BY
PRINCETON ARCHITECTURAL PRESS
37 EAST SEVENTH STREET
NEW YORK, NEW YORK 10003

FOR A FREE CATALOG OF BOOKS, CALL
1.800.722.6657.
VISIT OUR WEB SITE AT WWW.PAPRESS.COM.

FRONT COVER: LINDA EMOND, PHOTOGRAPHED
BY GREG MILLER
BACK COVER, CLOCKWISE FROM TOP LEFT:
PHOTOGRAPHED BY JAY MUHLIN, BRIAN
KENNEDY, GREG MILLER, JAY MUHLIN, GREG
MILLER, AND MICHAEL SOFRONSKI

EDITING: CLARE JACOBSON
DESIGN: DEB WOOD
EDITORIAL ASSISTANCE: TIFFANY WEY,
DOROTHY BALL, LAUREN NELSON

SPECIAL THANKS TO: NETTIE ALJIAN, NICOLA
BEDNAREK, JANET BEHNING, BECCA CASBON,
PENNY (YUEN PIK) CHU, RUSSELL FERNANDEZ,
JAN HAUX, JOHN KING, NANCY EKLUND
LATER, LINDA LEE, KATHARINE MYERS, SCOTT
TENNENT, JENNIFER THOMPSON, PAUL
WAGNER, AND JOSEPH WESTON OF PRINCETON
ARCHITECTURAL PRESS
—KEVIN C. LIPPERT, PUBLISHER

LIBRARY OF CONGRESS
CATALOGING-IN-PUBLICATION DATA
SCHLESINGER, TONI
  FIVE FLIGHTS UP AND OTHER NEW YORK
APARTMENT STORIES / TONI SCHLESINGER.
    P. CM.
ISBN-13: 978-1-56898-585-5 (ALK. PAPER)
  1. HOUSING—NEW YORK (STATE)—NEW YORK.
2. APARTMENT HOUSES—NEW YORK (STATE)—
NEW YORK. 3. NEW YORK (N.Y.)—SOCIAL
CONDITIONS. I. TITLE: 5 FLIGHTS UP AND
OTHER NEW YORK APARTMENT STORIES. II. TITLE.
  HD7304.N5S355 2006
  974.7'1—DC22
                                    2005032673

INTRODUCTION

How did I end up in so many living rooms?

It started one freezing January day when I went to see Don Forst, editor of the *Village Voice*, about a job, and he looked up at the ceiling and said, "We have something, but you probably wouldn't want to do it. It's just a column on people, their homes, just this kind of Q & A." By saying it that way, he probably thought that I would insist on doing it.

I did say yes, but not because I wanted to go inside people's rooms and discuss their chairs. No, it was because I knew the power of the interview and the spoken word. I had long ago realized that prose is the past. It can put people to sleep (except for what I'm writing now). The spoken word is in the moment—it can shift and change. There is conflict. It is questioning, Socratic. As for the home-decoration part, I knew rooms were just a lot of stage sets, backdrops for the big event—the drama of the human soul. It is not the granite counter that matters for cutting up the carrot. It is the heart one must pay attention to.

What I did not know, and Forst did, was the drama implicit in the struggle for finding space and keeping a sense of home in the city.

My first "Shelter" column in February 1997 was about *Allure* writer Lois Morris, who lived in an East Village back house, the kind from the late 1800s when speculators stuffed European immigrants in buildings behind buildings without light or air, and people had to go to the bathroom outside, though Lois's apartment had been renovated. When she stood near her orange Formica night table and started talking about the 1980s television set that she brought from her parents' house in Glencoe, Illinois, I went into a trance. Years later, I still have not come out of it.

Every "Shelter" interview is like walking into a movie—the mysterious hallway, the story about the father, the boyfriend who got mad and threw a china elephant across the room. It is as if I am on the sea, carried far out on the waves. If people start bringing out family photos, the day is gone—the mother in Cuba standing in the half light, the Kodachrome print of a child with his brother on a hill.

But the most interesting aspect of "Shelter" is that, because there are no expectations, no need to overthrow the government or expose the Department of Sanitation, the column is not supposed to be anything more than a few moments in the afternoon, a conversation that is somewhat focused on where the people are sitting and how they got there. In this smaller situation, the talk can expand, grow large, so that it becomes a story of people's pasts, their parents's pasts, the city's past.

The singular repeated format has its benefits. The protagonist never grows old. Though, as in a serial, "Shelter" adventures have begun to take on a Nancy Drew aspect—the secret of the privatization of the old union co-op. But the formal sameness has made for infinite variations. A person can read aloud his electric bill. We can talk about Antonioni movies, steel structures. Anything about space, furniture, New York City is appropriate for discussion, not to mention people's hometowns, their dream towns, the situation of all the towns in the world. And anything about life—the invention of the light bulb, a mother's preference for beige.

People wonder where I find "Shelter" subjects. Like all reporters, I get on the phone. I meet them at parties, through friends. Sometimes people write me. I contact organizations. I cannot interview undocumented immigrants because they do not want the government to know. Some people do not want their parents to find out they are gay. Others do not want the world to see that they are living in an illegal sublet or a seven-room, rent-regulated apartment paying $500 a month or a loft that costs $1.5 million. That is one reason a lot of affluent people are not in the columns. There are no children growing up in doorways, as in a nineteenth-century Jacob Riis photo—no *Bandits' Roost* or *Five Cents a Spot*. Extremes of rich and poor are well reported elsewhere. It is the mysterious middle that has become the draw for "Shelter."

Not all the close-to-four-hundred columns to date could fit in this book. When I went through the "Shelter" archives in the *Voice*'s sub-basement in the building that used to be the Hartz Mountain birdseed factory—former *Voice* owner Leonard Stern's father founded Hartz after he brought over 2,100 singing canaries from Germany in the 1920s and the birds sold out—choosing the columns became a fierce and difficult task. I ultimately picked not only the great interviews but the ones that illuminated a particular part of the city or an unusual housing situation.

After working through the sometimes long, existential conversations, certain recurrent structural patterns became apparent: the monologue, often from one with a weight of life behind him; the conflict, between a couple or eight roommates—we got it in June, no we got it in July; the chorus, finishing each other's sentences following a burst of memory—we did the bathroom in blue because you adore blue; the odditorium—these are the monkey eyes and over here are the hair bows of the quintuplets; the secret—don't say I'm smoking, just pretend this bowl is for the clamshells; the Indian captivity story—the landlord who tortured us interspersed with a discourse on property is theft or the landlord as courtier, like Mr. Goldglancz in Williamsburg, who left little notes in the hall: "We removed the water tank off the roof....Live well & prosper."

There are a lot of interviews with boys in their rooms. Maybe because Manhattan is like Neverland—pirates and Lost Boys go round and round the island. Where Peter lived, nobody worried about grown-up things ever.

Then, too, there are the columns with my unstoppable monologues about a tree I saw on the corner and how it reminded me of a childhood moment staring into a wall of smoked glass.

Sometimes the encounter is uncomfortable. I pick up on a tension. We stare as if we are both wondering why the other is here. Often a column like that comes out the best, and no one would have guessed what happened behind the scenes. Then there is the surprise from the wings—a neighbor knocks, the phone rings, a child appears with a hamster, I bump my head on a light fixture. Or I will hear things that I didn't expect. The conversation becomes a separate person, going this way and that without anybody doing anything. In truth, sometimes the interviews are somewhat staged. You have a camel. Who knew?

Often I do massive research beforehand, wanting the interviewees to know that I know everything about the country they came from and they smile at me politely as if I've been reading a 1970s *Encyclopaedia Britannica*. Other times I go in with nothing and watch the cat walk across the room. I have learned not to stay too long, to keep the sketch to a sketch. Though sometimes I will go to a neighborhood early and explore because it is a strange and interesting place. Once when I went to Flushing I visited so many dumpling shops that, by the time of the interview, I had to lie down. They gave me soy milk.

I do not use a tape recorder. I write down only what I want to remember—ultimately the test of what is interesting. I do not want to relive the conversation, analyze it. The "Shelter" column is an impression. There is an emotional component to what is going on. I try to get it onto the computer right away.

I learned to ask photographers to come after the interview because people get overexcited when a photographer walks into a room. The power of the visual image always precedes the text. Even the most intelligent, reflective, soulful people will get distracted and worry about their hair.

I like photographs of people in the process of doing something, so it is as if one is looking through a doorway as in a Dutch painting or at a movie.

But photographers do not always want to be cinematographers. They want to celebrate the stillness, heighten the photograph to great portraiture. With great photographers, like all great collaborators, not much has to be said other than, "Let's try to get the miniature monsters on the shelf, but if they don't read, just go with the goldfish."

When people see New York apartments on television, they think that they are big. Even Ralph Kramden's room looked spacious, though he and Alice only had that refrigerator and the table where he would sit in his bus driver uniform. Tenement rooms are small and old; Tenement buildings are estimated to number over two hundred thousand in the city. Of the city's existing housing stock nearly two-thirds were built before 1947. For a city so full of ambitious people preoccupied with moving ahead, New York looks so crumbling.

People have to crawl up flights of stairs to get to their apartments. Elizabeth Bishop once lived five flights up, subsequently the name of her poem and the title of this book. I hope she does not mind my using it, as she wrote a lot about space and home.

The economy of a rent-controlled or rent-stabilized apartment will keep a ninety-year-old woman crawling up with her plastic grocery bags until she passes on. Another incentive to the climb is that she will be able to pass on the apartment to her child, so in effect, it becomes an estate. Though some just want to stay because it has always been their home; they have never lived anywhere else. New York has strong, small villages, almost invisible walls in the European sense. In one half of a block there is the restaurateur, the waiters, the deli owner, the antique-store owner, the patrol woman, the priest, the nun, the neurotic, the dog owners, the old men. There is comfort in the containment.

Many who end up in these rooms at the top of the mountain have come to New York to be giants. They have come to get the best parts, write the greatest books. But then they have to come back to these little rooms that look like the ones in mid-century movies where someone's sitting around waiting for Ma and the dough. Many in New York are living in the rooms alone—almost one half of Manhattan households. When they go outside, the city's big numbers—200,000 acres of land, 12,335 bus stops, 353 salt and sand spreaders, 25,000 tons of garbage a day—can make them seem even smaller. There is nothing worse than feeling like an animal cracker in a city of more than eight million, walking along, kicking a pebble, then maybe having risotto in the rain. But the next day, a person can feel like a giant marshmallow.

The "Shelter" column has changed over the years as New York has changed. There seem to be fewer filmmakers living in small East Village rooms and more in windowless factories in Brooklyn. Rent-regulated apartments are slowly disappearing. In the early 1960s an estimated 77 percent of apartments were regulated; now the percentage is 51.5. Laws passed in the 1990s allowed landlords to deregulate an apartment if vacancy or renovation increases pushed the rent over two thousand dollars.

Rent regulation is what made it possible for people over the years to go on living as artists in New York—painting in bed, having smoky conversations. This celebration of bohemian life and political resistance is vanishing or is being pushed to the outer perimeters of Queens and Brooklyn, far down from the top of the mountain. Mean glassy towers have been going up on the Bowery and all over the Lower East Side and filling up with people in the business of money.

Hopefully this tower business is just a phase. The Moroccan carpet will be back, life in the black light, and long afternoons of making protest signs.

One final note: all the interviews in this book are as they appeared in the *Village Voice*. A few words here and there were changed for factual reasons. Some were cut down for space. As for what happened to everybody, just know them in the moment. Though all who could be contacted recently explained they had gone on to bigger and better lives.

Look at that building. The streetlights make shadows from the fire escapes. A curtain is blowing. The windows are dark. Wait, a light just went on in the one with the shade pulled down. There is the shadow of a person…two people.

A man is inside. He is so big. He hardly fits in the room. When he holds out his arms, he can touch both walls. It makes him very tired. If he sneezes, everything blows off his table, which is also his bed. It makes his girlfriend tired, too. She has to ride on his back because there is not room for two of them to stand. They are yelling at each other.

"Ouch, your elbow."

"Don't step on my foot."

She says they should move to Brooklyn. He says it's not much better there. Why be shoved inside a ten-foot-wide subway car with two hundred other people twice a day and stare at a linoleum floor and watch the conductor stick his head out of the little window and say absolutely nothing?

Then they yell some more. When the big man and his girlfriend walk outside, they separate. There is a great flapping and beating of wings. They do a dance around the Empire State Building. Until later when they have to fit inside the apartment again. They order in. The man in the door speaker says, "Delivery."

MINIATURE

PODS

LOCATION
Bushwick, Brooklyn

PRICE
$1,700 (market)

SQUARE FEET
735 (live-work loft in
former sweater factory)

OCCUPANTS
Joel Rapp (interior designer),
Brian Blessinger (writer, flavorpill.net),
Peter Phunstsok Wongdi Azubah
Lauenstein-Dejonga (tour director)

You sleep in space pods!

[JOEL] Yes. I moved in two years ago. I answered an ad from two models who used to be Miller Lite girls together.

Miller Lite girls.

One was staying with Josh across the hall, who's also a model and has a skateboard half-pipe in his house. The Miller Lite girls found this loft, which was completely raw, and of course they're models, not carpenters. They advertised for a man who is handy. They really wanted a roommate capable of building rooms but were afraid to say so. I walked in. I said, "Perfect!" I drafted them three separate ground plans. I called this one "The In Out." Everybody's space is divided twice. The opaque ones are their bedrooms. The office spaces are made of corrugated fiberglass, like roofs of backyard sheds of houses in Connecticut. When I stay here...

Where else do you stay?

My best friend works for the State Department, vice counsel to the Bahamas, so I was just there for six weeks. [*Joel calls Brian, who's at brunch.*] Find Azubah. Hurry. [*To me*] Azubah's a monk.

Does he wear monk clothes?

Occasionally. His parents met because his father was a favored monk of the queen of Sikkim and she sent a sect to Brown. She's American, kind of like Princess Grace but in Asia. We had a party once that had five Buddhist monks and a queen.

Your neighbor pays $2,200. He said a lot of rich kids are here.

There is a new trust-fund contingent since the miniwave of microgentrification. Next door, they're eight people. If you go in when they're sleeping, it's like Gettysburg, bodies on the floor. They're all twenty years old—managers of Abercrombie & Fitch stores. Wait, one's a busboy at Coffee Shop. [*Azubah never arrives. Brian comes in, and the conversation drifts.*] [BRIAN] My ex-girlfriend is dating a Mr. Buttinger and we have the same birthday.

Did you meet him?

Oh, I met him on Monday.

[*Later I call Azubah.*] Do you wear a monk robe?

[AZUBAH] No, my *dad's* the monk. My dad's not celibate, obviously. He has long hair down to his butt. My grandfather was a death astrologer and my grandmother was a poisoner. It was a little village. When everyone knows who the poisoner is, it's not as effective. The women have many husbands. This woman married a band of brothers.

She must have been exhausted. What's it like in a pod?
Each of us thinks he has the best pod. I do. I don't have a mattress. I sleep on a sheepskin and a kangaroo skin. I love science fiction. I'm a future retro man. I found this when Joel wrote an ad. I was one of seventy-five who responded. Instead of having personal interviews, he had a party on the roof. I knew from the description—"no straight lines"—that it was something cool. I wanted it. I didn't get a call for four days and I was in total agony. Also because I had such a good time at the party. I knew my life had to start with this thing. My mother and dad happened to be stateside. I went home to Massachusetts. I emailed Joel twice and left messages. I made this little card, a tenant profile. It gave the invisible perks of living with me. When he didn't call me, I thought, "He thought I was a freak! Why did I do that?" I get home and my dad pulls out this tiny bag of yellow rice. He said, "Put this wherever you want to live." I said, "Dad, first of all, you're crazy. Second of all, you're too *late*." I'm totally torn up about it, totally depressed. Joel is such a cool guy. He worked for Club Med. On the night of the third day, I have a dream where I'm in the apartment, kind of floating around and throwing this yellow rice all over the place, and then a day later, Joel finally calls. I don't know what took him four days.

March 30, 2005

BRIAN KENNEDY

FOUR AND A HALF INCHES

LOCATION
East Village, Manhattan

RENT
$412.22 (rent stabilized)

SQUARE FEET
240 (studio apartment
in tenement building)

OCCUPANT
Mark Kirk (painter; sales, Ligne
Roset Furniture)

I happened to be at the showing of Alan Sklansky's furniture when my friend Dian said that you have the smallest apartment in all of downtown. Dian should know. She's been going to bars in the East Village since she was twelve. Her parents are artists. They met in Paris in the 1950s at the atelier of Fernand Léger. Actually your apartment just seems small because there's a lot in here.

When I moved in, I said maybe it'll just be a couple of years. Now it's eighteen. I've lived here longer than anywhere, including my parents' home in Baltimore.

You're at a critical storage point? Whooah! An inch can make a difference!

I don't keep books anymore. When I'm done, I put them on the street. See, I can't

move. I've got a rent-stabilized apartment in a neighborhood I really like.

If you got rich, you wouldn't want to live in a pink Italianate building on the Upper East Side?

No.

Me either. Though sometimes I have long discussions with myself about it. The buildings are so beautiful. But the streets are so empty. I wonder about the people behind the doors. Are they wandering from room to room with the wind blowing? Is the doctor who removed their polyp their only friend? Let's talk about your Pez dispensers. You got excited when I said "Pez" and sat forward on the couch, I mean the bed. You looked over at the dining room cabinet that you call the Pez-O-Leum.

I'd say I have a world-class Pez collection. I have about 200 to 250 dispensers. And at least 100 other Pez-related candy dispensers.

What makes a Pez a Pez, aside from being plastic and four and a half inches high?

Things too complicated to go into here. Pez was invented in the mid forties. These are my Pez trucks. The cab and the trailer of each truck come in red, blue, green, or yellow. Oh, wait, the trailers are never yellow.

You're holding a box in front of my eye. Hungarian Pez vitamins!

That's how a Hungarian gets his vitamins, from a Pez dispenser.

GREG MILLER

You have a big bowl of Pez refills!
I have a mint Pez before going to work every morning.

Where is Pez headquarters?
The Cookie Jar, in an antique building in Chelsea. There are about five Pez conventions a year with Pez auctions, Pez bingo. My best Pez pal is in Mississippi. She plays the violin for the Jackson Symphony. Once, in Hungary, I was trying to get two of everything Pez, one for her, one for me. There was this one Jerry Pez, of Tom and Jerry. I kept it. Word got back to her. I think her boyfriend told.

Did he whisper to her in a cafe?
I don't know. See the strip lights in the Pez-O-Leum? I did them myself. When I go out in the evening, I just leave the Pez lights on. But I used to have horrible disasters when a truck rumbled by. I'd come home. The Pezes would be on their sides. Then I discovered Fun-Tak. Oh, do you have to go now?

Yes. Oops!
You walked into the closet. It happens a lot.

December 23, 1997

DAS BOOT

LOCATION

Lower East Side, Manhattan

RENT

$1,024 (rent stabilized)

SQUARE FEET

250 (studio apartment in
tenement building)

OCCUPANTS

Adam Nelson and Jake Gwyn
(computer systems administrators)

**How can you live like this! You're like
two men in a shower as opposed to
three men in a tub—crushed together
in this submarine, a dark, narrow room
with a shower stall in the middle. *Plus*
you work together all day.**
[ADAM] We used to sit next to each other
at work, but they moved our desks fifteen
feet apart. [JAKE] We do have an hour and
a half apart when we wake up. [ADAM] I
start work later. Basically it's like *Dukes of
Hazzard*, two cousins riding around in this
hot rod, dodging cops, scoping girls. [JAKE]
The cousins only have one car, so they have
to do everything together. [ADAM] As for
girls visiting… [JAKE] We have a time-
share system. [ADAM] We've known each
other since high school—we're twenty-four
now—Sayville, Long Island. Jake wasn't
going to high school, though. [JAKE] I was
there because I ran away from home. I
was renting a room from a Polish POW
survivor. He was a friend of a friend. I'm
from Gadsden, northeast Alabama. I was

born on a commune in Summertown,
Tennessee. My family moved around a
lot, every two years. I was the second of
eight boys—I'm used to close quarters and
sharing. There was a room in our house full
of nitrogen-packed food, big white plastic
buckets of texturized vegetable protein to
feed all of us. When I decided to leave
home—my mother remarried, became a
Mormon, and I was going for the most
remote place from my stepfather—my
father's friends said if I was ever in trouble
to call them. They were pagan, like witches.
It's a modern movement of observance of
various ancient European rites. The high
priest had a friend in Long Island, though
he wasn't a pagan, and they sent me there
with $1,000 in my pocket. I got a job off
the books working for a tree surgeon.

You met Adam while treating an elm?
No. I was lonely and I was invited to a
school play by two girls from the local
library. I think it was *The Imaginary Invalid*,
Molière. I met Adam at the cast party.
[ADAM] We lived together then, too, at my
parents' house—they're teachers—after Jake
got kicked out of the POW place where he
was staying, because he was sleeping with a
girl. I guess they made too much noise. The
girl he was sleeping with was my girlfriend.

**Jake's like Hal in Inge's *Picnic*. He comes
into town and nothing's the same. But
Adam, weren't you upset about your
girlfriend?**
I didn't know.

What happened to her?

She went insane. So I go up to Albany to school. [JAKE] I went back to Georgia with the people who helped me escape from my stepfather. I started massage-therapy training, later I moved to North Carolina with my girlfriend, a different one. We made an entirely organic two-story cypress log cabin insulated with organic cotton, no fiberglass. All natural varnish. We were there three years. I did my massage therapy, acupuncture, kinesiology. [ADAM] It's hippie talk. [JAKE] I got an invitation from someone I knew in Brooklyn. I planned to come for a week. Adam had just gotten this apartment. I said, "Well, I'll stay."

What about the girlfriend in the organic cabin?

She was furious. But see, there's another thing. [ADAM] Tell her. [JAKE] She was thirty years older than me.

So did Jocasta, I mean whatever her name was, didn't she get upset?

Yes. I didn't say I was leaving. I took a large backpack, a gym bag. [ADAM] For *one* week. [JAKE] That's how I left home, by the way. With a gym bag.

February 27, 2001

BILYANADIMITROVA.COM

MAID'S ROOM

LOCATION
Upper East Side, Manhattan

RENT
$0

SQUARE FEET
128 (maid's room in Park
Avenue building)

OCCUPANT
Mark Noonan (PhD student,
CUNY; founder and editor, *Columbia
Journal of American Studies*)

I walked into this fancy building and the doorman whisked me off to the servants' quarters where the floors are linoleum and you live in one of the ten tiny maids' rooms like Cinderella. Though she didn't have a photograph of Sylvia Plath and Ted Hughes, a poster from *Faster Pussycat! Kill! Kill!*, and a Brooks Brothers cranberry silk vest with thin gold stripes in the closet. In exchange for free rent for the last two years you drive a CEO, who owns a co-op in the building, to work. Do you wear a chauffeur's hat like Sabrina's father?

Nothing uptight like that. The kind of person I drive is the kind I enjoy hanging out with. I just drive him in his Mercedes to Midtown. It works perfectly with my student needs.

Don't you have to drive him *anywhere* else?

No, he likes to come back on the subway.

It puts him in touch with the strap holders. This apartment size is quite a shock to some people. It's literally an eight-by-sixteen-foot room. There's no kitchen. It's quite a test in determination and character to do this. But it's for the cause of literature. My father tells his friends I sleep standing up. I'm also a book dealer, you see. Though because of the size of my apartment, you wouldn't know it. I keep my books at my parents' house in Connecticut. Basically I'm pretty active, so I'm always out. That's how I deal with this apartment, going to events. And, being a writer, I have an imagination. That can make a small space seem bigger. Though I've learned size does matter. Umberto Eco hates getting a book from someone. He says if someone sends him a book, it costs him rent money. It's a space-taker-upper. I got this apartment when I was studying at Columbia. I saw a sign advertising a free apartment on Park Avenue. The competition was fierce.

You have a little bathroom down the hall with peeling walls. Your Exercycle is pressed up next to the tub. It must be so depressing to sit there pedaling.

That's New York. You grin and bear it until you become famous.

I've heard stories about these maids' rooms. How a wealthy person might keep a beautiful young poor person in one—pretend she's the baby-sitter—and then sneak down ten times a day and say, "Oh, hi, could we discuss how Billy feels about his stuffed rabbit?" I don't suppose that goes on in this building.

Oh *no*, not here! One of my neighbors works at *Mad* magazine. She cooks turkey burgers for the family I drive for. The reason we both do this is the family is flexible and doesn't ask for much of our time. We like them.

Isn't it stuffy here in the summer?
Yes, but I go out to their East Hampton estate and water their roses. I have an apartment attached to their estate. The guy I work for is so cool.

Maybe you really are the guy and you keep an apartment down here so you can lead a double life as a hopeful student.
If I were the guy, don't you think I'd rather play charades in a full-size studio?

No, the extreme is always more erotic.

June 23, 1998

GREG MILLER

SMALL BED

LOCATION
East Village, Manhattan

RENT
$817.89 (rent stabilized)

SQUARE FEET
192 (studio apartment in
tenement building)

OCCUPANTS
Michael Quinn (visual merchandising
manager, Armani Exchange), Kevin
Burke (visual stylist and illustrator)

You're both so tall and the bed's so small.

[MICHAEL] Sometimes we don't even touch. Lisa, our cat, sleeps with us, too. The twin bed's collapsed like three times. It was my bed from my house in Long Island. My parents always said, "Don't ever get rid of that bed. It was your great-aunt's."

Do you think she was lying there at the end, tightly holding a Bible or maybe a locket?

I don't know. At that time I wasn't that interested in thinking about my great-aunt. The bed collapsed in high school. My father said it was because I'm abnormally large. My family's all five-feet-something. I'm six-two. So is Kevin. When it collapses here, everyone handles it pretty well.

Did you ever consider getting a larger bed?

[KEVIN] Actually we talked about it for

a long time. [MICHAEL] We've been sleeping on it for three years. [KEVIN] Our friends say, "You're *both* on a twin?" [MICHAEL] "Like, you're both so *big*." [KEVIN] Our friends get queen and king beds just for themselves. [MICHAEL] They're so *little*. They have these giant things. One of our biggest naysayers, Lauren, came over. We were all on the bed watching *Nightmare Before Christmas* and we all fell asleep. She admitted under duress that it was very comfortable.

Maybe it's a magic bed. It expands while you're sleeping, but in waking life, it just looks small.

Like in *The Nutcracker*—Marie comes down and the furniture grows huge. I really only know *The Hard Nut*, Mark Morris, the battle between the rats and the G. I. Joe's.

How did you meet?

I was working at Emporio and Kevin was hired to freelance and we were going to arrange the merchandise in the outlet in Woodbury Common. At lunch, Kevin said, "Do you want to go to K-B and look for Real Monsters?" We have those in the bathroom here. Then a week later, *Elle* has a party. Kevin shows up with gold teeth. [KEVIN] Those are my party teeth.

We haven't discussed how this tiny one-room apartment is covered everywhere with hundreds of small, perfectly placed things: paper stars and roses and owls and jack-o'-lanterns and Japanese dolls with eyes that change color and skeletons with glitter eyes. Everything's pink and red and gold, but also other

JAY MUHLIN

colors. So joyous, like the apartment is singing.

[MICHAEL] We both love stuff, arranging things. My mom always said—Kevin's mom said it about him, too—that I never played with toys, I just liked to set them up.

Now you have a kingdom, together.

[KEVIN] Look at this picture on the refrigerator. I found it years ago in *Jane*. It's the outside of a tenement. I kept the picture because I really liked it. Then I met Michael six months later. His apartment was in the *same* building that was in the picture, of all the places in the city. [MICHAEL] Kevin got this apartment before I met him. My mom made these baskets. She took a course on Long Island. She has my dad mix up the stains. My dad's a high school teacher. He's also a hunter. He has decomposing deer bodies in these vats in their yard. They're in a lye solution to clean the bones.

And that red wall behind the bed—we used to have two Keane paintings—those big-eyed kids, a boy and a girl. Last Valentine's Day, Kevin made reservations to eat at this place called 26 Seats on Avenue B. The reservation was very late. So we both stretched out for a nap first. Lisa was infuriated by our lethargy. She started weaving in and out and went on the headboard and rubbed against the boy painting and it fell and its sharp point slammed into Kevin's forehead. It sounded like a gun going off. Kevin started screaming, "She split my head open!" Blood was running down his face and we spent the night at St. Vincent's. Kevin got stitches. After that, we made this pact: nothing over the bed.

January 22, 2002

MUSÉE DE BARB AND BETH

LOCATION
East Village, Manhattan

RENT
$781.02 (rent stabilized)

SQUARE FEET
240 (studio apartment in tenement building)

OCCUPANTS
Barbara Monoian (artist; commercial fisherman), Beth Monoian (artist)

You have a twin!
[BARBARA] Beth lives with me part of the time. She commutes from Pittsburgh. [*Beth nods.*]

Where are the hog parts?
OK. [*Takes a breath*] The hog intestines are these pieces.

You have the work of ninety artists in here!
I've started a museum. That's Beth on the video.

Beth is in a pink tutu.
Tutu and you.

When did you turn your apartment into a museum?
Last month. We have open hours.

Where do you keep your clothes?
In a plastic garbage bag.

Are you sure you really live here?
Yes! I've been here since 1996.

Where do you sleep?
Beth's on the couch. I'm on the floor. It's like sleeping on my boat.

Ah yes, the fishing boat in Alaska.
OK, my boat. [*Takes a breath*] I've got a 1930 wooden hand troller. [*She shows a picture.*]

It's like a boat in a murder story or where they smuggle things.
[BETH] It's not *quite* like that. [BARBARA] I bought it in Hoonah, a Tlingit village I love near Juneau.

What do you catch?
Salmon, crab, herring.

What's your best catch in a day?
Those are difficult questions. OK, it's sold by the pound. All the fish are cleaned by hand—by me. Sixty silver salmon in a day would be fun.

Beth, do you help with this?
[BETH] No. I fished once when I was eighteen.

Beth, you're slapping a pit bull on its behind.
Barb is an exceptionally tough person. [BARBARA] I'm thinking of going back in December. The northern lights are out, lots of dark nights. Last year I drove across

Canada, alone, in a week. Usually I sleep in the car.

In the middle of Canada, my God. I got inspired when you talked about being in Alaska and there's this story in Outhouses of Alaska about a woman who accidentally peed on a grizzly bear and then I started looking at those thousands of miles of empty snow and I thought about the Gold Rush and the people who climbed up and down the Chilkoot Pass, forty miles up and forty miles down, and the avalanches and scurvy.

They brag about that.

Oh, what gold will do to a person. Anyway, back to the snow, and the shifting polar ice cap and the thought of being abandoned, lost alone in that empty whiteness. Once on The X-Files, this man fell through an ice hole into the earth below Antarctica. I can't think of anything worse.

[BETH] It's not quite that way.

Are those more hog intestines over there?

[BARBARA] Rawhide. It's a piece I did after September 11. After seeing a deer hunt, twenty deer hanging by the neck… [BETH] She has this photo of deer splayed. You should show… [BARBARA] No, they're too graphic.

TINAZIMMER.COM

These hanging bladders?

This is a hunk of sausage casing.

Look, a haunted roller coaster. Such a brilliant work. Why did you go to Alaska?

My grandparents are in Ketchikan. The other grandfather's Armenian. He's in Washington State. [BETH] He was a hop farmer. [BARBARA] We're from Yakima.

Is there a large Armenian community in Yakima?

[BETH] Just our family. Our grandfather escaped the Armenian genocide. [BARBARA] Hitler used it as a model. [BETH] Our other grandfather is part Cherokee. [BARBARA] My mom's health-care clinic is in the top six in the country.

Who else lives in Yakima?

There's Mr. Paddock. He's important.

November 17, 2004

13

ALL I CARE ABOUT IS LOCATION

LOCATION
Upper West Side, Manhattan

PRICE
$69,000 in 1993
($562.49 maintenance)

SQUARE FEET
280 (studio co-op apartment
in 1925 building)

OCCUPANT
Ray Sakata aka Buck
(adult/fetish film actor)

Could you just talk a little about your line of work?

I started in 2001. When people hear 2001, they always think, "Did you do this because you could go at any moment?" It was before 9-11. I went to one of the bondage clubs on Yahoo. I found out about the director, Todd. He emailed me.

In your latest film, *Physical Education*, you play a coach chloroformed by his students after you torture them on the track.

My debut. It was one of the top sellers by Todd.

The Dead Guys Cinema Web site says, "This movie...contains graphic images of implied rape and murder." Is this like *Demonlover*, where everyone wears French clothes and goes to Mexico on a secret plane to be filmed in a jail cell wearing a hood?

We made *Physical Education* in New Jersey. We're not making them in Russia and killing people. It's all implied. There's no penetration. I'm usually nude. I've developed a cult following because of it. People recognize me on the streets. Before, I was a manager at Saks—DKNY. I've been in retail mostly. I worked at Charivari. I was a salesperson there after Marc Jacobs. I worked on 57th, then ended up on 72nd.

Your mother found you your apartment in a Japanese newspaper.

OCS—the *New York Post* or the *Times* of the Japanese world. They have a real-estate section. This Jewish couple was trying to sell their apartment on the Upper West Side. My mom said, "Great apartment, affordable for you." I said, "Mom, let's just get it, I don't care." I walked in. I went, "Oh my God. It's too small." When I walked out on the terrace, I said, "I don't care if it's small." [*The hallway is so narrow, only one person can fit. The kitchen has two burners over a small refrigerator, no stove.*] All I care about is location. I said, "I'm going to live on John Lennon's block." I was born and raised in Dayton, Ohio. My mom's Japanese and she was born in Hawaii. She met my father—they were part of this pot-smoking vegetarian commune, anti-fur, trying to be all about one with earth. Then my dad went corporate and went to work

at the Mead notebook company. They got
divorced when I was five. My mom moved
to Jackson Heights. A lot of my fun years
were there. But it was time for me to move
on. I lived in SoHo with Caroline, who was
a director's assistant on *Ishtar*.

Look at all your photos!
These are all me. I painted this apartment
like Monica's on *Friends*. She had it lavender
and then the moldings were green. The
ceiling was like a fuchsia. I took the same
three-color scheme but did it yellow, green,
periwinkle blue. Everyone said it would
make it look small. But I love the colors.

**The building has an elegant marble and
brass lobby.**
It's a very peaceful building. No one's nosy.
There are lots of old folk who've been here
over fifty years. Now there are new people.
They have lots of children. It's wonderful.
No, they don't know what I do. I know
how to differentiate my fetish world from
my real world. Sigourney Weaver lives in
the building next door. Tour buses pull up
all day long. People are more respectful
up here. Downtown is more celebrity
ridden—"Is that so-and-so?" Here, no one
acknowledges you. That's a nice thing, when
you can live on a block peacefully.

KATE LACEY

You're thinking of moving someday?
I'm thinking about Long Island City, where
Silvercup Studios are. That's going to be the
next Hollywood. All the movie studios are
coming there. De Niro's studio is supposed
to go there. Heaven knows if I stay here or
Queens, where mom is.

January 14, 2004

WE FIT TWO HUNDRED

LOCATION
Park Slope, Brooklyn

RENT
$494 (rent stabilized)

SQUARE FEET
700 (two-bedroom apartment in 1903 landmark building)

OCCUPANTS
Mary Agredo (artist; retail sales),
Javier Agredo (painter; disc jockey),
Marisol Agredo (tenth grader,
La Guardia High School),
Adrian Agredo (eighth grader,
The Museum School)

With the beads and the blinking lights, it looks like the inside of a Day of the Dead exhibit in here.
[MARY] I like stuff. I'm hopeless.

You are from Queens. Javier is from Colombia. You met at the High School of Art and Design in 1976, got married, and moved here in 1980. You said you would not have been able to go on in life had you not filed a rent-overcharge complaint in the mid 1980s.
We sent in the papers, and a long time later we got a letter from the Division of Housing and Community Renewal saying we were overcharged. Then we had to go through

this tennis game with the landlord, filing papers back and forth until the landlord agreed. Our rent went back down from $450 to $325, which it was when we moved in. Because our rent is so low, we've been able to be artists and raise our children. My parents are artists. I grew up in a small four-room house with four kids. [JAVIER] I knew I would do nothing else but art.

Why Park Slope in 1980?
[MARY] We'd looked downtown. We only saw these dangerous buildings. We had friends in Park Slope. It was mostly Spanish, Irish, old Brooklyn families. Now everybody's here. The South Slope is one of the few places in the Slope where you can still get a $500 apartment. [JAVIER] But it would have to be very small.

How do four of you live and work in this space with the 8,000 record albums, 2 conga drums, 6 DJ speakers, and 250 stuffed animals? Your entire studios are on two small work tables next to each other in the master bedroom! And there's a giant orchestra gong in here, too. Do you work in shifts?
We work together. We all sleep on shelves. When we have our annual Pisces party, we fit two hundred people in here. Seventy-five people are in the bedroom alone, with five musicians jamming. One friend swears the house expands for the party.

The walls slide out. Then Rod Serling comes in and puts his hands on your shoulders.
[MARY] Yes. Did you notice the dicks?

The what? Oh, the wooden penises hanging from the ceiling.
They're for prosperity. They're mostly from Bali. My favorite is from Colombia. [JAVIER, *looking around the room*] There's nothing from Colombia. [MARY] He's a little slow!

Now, let me speak to the children. They have purple and orange hair and some piercings. How do you see your future dwellings?

[ADRIAN] Somewhere not far from here. I'll just have a pair of skates and that will be it. [MARISOL] I want this apartment—Mom said I could have it. [JAVIER] The plan is to leave her this apartment because we can leave it to a relative. [MARISOL] I want that red velvet chair. Only I'm going to put taxidermy specimens on it.

November 11, 1997

GREG MILLER

1,000 ROOMS

LOCATION
East Village, Manhattan

RENT
"I don't know how much it is, because my accountant takes care of it, but maybe it's a couple of hundred." (rent stabilized)

SQUARE FEET
"I have no idea." (four-room apartment with 1,000 "rooms")

OCCUPANT
Beauregard Houston-Montgomery
(contributing editor, *Doll Reader*, collector)

In four small rooms, you have a lot of doors and windows and elevators.

I have hundreds of dollhouses and play sets and a skyscraper. And I have lots of fashion dolls. But I try not to buy Barbie. Barbie's a racketeer. I keep the five hundred elves and lawn ornaments at my father's retirement house in Sagaponack. My father collects pedal cars and political buttons.

If all the dolls were to join hands, how far would the line be? With their little arms spread out?

Oh, if they were doing splits, they'd reach all the way to Paterson, New Jersey.

You have more doll furniture than regular furniture, though there are two adult chairs in the bedroom near the 1950s tin dollhouses.

All this is the result of being a neglected housewife over the years, which is the lowest thing you could be. I had this husband who—well anyway, instead of going into Valley of the Dolls I would go to Kiddie City every day. Instead of living it for real, I lived it on the doll level.

It just occurred to me that you have no kitchen.

Not even a hot plate. No. A person could have a glass of water if they wanted it. Of course, I'd have to find the glass.

Do you dust with Q-Tips?

I prefer tungsten feather dusters. Really. I don't need a maid. I need a curator. Oh God, the intricacy of this place! The other day I had to find Elizabeth Taylor's fur coat and it took two days to put the apartment back. It's like a Rubik's Cube.

You mentioned that Elizabeth Taylor lives in the twenty-five-room shoulder-high mansion with the African rumpus room, screening room, solarium, grand staircase, cash machine station, escalator, and harp.

Yes. Elizabeth is in the master suite on the balcony wearing only her mink. She's talking to Fran Drescher, who's visiting her on another balcony.

You're so literal.

I'm too busy making sure their faces are clean. Right now I have all the male rooted-hair dolls out because I'm doing sociological research.

GREG MILLER

Your little office has a TV, a human-size computer, and rows of miniature summer homes.
It's the Hamptons.

The bulging turn-of-the-century walls are painted shiny pink and cream like an ice cream parlor.
Pink to offset the awful Barbie pink. This building used to be a boardinghouse. I've lived here forever. I've been excavating. I discovered a secret hallway. It's very

Rosemary's Baby to find an undiscovered space. It's the New York dream. I use it for storage. I have more miniature filling stations...

What a big real-estate mogul you are.
And you're a doll.

Oh, you say that to everyone.

March 11, 1997

The Empire State building is all green. The rivers do not move. There are no waves, even in the Narrows. Manhattan is only fifteen by seventy feet. The Bronx is forty by forty, and the Verrazano Bridge is five feet eleven. I am standing with the other visitors on a ramp at the Queen's Museum of Art, looking down at the Panorama of the City of New York that was originally built by Robert Moses for the 1964 World's Fair. Back then, Lowell Thomas narrated the pretend helicopter ride: "Hi there. This is Lowell Thomas....Let's get ready for takeoff." A photograph from 1963 shows all these men standing at jigsaws making the one-inch tenements. One in the back is smiling at the camera with a cigarette in his mouth.

The Panorama was supposed to be an urban planner's tool after the fair was over. It was updated in 1994, though it's hard for them to keep up with all the new development. It is a 9,335-square-foot, 45,000-pound scale model; one inch equals one hundred feet, with 895,000 some buildings and all the bridges and everything glued down.

Moses, New York's biggest giant, never did anything small, except for the Panorama. "Vroom, vroom, this bridge goes over here. I'll put another one here." He masterminded the building of 7 real-size bridges, 14 expressways, more than 650 playgrounds, 288 tennis courts, 673 baseball diamonds, a few zoos, Lincoln Center, the U.N., Shea Stadium, Co-op City, Jones Beach. He destroyed Penn Station. When he built the Cross Bronx Expressway and all his other public works, he pushed close to half a million people out of their homes.

A guard on the Panorama ramp is whistling a mysterious birdcall to another guard. I've been standing there a long time waiting for the sun to go down. It's supposed to be a nine-minute day-to-night cycle. It's now been twenty. I had to sit down in the guard's chair. I said, "The sun's *not* going down!"

"I better check," the guard said. "Oh right, it was on manual."

The black lights went on, the ultraviolet paint outlining the buildings lit up. Onlookers gripped the rail.

GIANT

BIGGEST BALL

LOCATION
Upper West Side, Manhattan

RENT
$1,023.76 (rent stabilized)

SQUARE FEET
300 (studio in prewar
elevator building)

OCCUPANT
Zack Hample (writer)

Your walls are all covered with magazine pages.
Every inch! Almost every page is the same size. I've cut my pictures perfectly to fit around doorknobs and light switches while I keep them in even rows. Everything either has a face or a person.

You're waving a mysterious red light.
I always use a laser pointer when I'm pointing stuff out. There are maybe a thousand people in here. We could count the rows and columns and multiply—261 are probably just on that wall, more than 1,000 total. I do have some naked ones, a lot of pictures of people that some would find offensive.

I can't see any, just Jack Nicholson. Oh, I see one. She's holding his...
Here's my rubber-band ball. It's 129 pounds, about twenty-one inches in diameter. I've done it since I was four, about twenty-two

years. I add to it when I have to. See, rubber bands rot and break from being exposed to the elements and being constantly stretched to capacity. I do see a broken one every now and then. I put on a fresh layer when I have to. There will come a day when I won't be able to get the ball out my apartment door.

Do you have rules—only new bands, or same-color bands?
Color or not is fine. As time goes by, you need larger and larger bands to fit around the ball. [*He holds up a very long rubber band.*] This is probably bigger than any rubber band you've even seen. Without being stretched, it's about a foot long.

When was the first moment that you knew you had a ball?
Show-and-tell at school. It was already basketball size. It was too big to fit in my locker. My teachers let me carry it around all day. It was a famous ball even then.

Is yours the largest in the world?
I've heard there is one much bigger than mine. I contacted Guinness World Records in the mid nineties to inquire. They once decided to have either a string ball or rubber-band ball and they decided the string ball was more popular. I'm already trying to get in my baseball collection. They're at my parents' place. I wrote a book, *How to Snag Major League Baseballs*. See the fridge door.

"2,131 BALLS IS A LOT OF BALLS" spelled out in alphabet refrigerator magnets.

BRIAN KENNEDY

Every time I come back from a game, I update my magnets and my Web site. Almost every day I used to go to games in high school, Columbia Prep. I went to Friends Seminary for a few years. There's my grandfather on the wall. [*The laser pointer flashes on the grandfather.*] On the cover of *Newsday Magazine*, 1990. He started Argosy books in 1925. Now my mother is part owner. Baseball was once my only interest.

You're whistling as we look at your Web site.

I always have a song in my head. My grandfather taught me how to play the violin. My grandmother still lives on Park Avenue. Is the apartment great? I think my parents' is better. They bought it in the late seventies. [*We look at the screen as a camera tracks through a huge, beautiful apartment on the Upper West Side.*] My aunt's boyfriend owns this building I'm in. I got the apartment over a year ago—I got a little bit of a rent break. The rent would be $1,574.34.

Is there the smell of ether or something?

No. Here's video of my baseball collection. Are you ready? There they are. [*Every can, drawer is full of baseballs.*] Here's a video of my dad carving a turkey using a screwdriver. He's a writer—you know *Children's Letters to God?* [*His father speaks on the video: "Ciao bambino, sayonara, shalom shalom." Then he sings like Jimmy Durante. "Do I do, adieu."*] There's a lot of laughs if you're a Hample.

November 26, 2003

BIGGEST HALL

LOCATION

Washington Heights, Manhattan

RENT

$726.75 (rent stabilized)

SQUARE FEET

About 750 (two-bedroom apartment in prewar sixty-unit building)

OCCUPANTS

Daniel Gwirtzman (choreographer, dancer, and artistic director), Xilef Aletrop (painter, installation artist)

You say you're excited about your hallway. I can see why. It's as long as seven six-foot men lying head-to-toe. Forty-two feet!

[DANIEL] All our friends fetishize the hallway. Everyone has an idea for it. One person said, "You should put a different photo in each wall panel." Another said, "You have to paint the door purple." But we thought by keeping it entirely neutral, it would always have this realm of possibility. Though for Halloween, we are thinking of making it a haunted hallway, all dark. People will walk in and they just won't know what they're walking through. Though maybe we'll light small candles.

Your kitchen is a nice size. There's even a table in it.

A kitchen was a big thing, because we do cook a lot. But on the wall is a photo of our dream kitchen.

The dream kitchen is all white with an island in the center. Why do people get dreamy over an island in the kitchen? I see there's no furniture in the living room.

We don't have any. The plus side is I'm able to use it for my dance studio.

Did you move out of your $832 two-bedroom rent-controlled apartment in SoHo just because it was smaller?

Not entirely. SoHo is definitely overrated. The mallization! I was there two years. Before that, I subletted everywhere from Westbeth to the East Village to the West Side to the Upper East Side. This was my eighth apartment and the first with a lease in my name. I used to think New York existed only below 14th Street. It's been very eye-opening.

Because it's late at night, I took a cab up to the 180s. I got to look at the Academy of Arts and Letters, so Beaux Arts! And the American Numismatic Society, with its changing displays of the world's coins.

This area is so rich historically. Here you not only gain space, but natural beauty. The Cloisters—we're blessed! Rockefeller paid for ten miles of coastland so that it would never be developed. Further north you can see caves where Algonquin Indians lived. When the Indians sold Manhattan, it happened in Inwood, north of here.

GREG MILLER

How far north would you be willing to go?

I suppose my destiny is pulling me back up toward Rochester, where I grew up. But really, there is this prejudice and fear about leaving what people consider to be Manhattan. It's unfortunate. There is so much here. The Coliseum Theatre down the street. The mix of people. There's still an enclave of Jews who came after World War II, but east of Broadway it's almost completely Dominican. Everywhere there are wonderful Caribbean fruits and vegetables. Like this plantain.

You just held up what looks like the hugest green banana in the world!

Like I said, we came up here for more.

June 10, 1997

ALL THE WORLD

LOCATION
Carroll Gardens, Brooklyn

RENT
$1,300 (market)

SQUARE FEET
450 (one-bedroom renovated apartment with terrace in four-flat house)

OCCUPANTS
Birgit Garland (girl Friday), Thomas Garland (architect, ABS Architects)

Where is he? I'm so anxious to see him. Oh, that's him.
[THOMAS] He's a phenomenon. [BIRGIT] People have heard about Hegeloff. [THOMAS] Without even meeting us. [BIRGIT] They come up and say, You're the guys with Hegeloff.

Let's see, he's about...
[THOMAS] Four inches. [BIRGIT] Twelve and a half grams with a big bottom. He gets refurred every year.

Is that a common German name—Birgit being from Munich and all?
[THOMAS] No, it's an ex-girlfriend who's French and she couldn't say "hedgehog." [BIRGIT] His full name is Roberto Paulo Hegeloff. There are two stories. One is our story and one is his. Ours is that Hegeloff was in a group of little furry toys in the sixties given by Thomas's father to Thomas's mother. Hegeloff was the only one who survived the cat. Then he stayed with Thomas. I saw him at Oxford, at the architecture school, where we met. I said, "Oh, what's that cute little thing?" Then Hegeloff became alive.

Eight years ago.
Now he is always with us, traveling—New Zealand, England. We know a guy in Wales who was living in a gatehouse with a big tower and he just threw Hegeloff down, one hundred stories, and said, "You can look for him tomorrow."

How cruel.
We had to look for him immediately. We didn't have a torch. We had to go down with candles.

Where does he sleep?
With me, in the bed.

Thomas is there, too?
Yes.

What is Hegeloff's story?
[THOMAS] He comes from Brazil, a little village. [BIRGIT] In the Amazon with a lot of little Hegeloffs. You have to see Thomas's drawings.

Are you going to make a book?
This year, Thomas, or I kick your ass. Hegeloff's married with kids but he left them. We think he's gay because ninety-nine percent of his friends are male but he doesn't mooch about. [THOMAS] He's into SpongeBob. Here's his passport.

So tiny. My voice is getting higher.
Here's a photo of us getting married in
Vegas with Hegeloff. This is his goblet, bowl,
cheese grater.

**So anything smaller than Hegeloff is his.
Who carries him?**
I do. I put him inside my sweater, under
the neck. I take him to the office every day.
He saw 9-11 from my office.

**Would you let anyone else carry him?
No? I was reading Winnicott before I
came over. I was going to discuss the
transitional object.... You're looking at
me coldly...never mind. What about
that first French girlfriend?**
[BIRGIT] She just saw him. That's all.
[THOMAS] Don't you want to write about
the apartment?

Right! How did you find it?
Boccie ball. [BIRGIT] We were living in
Chelsea. We were evicted. The guy we

were subletting from owed the landlord two
weeks' rent. He was very apologetic. He
said, "Take all my furniture." He was living
somewhere else with his girlfriend. We paid
him rent but he didn't pay the landlord.
It's a complicated story. The sheriff came.
[THOMAS] No, the city marshal. [BIRGIT]
He hired a moving van for us. We share a
boccie ball court here with a lot of elderly
men, Italian men. They are the masters. I
wanted to live here because all our friends
are here. I came to look with a real-estate
agent. Dominic from the court is sitting
there. He said, "What are you doing here?"
I said, "I'm looking for an apartment."
[THOMAS] A one-bedroom. [BIRGIT]
Can I tell this story? I was there. You were
at work. [*Thomas is quiet, as is Hegeloff.*] I said,
"I'm looking for a one-bedroom." He said,
"Forget the broker. Come with me. I have
one with a terrace." I said, "Don't give it to
anyone."

February 23, 2005

CARY CONOVER

PAY BY THE INCH

LOCATION
Williamsburg, Brooklyn

RENT
$850 (market)

SQUARE FEET
800 (top floor of three-story house)

OCCUPANT
Daniel Nardicio (event planner)

Do your assistants always work in their underwear?
Yes.

You're preparing for the convention!
We're doing a Republican National Sex Party at 13 Little Devils. There will be the Oral Office. [*His phone rings.*] I'm going to help Kelly get her bike upstairs. She can't afford a lock yet. [*Kelly, a belly dancer, enters and goes to work on Photoshop on a picture of the vice president penetrating the president.*]

Will there be a desk in the Oral Office?
Of course—a penholder, maybe a Declaration of Independence. That's August 29. The Go-Go Boys will be naked as always. I pay them $13 an inch. Dick Slick makes $130 dollars a night. You do the math. The boys in the other room are making a sign for a seventy-year-old drag queen in a kissing booth.

I'm pretty excited about those two hundred bomb-sniffing dogs coming into town. I wonder where they're staying. So, along with the expected 50,000 conventioneers, 250,000 demonstrators, 15,000 reporters, the Broadway "Mouse Bloc," the pre- and post-convention protests, the monologues, the puppet shows—your team will join the swell. Is Paul the one in the white underpants?
Yes. Chase is in the blue. I'm from Painesville, Ohio. [KELLY] The pain! [*Knock at the door*] [DANIEL] It's the pizza. Justin Bond [*Kiki, of Kiki and Herb*] and I used to be roommates. We had an apartment down the street. We moved to New York at the same time, ten years ago. I came from Berlin, he moved from San Francisco.

Who's the man in front in the lawn chair—bright yellow cabana shirt, big hands, gold watch?
Pete, my landlord.

What does he think with everybody coming in and out?
He's hard of hearing. The other night, I overslept. The people at the bar where I do events sent a kid. The landlord saw him yelling at the window and called the police. Everybody thought I was dead. But I was sleeping in a sarong.

It's nice how he cares.
He worries more about himself than he does me. [*To Kelly*] I got you a health bar. [KELLY] I was in the cookie gutter and one day I said, "I have a lot to do

in my life." [*He tosses her some underpants.*] [DANIEL] I used to work in opera in Berlin, *Porgy and Bess.*

What are Paul and Chase chatting about in the other room?

Chase just moved here to be an actor. Paul's in *Short Bus*, the John Cameron Mitchell film. [PAUL, *as he runs in and adjusts his underpants*] We're working on it improvisationally, like Cassavetes. It will involve real sex. [DANIEL] I also have land in Nevada, six acres in Elko. My brother left it to me when I was ten. He bought it in the back of a magazine, like five dollars an acre. He died of testicular cancer when he was twenty-seven. He was like a real hippie, traveled all over. I said to my aunt once, "Was my brother gay?" She said, "Well, he was AC/DC." [*We join the boys in the other room while they paint their sign on the floor. Chase is counting a big box full of cash.*] Chase, it's illegal to write on money. [CHASE] Like President's Train money.

What's President's Train money?

You'd set a quarter down on the track. And it would be run over by the president's train. Like if there was a train going through town with the president on it. [DANIEL] He's from Ohio. He just graduated from high school. [CHASE] I've had a boyfriend since I was fourteen. [PAUL] He's still putting those coins on the track, hoping you come back. [*Paul underlines the words on the sign.*] [DANIEL] Now I want the word "kissing" in *quotes.*

You're the mad genius and they're ready to carry it out. I feel like I'm the baby-sitter—the boys on the floor in their underpants. God, what am I sitting on?

Chase's cell phone. It's vibrating.

August 25, 2004

CARY CONOVER

CRASHING THE WALLS

LOCATION
Long Island City, Queens

PRICE
$60,000 in 1994 (maintenance $203)

SQUARE FEET
1,000 (one-bedroom condominium in former warehouse)

OCCUPANT
Jerome Audureau (co-owner, Once Upon a Tart, a bakery in SoHo)

You have an exciting economic story to tell!

Every month I pay half—in mortgage and maintenance—of the three hundred I used to pay when I rented this apartment for five years.

***C'est merveilleux!* I said that in French because it is your native tongue. How did this good fortune happen?**

The man who owned the building died. Before he died, he offered the tenants the opportunity to buy their apartments.

Because you are from France, I imagine you living in Paris near La Musée des Arts Decoratifs or perhaps in Lyons near the church where Madame Bovary secretly met Leon. Yet you actually live near the big blue Citibank building in Queens.

When I first came to New York, I was working for a French hotel. The first person I met used to live around the corner from here. When I'd visit, I would love the way the train circled around, and there was this incredible view of Manhattan.

The view from your loft does look like the opening credits of every film set in New York.

I lived in three different apartments in this neighborhood before I found this one. This is where I started the bakery. The fire escape was the refrigerator in the winter. I was making vegetable tarts in three ovens. It was completely illegal.

You said you spent about $20,000 on the renovation. It would have cost $60,000 if you hadn't done it yourself.

My friend Ivan and I have been working for a year. I was living in the basement of this building for the last few months. I was so depressed.

You changed everything. You even made an opening in the bathroom wall for goldfish. How many fish are you going to have?

I have to talk to my cat and see how many he wants.

But if the fish are inside a glass panel in the wall, how are you going to feed them?

It's a little detail. I don't exactly care right now. I just want to put my bed back.

GREG MILLER

You redid the floors with twelve-inch planks of hard pine.
I wanted the effect of a barn to go with the cat and the fish.

It creates an exciting tension with the model airplanes, the Cuban music collection, and the black leather Corbusier furniture. I'm taking a welding class to design my own furniture.

How did you come up with the idea for recessed wall panels?
Red wine.

Then you did the big bust-out! You crashed through all the interior walls— two bedrooms worth. It reminds me of a room installation I once saw called *The Man Who Flew into Space from His Apartment* by the Russian artist Ilya Kabakov. A lot of people want to dynamite out of where they are. How did you get rid of the walls?
With a knife. I cut through the sheetrock partitions. It felt so great. Then I had a party. Seventy people drinking and dancing until nine in the morning. There was a lot of mambo music.

July 8, 1997

MANSION

LOCATION
Harlem, Manhattan

PRICE
$400,000 in 1997

SQUARE FEET
7,500 (five-story 1888 brownstone)

OCCUPANTS
Dimitri Katsarelias (deputy director, Foundation for Hellenic Culture; Byzantinist), Vasili Kontakos (worker in family restaurant businesses), Ari Economides (microbiologist)

[DIMITRI] She just comes to dust. We do the rest. The house is from 1888. We found a brochure about it in the Museum of the City of New York. It was built for a doctor. Most of these houses were built for upper-middle-class New Yorkers who did not like immigrants moving into Midtown. I'm quoting from a history book of Harlem. The area didn't stay wealthy for very long. I don't think these houses could sustain themselves. It was too expensive to keep a place like this in top shape. Families moved out really fast. Later, with poverty and depression, the whole thing went down the drain. All this gracious living only lasted a very few decades. These places were rented out as rooming houses.

The first time I was here I thought you lived in an embassy. There was this grand party with hundreds of people— royalty, an Auchincloss, and *all* the big names in the landmark world. People drifted through rooms with fifteen-foot ceilings lit by hundreds of candles. Some guests perched on the persimmon velvet side chairs near the andirons. Others threw back their heads and laughed near the pink-and-white–striped satin chaise. Then of course there were those who stood under the oak-coffered ceiling in the dining room nibbling almond paste cookies among the autumn arrangements of hydrangeas and the gold silk drapes that spilled onto the Oriental rug. You said you have one cleaning lady once a week to care for sixteen rooms, two kitchens, and five bathrooms. She must go into collapse.

You moved to Harlem over one and a half years ago.

I came by accident one day. My foundation had some work here with the Children's Storefront—we were giving them money to teach the kids ancient Greek. I passed Mount Morris Park and that was it. It sounds like a fairy tale, but when I see what I want, I go after it. So we started looking. We didn't want anything this big, but we came in just before the market got really crazy. Now there are not many buildings left to buy and prices have gone up a lot. The guy around the corner bought his about the same time we did. He works for an investment company. A lot of friends think we're completely crazy to move up here. I think what people say about Harlem is highly exaggerated. I lived on the Bowery, in Chelsea, East 13th Street. That neighborhood has lost its edge. We've only done basic renovation on the house so far.

SANDRA-LEE PHIPPS

The lawyer who lived here before did most of the dirty work, tearing down walls. As a historian, I want to make it livable without interfering with the fabric of the house. We don't need air-conditioning because the skylights always create a draft. Also, I don't want its years as an SRO to be lost, the imperfections in the doors because of fights.

The bedrooms upstairs are *huge*. There is a big open dressing room connecting two of them, with high cupboards full of all your jeans and T-shirts. I bet they used to be full of waistcoats and petticoats in 1888. You have fabrics on the walls with red and blue and gold embroidery of boats and little people waving.

They're nineteenth-century textiles from Skyros, where I'm from—an island known for embroidery and those little horses that look like ponies. Here is an eighteenth-century bridal bedcover. If my mother knew these things were here, she'd decapitate me.

By the way, they were making a movie in front of your house when I came in—*50 Violins* with Meryl Streep.
They make movies around here all the time. A guy was trying to convince me to use our house for a minimal fee. He said, "So-and-so, the actor, will be here. We'll make you famous." I said, "Look, I don't care if it's the Queen of England."

January 26, 1999

The Indian gold in the window is blinding—tiaras, anklets, nose rings. Women in pink saris are locking up it up for the night, taking it out of the store window and putting it in cabinets. They are talking but I can't hear what they are saying. They are on the other side of the glass. Down the street are the fabrics, floaty chiffon with pretend diamonds and thousands of mirrored sequins that look like gold.

This is just Jackson Heights gold. There is Fifth Avenue gold, Tiffany gold, medieval gold, Trump gold, Babylonian gold, and the largest vault of gold in the world behind a ninety-ton cylinder, eighty feet underground in the Federal Reserve Bank. Rumpelstiltskin is jumping up and down. New York is all about gold. Except for the top of the Chrysler Building and cell phones, which are silver.

New York is the most expensive city in the country to live in. Why is this? Of course, supply and demand. Everybody wants to be in New York (Manhattan's density is 871 times that of the U.S. as a whole) and then when they get here, people who thought they were middle class learn that they are just barely because so many New Yorkers are so rich. More than 13,000 taxpayers in 2004 were estimated to have annual incomes over one million dollars. Almost 720,000 had incomes under ten thousand dollars, according to the city's Independent Budget Office.

But those are just earnings. The city's foundation rests on trust funds. One artist said of another, "Oh *sure*, she had all that sound equipment. *Her* parents had a circular driveway."

For the other crowd, there are bargains: three pairs of socks for $2, an aqua brassiere for $3.99, Lysol for $1.99—sale, sale, sale. You can buy a Gucci handbag on the sidewalk. But apartments do not fall off trucks. Over a quarter of all New York City renters pay more than fifty percent of their gross household income for rent, according to the Department of Housing Preservation and Development.

One painter lives in a tiny apartment way out in Queens, paints in his room, but still has to have a day job. He would never tell what it was. He would only say, "It makes people happy." A friend whispered, "He makes false teeth."

I go to the Jackson Diner to think about all this, sitting next to a woman who has gold nail polish on one finger and her boyfriend who has his hair in a bun on the top of his head and a T-shirt that reads, "Beef Kills." I order a murg tikka palakwala and then walk along 74th Street, pondering the business of animal, vegetable, and mineral. A man just walked by the toy store. He has a hook for a hand.

MONEY

EVERYBODY PAYS

LOCATION
Williamsburg, Brooklyn

RENT
$2,500 (commercial)

SQUARE FEET
6,000 (loft in five-story nineteenth-century building)

OCCUPANTS
Andrew Tarlow (painter), Sue McLean, Mark Firth (writer; manager, bodega), Martin Cohen (mosaic designer), Matt Dunphy (painter)

This looks like early-eighties Berlin with the big ruined buildings in Kreuzberg where kids with pink hair had rats on leashes and sprayed German poems on the scabby walls. How did you get so much raw, throbbing space with the Williamsburg Bridge looming up outside the window?

[ANDREW] We found it through the newspaper. Mark and I met working at the Odeon. First we rented out a quarter of the space to a restaurant-construction company to help pay the rent. The place was pretty derelict. Three of us fixed it up. Now there are five. But the deal is, we always divide the full price evenly by the number of people— no matter how many in a bed. Even my girlfriend pays.

How derelict was it?

All the windows were boarded up. We knocked down the walls, cut glass to fit the windows, recycled almost everything. We got the gas pipes for a price. My mom in Long Island traded one of her own paintings to pay for the $1,000 Sheetrock and lumber bill. We only spent about $5,000 total.

You're so handy.

You don't know the half of it.

You have a Shelvador Automatic refrigerator. This 1930s globe is great.

You can have it for $150. [MARK] The globe belongs to me! [ANDREW] So, do you want to buy it?

Last year you rented the loft to a Japanese production company to film *Artful Dodgers*, made by a former NYU student. It's an eroticized thrill ride about a Washington Square portrait painter, a Times Square street guitarist, and a soft-porn Internet writer. The painter runs into a girl he went to kindergarten with in Japan because her parents sent her to New York to find her older sister who had disappeared. The older sister had been in the corporate world in Japan but had broken down under all the pressure and her parents were at a loss about what to do with her so they sent her to New York to recover. Everybody in the film lives in a loft. How was it being in a film set?

We got about $2,500 for a few days. But a few days turned into five or six. They

GREG MILLER

tell you there're going to be loads of people. Somehow it doesn't sink in. We had to stand in line with the crew for the bathroom. I'd say there were about fifty here. It was chaos.

A location scout once told me that when they're shooting on a street, some people will play music really loud to extort money from the crew.

What an idea! Now, across the way, there's an old cobblestone street that's ideal for

making movies. But people in the building painted horrible colors on the outside so people *can't* make movies there.

Would you rent your loft to the movies again?

Only for more money.

September 30, 1997

THE PRICE OF NOISE

LOCATION

DUMBO, Brooklyn

RENT

$2,900 (rent stabilized)

SQUARE FEET

1,800 (renovated loft in former warehouse)

OCCUPANTS

Reeves Carter (litigation associate, Ladas & Parry), Karla Olivier (corporate and real-estate attorney)

Every time I talk to you, it's something else. This situation is like a writhing mass. This is our twentieth discussion. Let's review: You moved into this large, elegant loft—steel refrigerator, marble sink on silver poles—in February 2000. You put in South Asian–inspired furnishings, a dining table made of Indonesian wood, chairs with Thai designs, sparkling pillows from India. You'd just married after meeting at the Justice Department—Karla was representing a Somalian refugee. You were happy! You loved blossoming DUMBO, one of the fastest-gentrifying industrial neighborhoods in the world, with the Walentas family developers giving specially picked businesses free rent for a year. You loved the chocolate shop in your building with the rabbits wrapped in cellophane, the park, the people. But then, last summer, they began building a bar downstairs— building, you said, "nights, weekends, Christmas Day." On Martin Luther King Day, you came home and "the apartment was filthy with dust from sandblasting." Brian, one of the bar owners, put you both up in a hotel and paid for an industrial cleaner. Everything was OK for a bit, but then, on St. Patrick's Day, the bar opened.

[REEVES] The floors were shaking. [KARLA] Everyone came out of their apartments. The bar had a band. [REEVES] Oh the *band.* I invited Brian up to my apartment. He said, "We have the best soundproofing in the city." I said, "You have to get your money back." He said that Walentas's Two Trees Management Company was one hundred percent behind the bar and we should move if it bothered us that much and he'd help us find an apartment. [KARLA] He hasn't given us any leads. We're on pins and needles at night. I dread my weekends. And the smoke! I wake up feeling hung over as if I've been at the party. You smelled it coming up in the elevator.

Then the Two Trees property manager, who you said is "in cahoots with Brian"—well, she is his sister—showed you apartments in other buildings. Smaller, more expensive. [REEVES] Our response is, "Why should we move?" [KARLA] Her response is always, "Why are you here?" [REEVES] This is the same building that made a tenant get rid of a dog that barked. [KARLA] We don't want to come across as these privileged people. [REEVES] We love our apartment; we want to sleep in it. [KARLA] Everything else about DUMBO is very nice and upscale. So many people in the building have babies. And you know the artists aren't going to *this* bar. *They're* going to Superfine.

You contacted the council member, the borough president. You got the tenants together. You wrote letters. The building owner's son, Jed Walentas, came to hear the sound. In April, you and two other tenants went on a rent strike. The Department of Environmental Protection, which came in March, said the noise was within the legal range. But what I heard while visiting you on a Sunday at 7 p.m. would make me jump out a window. Anyway, you started spending weekends at the Brooklyn Marriott for $179 a night so you can sleep. Two Trees sued you for withholding rent. You're getting digital sound equipment to gather evidence. Your defense is, "Two Trees did not provide us with the apartment we've been renting for two and a half years. We won't pay until we get back the full use." Meanwhile Two Trees says smoke and sound will be corrected by the end of June. You don't see how they're going to solve this by then. You already "feel betrayed. They say they're going to set sound levels, then they don't." I told you about a woman who poured ammonia down her porous loft floors to shut up a tenant below, and, well, that is extreme. Anyway, on May 11, there was a fire in the back of the bar. You were in the apartment folding laundry at the time, but you are a "strong believer in karma." This is all we have room for today. Keep calling with reports.

May 28, 2002

SUSAN EGAN

WALL STREET

LOCATION
Financial District, Manhattan

RENT
$2,200 (market)

SQUARE FEET
804 (one-bedroom apartment in 1959
former office building)

OCCUPANTS
Joanne Hunt (marketing services,
Clinique), Marc Brotherton (teacher,
St. Ann's School; artist),
Lucas Brotherton

Lucas is upset and crying.
[JOANNE] He has a little fever, from his
day care. There's a big germ in that place.
[*Ding-dong, ding-dong*] The bells are from
the Catholic church. [MARC] The echoes
down here—you never know the direction
anything's coming from. It's like a canyon
with all these sounds bouncing off the
buildings. [JOANNE] We hear jackhammers,
horns from all the livery drivers picking up
people at the stock exchange.

You have a forty-one-page lease.
There's a paragraph about bioterrorism.
We got a $250-a-month grant back from
the Lower Manhattan Development
Corporation to live down here, a total of
$6,000 over two years. They stopped it
last May. Then with a two-year lease, we
got two free months from the landlord and

another $750 grant for having a child. We
could buy diapers for a couple of months.
We saw the apartment in a classified. It
was advertised cheaper—$1,600. We were
living in Greenpoint then, $1,000, small. It
was cheaper to move to Manhattan than
to Williamsburg. I told Marc, if we get this
place, we not only save on cabs but on
gym membership. There's a health club
on the roof. I've been there twice since
we moved—April 2003. The war had just
started—our going into Iraq. I was nervous
signing this. At the stock exchange, some
days there are armed guards out there
with machine guns; other days, one guy's
standing there.

Your parakeet is so green, tropical.
He showed up at our window in
Greenpoint. He was all mangy. His beak
was all twisted. With a little love, thank
God, we never had to go to a vet. It's nice
to hear happy chirping in the morning.
I had an iguana for seven years. He ate
some change—eleven cents. He had to
have surgery to remove his change. He
died the day after I spent $1,200. This was
in Greenpoint. I met Marc in Dallas when
we were nineteen. He moved to Chicago, I
visited him there. We went to a pet store. I
saw thirty iguanas in a tank. I felt sorry for
them, all piled on top of each other in this
overcrowded store. I didn't really want him.
I spent all my money on this lizard. I think
you live and learn.

**Your neighbors are a few other families
and a lot of NYU students, you said.**
Across the hall, the apartment has five
bedrooms. It's all kids.

There's been so much commotion in this building. By the mid nineties, when it was vacant—Wall Street wasn't as hopping then—Rockrose converted it to 435 apartments, rented it in four months. Then Giuliani had his $1.4 billion "Christmas present for New York" idea—expand the stock exchange, build a trading complex, a fifty-story building. The city was going to buy this building, tear it down. Rockrose began to vacate, but after 9-11, the deal was off—criticism of the $1 billion public subsidy, city's budget problems, post-9-11 nervousness. Then it went back to Rockrose and they rented it fast. There have been a ton of conversions down here. The buildings are so classical revival—all the Doric columns. Then, of course, the historical violence. In 1920, an anarchist ignited a wagonload of explosives at the former JP Morgan. Thirty-three were killed and four hundred injured. In 1891, the financier Russell Sage was almost assassinated at the Empire Building, but he threw his male secretary at the bomber. It gets so rough when money's involved. Who's reading Emerson? Did you read "Self-Reliance"? A friend recommended that I read it every day.

[MARC] Yes. I started reading him because Nietzsche was influenced by Emerson. [*We go into the hall, which looks sort of in between a hotel and an office building, to go up to the roof deck.*]

When you walk here, down Broadway, it's at Liberty Street that you can see the light of the water beyond. The city opens up, all life has possibility. Then I saw the tulips in the Trinity Church yard, open to the sky, all white and purple, belting out a song for spring.

May 19, 2004

BRIAN KENNEDY

THOSE FEARLESS FOSDICKS

LOCATION
Stuyvesant Square, Manhattan

PRICE
$3,000 in 1974 ($500 maintenance)

SQUARE FEET
650 (four-room co-op apartment
in early-twentieth-century
walk-up building)

OCCUPANTS
Pauline Goodman (activist), Bernard
Goodman (painter; former tenant
adviser, Legal Aid Society)

We have to have a two-part "Shelter" column because of all your housing battles. Pauline, you're seventy-nine; Bernard, ninety-two. You've lived in the neighborhood since...?
[PAULINE] The Third Avenue el was up. We raised our daughter here. When the el came down, speculators came in. "*This* house should go down," they said. "*That* one." A real land grab.

You took up the sword. Where were you born?
East Side. My family lived in a lot of places. In those years, immigrants didn't have enough to pay the rent. When they couldn't pay, they moved to the next apartment. Bernie was raised in an orphanage.

[BERNARD] The memories are baggage I don't want to carry with me. [PAULINE] Where did we meet? I don't know. We were socially conscious people. We met at some working-class hall, maybe Webster Hall, sixty-two years ago. We fell in love in three weeks and got married. We both wanted a better life, better people, better everything. Bernie was a merchant seaman. He said he'd have to go to sea. It was 1940. He went to San Pedro, California. I went with him. I was an organizer for the fish cannery union. People were making sixteen cents an hour, wearing heavy boots. When the fish came in, bells rang. We had to run to work or the fish would rot. Then we decided to come back to New York. I got a cold-water flat on First Avenue, 1942. It was hard to find a place. Then we got an apartment in the building next door to here. Then came the march of the monoliths, the late fifties. The el's down. Speculators say, "Why do we need three stories when we can have twenty-four?" They threw down the working-class houses. [BERNARD] A *terrible* thing—the beginning of the homeless problem in New York. [PAULINE] Lo and behold, speculators bought *our* building. Yes, we had rent-control protection. But it was like today. They'd harass people out of their houses—fires, floods. Thugs would come knock on doors.

What were you paying back then?
[BERNARD] Forty dollars a month. If we had had to move, we would have had to pay a hundred dollars. We were having a hard time. [PAULINE] I was a part-time waitress. We needed dental work for my

child, piano lessons. [BERNARD] A lot of our time we gave to social causes. McCarthy destroyed our ability to make a living. I was blacklisted after twenty-five years as a merchant seaman. [PAULINE] Bernie was secretary of the joint strike committee, the Seafarers Union. [BERNARD] I had to make a living. So I did house painting. I got involved in tenants' rights because six different landlords tried to buy these properties and force us out. [PAULINE] We were able to knock down *each one*—ten years, six different owners. It took five years to fight the last one, who said, "These people are ruining me. They're costing me hundreds of thousands of dollars." [BERNARD] I was working for Legal Aid at the time. The landlord owned this building and the one we were in next door. I said, "The way out is to let him have the other building. We'll fit all the tenants from both buildings into this one." [PAULINE] There were only eight left in this one. The others fled out of fear. [BERNARD] We got the city to advance us money for what he paid for this building—$250,000. [PAULINE] The city gave us a mortgage at a low interest rate. [BERNARD] We had to set up a co-op corporation. [PAULINE] We had a big, round table with lawyers. [BERNARD] *No*, the lawyers were *not* at the table. [PAULINE] There *were* lawyers. [BERNARD] In the next twenty years, we paid the mortgage off. Some couldn't pay. We helped raise a lot of money for two elderly people. It was one of the few successful co-ops back then. But they should have given people *expert* advisers. There were properties the city had taken over. [PAULINE] *Loads!* [BERNARD] The city

only chose a handful to turn into co-ops. [PAULINE] The amount of pressure we put on City Hall was unbelievable. Now we get to Esther Moscow! Esther was relocation director for the city. [BERNARD] Esther was throwing all these old people out of their homes. [PAULINE] One day I said, "Where does this Esther live?" Rent-regulated, tax-abated Stuyvesant Town! She had the best of *everything*. [BERNARD] Once she allowed people's relocations, old people lost their doctors, their friends; they *died*. [PAULINE] Our landlord here got relocation orders for everyone in our building so he could "renovate." We went to look at the apartments in the Bronx where they were relocating people. [BERNARD] We were *horrified*—rats, roaches. [PAULINE] We decided to do a big *job* on Esther. We picketed her out of her skin. Everybody came from all over the city. [BERNARD] I want to emphasize— [PAULINE] *Don't* cut me off. Bernie has a tendency to cut me off. Bernie organized the tenants. It was great. *Oh, go ahead,* describe your organization. [BERNARD] In this continuous battle, we realized there were four million people in New York who paid rent. They should be masters in their own houses. Koch was congressman at the time. We told him tenants were getting a terrible deal. He said, "That's not my field. I'm on the House Banking Committee." We stormed out of his office. We organized the Tenants Party, a party no tenant could resist, for reinstatement of rent control, rollback on rents. They ran me against Koch in the congressional race. We got six thousand signatures. We presented them to— [PAULINE] *You know who? David*

Dinkins. [BERNARD] Dinkins looked at us and sneered. [PAULINE] Could I cut in? Dinkins worked under Koch. [BERNARD] Dinkins said, *"You'll* never be on the ballot." Two weeks later, Koch challenged our signatures. The *Village Voice* arranged a debate. I debated Koch directly. [PAULINE] It was *very* powerful. Jack Newfield was there. But then Koch found Josie, the little old lady in front of the supermarket. She'd witnessed our petitions. [BERNARD] Koch found out she'd been gerrymandered out of our district, and I was knocked off the ballot. [PAULINE] What a job! [BERNARD] We wanted to go to the feds to get some justice.

Meanwhile.
[PAULINE] Mickey Schwartz, our landlord's lawyer, kept giving us eviction notices. He actually told someone down the street he couldn't take this case anymore because Bernard Goodman was driving him crazy. [BERNARD] I used to organize tenants from one end of the city to the other. [PAULINE] One night, Bernie had a meeting. I said, "Bernie, I have a feeling they're going to harass the older people." I'm outside the place. Here come these Fearless Fosdicks, two characters, walking in the building. I start blowing a whistle. I really made a big fuss. [BERNARD] They were thugs. They started running down the street. People surrounded their taxi, pushing it back and forth.

We never got to the paint-box part. How you bought Bernie one for his eightieth birthday, and now he has shows everywhere. Anyway...
[PAULINE] Housing shouldn't be part of the profit system. [BERNARD] Housing expenses should be on the sliding scale. The city has buildings that could be turned into co-ops. If people owned their housing, they'd take care of it.

Have you formally retired from the struggle or are you still dabbling?
[PAULINE] We can't stand it anymore. When we took this building over, we were so busy renovating. Bernie put in thirty-six sets of windows—with his own hands. Then we were up to here in the civil rights movement. Now we're waiting for the young people. *But* there's a new generation called "yuppies" leaving social questions behind them. [BERNARD] No, they are acting out of their economic status, *not* greed. If times are good, you get the selfish. [PAULINE] No, young people today— *Bernie, let me finish!*

March 5 and 12, 2002

JAY MUHLIN

SCHOOL
OF
BUSINESS

LOCATION
Chelsea, Manhattan
RENT
$2,735 (market)
SQUARE FEET
700 (one-bedroom apartment in 2002
80/20 building)
OCCUPANTS
Bryan Sloane (futures trader), Leslie
Fuchs (assistant to the president,
Gourmet Advisory Services)

How did you come to be here?
[LESLIE] I moved in in July. [BRYAN]
I used to have a roommate. [LESLIE] I
spent ninety-nine percent of my nights
here. [BRYAN] I graduated from NYU in
2002. It was no-man's-land here. The only
place around was Whole Foods. [LESLIE]
Restaurants are finally catching up.

What was here before?
[BRYAN] A parking lot. Rockrose was the
developer.

What did your roommate do?
[LESLIE] They both were from the Stern
School of Business. [BRYAN] He and I
looked all over. We looked on Lex. I refused
to live there because there was dog poop

all over the street. We also looked on 21st
between Seventh and Eighth. There was...

Yes, got it.
It's the broken-windows theory. If
there's dog poop today, there's dog poop
tomorrow.

How did you meet?
It was the fall of 2002. [LESLIE] He didn't
have cable hooked up yet. My landlord
gave us a free black box. All of a sudden
we were stealing cable. My friend from
college came over and said he was bringing
a friend. He came to watch *The Sopranos*
and he never left. It was an L-shaped sofa.
When you'd sit here on...

**You're diagramming this on your
tabletop made of...**
Stainless steel. When you'd sit here,
on the end, the view was awful. As the
months went on, he kind of moved up on
the couch. We're going to Brooklyn this
afternoon to pick up...[BRYAN] We've
been great at buying distressed Internet
assets. These chairs we're on sale for $250
apiece. I offered the people $150 for all
four. We find people who have to sell. They
have to move.

You've got a lot of boxes still unpacked.
We've been so busy. [LESLIE] Work and
life. Today we're getting a brushed-steel
lateral file cabinet. [BRYAN] Let me tell
her the events of last week. [LESLIE] I
do event planning. [BRYAN] We are very
busy. [LESLIE] When I was growing up,
I was going to be a lawyer, and my best

friend was going to be a finance person. We were going to liberate women from their awful marriages. My friend's mother said, I do divorce and I do real estate. When I do divorce, it's so painful. When you do real estate, it's happy.

Always? [We think quietly.]
[BRYAN] Now she does forty-foot towers of seafood for bar mitzvahs. Part of the reason we like this apartment so much is the deck. [LESLIE] It's gorgeous. [BRYAN] We'd looked at Avalon Chrystie Place. [LESLIE] Before it was open—we loved it. [BRYAN] You want to live on Houston—then you go on a tour. You realize they have these special noise-proof windows. There are horns blaring twenty-four hours. [LESLIE] It was about $1,000 more a month. [BRYAN] Our friends who just got married…

Yes?
They moved to Hell's Kitchen and they're paying $2,350. Their floors are not level so you get vertigo. [LESLIE] They have one circuit. [BRYAN] You can't run the air conditioner with the toaster. [LESLIE] I am not such a walk-up-the-stairs girl. Of course they had all their wedding gifts sent here because we have the doorman. [BRYAN] Since I trade energy products, I'm acutely aware of the energy that goes into electricity. Last week after the hurricane, we cut back on air conditioning. [LESLIE] Natural gas was up twenty-five percent. What else can we tell you? [BRYAN] We got these lamps for fifty bucks. Seaman's was going out of business.

I forgot to talk about New Orleans. It's been on all our minds. [We discuss.]
We have a go-bag. [LESLIE] Where is it? [BRYAN] That's a good question.

Why do you have so many umbrellas?
When we moved, we didn't think we had any.

September 14, 2005

CARY CONOVER

RISE UP

LOCATION
Park Slope, Brooklyn
RENT
$625 (rent stabilized)
SQUARE FEET
250 (two-room apartment in
six-unit building)
OCCUPANT
Nazima Kadir (investigator, Civilian
Complaint Review Board)

You live near the Grand Prospect banquet hall with the marble fountains and gold-leaf toilet seats! I saw some yellow houses with blue and purple window trim, like Easter eggs.

I love the neighborhood—it's much more diverse, ethnically and racially, than the upper part of Park Slope. I was really desperate when I got this apartment. A friend who goes to the New School saw the ad on a board. The landlady kept asking me to call back in a half hour. She kept saying another half hour. Finally she says, "Come over." I get there. She says, "Oh, the person who lives there isn't there now." I was about to kill her. Then the woman came. I was in such a hurry to take it that I didn't see there was a view of all of lower Manhattan. I love my apartment, but not my landlady. We got along for a year, but not anymore.

That was the woman wearing the fuchsia flip-flop slippers downstairs near the mailboxes.

She won't give me a new lease. She thinks I'm a troublemaker. If she yells at me, I send her letters. She doesn't like letters. The heat's been a problem from last February on. I'd call and say, "There's no heat." I'd get into ridiculous conversations with her son—tiresome, obnoxious conversations—and then finally he'd turn it up. I'm obsessed with tenant rights. I grew up in a two-bedroom, rent-stabilized apartment in Flushing. Sixty apartments in the building, a lot of Afghani refugees, Latinos, Asians, *and* landlords who never gave us heat. My dad was a cook in a deli. My mom worked at home. My parents are immigrants from Bangladesh. They didn't really know their rights. Most of the building didn't. Sometimes we wouldn't have hot water for days. I had all this rage about the situation. I didn't realize until I moved here that there are so many laws that protect tenants. I went to Hunter College High School. In sixth grade, I took a test and got in. It's free, but all the Upper East Side kids who go to Dalton try to get in. I was too ashamed to bring kids back to my building.

Then Swarthmore.

In '97, I was out of college. I lived on the third floor of this big, gorgeous house in Ditmas Park, Brooklyn. I was interning at the U.N. My parents were so upset about me not living at home they wouldn't visit. But they would bring food over. They'd call and say, "We're coming over at 8:45. We're not going to come inside. We're going to drive by, and you should be standing there waiting for us. We'll honk and then you'll come over to the car window and we will hand you the food and leave." I said, "No, I'm not going to stand out in the cold. Come and ring the bell." It was this circuslike drama, anxiety ridden. Though now my mother visits me. In fact, she visits for three days at a time. She wants to come every weekend.

Back to the landlady. You called HPD [Department of Housing Preservation and Development], complained about the heat. They sent an inspector. She put on heat. No one else in the building complained?

No, because the landlady will yell. The tenants are not very empowered here. The landlady and her son like to make everyone think we're a big family. If they really were family, they'd turn on the heat. The landlady does whatever she wants because people are wimpy. They don't want to cause waves. You know, when Westerners view people in countries where human rights are violated, they say, "Oh, I wouldn't let them abuse me that way." If you don't have enough courage to tell your eighty-four-year-old landlady to turn on the damn heat, how do you expect people in other countries to rise up while they're killing the masses?

January 25, 2000

SANDRA-LEE PHIPPS

SOMETHING WONDERFUL

LOCATION

Harlem, Manhattan

RENT

$1,297.34 (rent stabilized)

SQUARE FEET

850 (three-bedroom apartment in 1909 building)

OCCUPANTS

Derek Agile Jones (singer/actor), Stephen Charles Nicholson (performer/teacher, Music Together), Robert Roland (naturopath)

Agile, you came to New York to be a big star!

[AGILE] Yes, from the heart of Denver, 1997. Stephen and I are from the Actors Studio. We got twenty other actors in the past five years to live in this building and its sister building—so many that James Lipton, host of *Inside the Actors Studio*, called this the "Actors Studio Uptown Residences." [ROBERT] I met both of them at the Yoga Connection in TriBeCa. [AGILE] Yoga's really a part of our lifestyles. At our school, if something wonderful happens, then everybody does it.

Every time you say something wonderful happens, I hear tinkling bells.

[STEPHEN] Show her your walking-tour map of Sugar Hill. [AGILE] People who

lived in the valley in Harlem would look up and say, "One day, I'm going to have the sweet life." A great number of intellectuals lived up here. Thurgood Marshall.

Cab Calloway. He would be directing his orchestra. Go, Cab. Some real toe-tappers. The lobby here is so grand, creamy marble.

I just got good news. The Parks Commissioner's office called, finally. For years, I'm always on the phone. "Fix my sidewalk. La, la, la." You saw the cracks. And the "Home Sweet Edgecombe" flag outside. We got the children to make it.

Now your building looks very tidy, yet your landlord, Baruch Singer—Harvard-educated son of a rabbi, owner of more than fifty buildings—reportedly ripped out the stairs of a five-story walk-up, leaving twenty tenants stranded, had another building that collapsed and killed three tenants, had two thousand violations in five buildings, it goes on. His pit bulls, Chaos and Mayhem. So, is he another wonderful thing happening?

I must say, I've never had a problem with the man. When we got the apartment, Stephen and I went down and did the charm thing on him. The office is on Delancey. It's a dump, everyone smokes cigarettes. He was busy. He said, "You look like good guys. I trust you."

You're having your monthly house meeting tonight.

[ROBERT] It's very liberating to recognize the power of communication. [STEPHEN] Last month the ceiling fell down in the

ROBERT HALE

bathroom. [AGILE] We really got some clarity. [STEPHEN] There was an overflow from the tub upstairs. [ROBERT] It was an interesting revelation in points of view. I was in the bathroom first. Since there wasn't water actually coming through—the ceiling was just buckling—I went to check my e-mail. [STEPHEN] I went in. I see the Sheetrock buckling down, seems like it's holding. I thought, "Oh rats," to use the "Peanuts" term. I'd done a lot of renovation with Sheetrock. I got my coat. Agile said, "Do you see the ceiling?" I said, "Yes." I walked out to go to work. [AGILE] Shortly thereafter, I hit the roof. How could they not take care of the ceiling? The cats could be electrocuted. I yelled at Rob, "Why, you inconsiderate s.o.b." I got the plumber. The whole ceiling was totally soaked. Da, da, da. At that time I was perceiving that they

were not giving a fuck, but when I kind of calmed down, I realized where they were coming from. Also, guys, please put the top of the toilet seat down. With it up, in feng shui, it represents your money going down the drain. Since I'm creating abundance, I'm making sure I take care of every angle. The exterminator is coming on Thursday. Can one of you be here as a backup? [ROBERT] I think I can be here. [AGILE] Just in case, if I were to get a gig.

Agile, the only things in your room are pictures of yourself on every wall.
[STEPHEN] He doesn't put any portraits of himself in the bathroom. He doesn't want himself to go down the drain.

January 1, 2003

THE ARRANGEMENT

LOCATION

Park Slope, Brooklyn

RENT

$700 (market)

SQUARE FEET

580 (one-bedroom garden apartment in early-twentieth-century brownstone)

OCCUPANT

Sarah Falkner (licensed massage therapist; co-owner, Opal Center for Massage and Applied Therapies)

Your landlord is your ex-boyfriend! Ooh la la!

Friends say it's very French. Others are like, "Are you fucking crazy?" We used to live in the upstairs apartment together. Now I rent the garden apartment. I have a separate entrance. It's only been since July that we stopped living together. It was his suggestion that I live here. I was looking for a place, but not for very long. I saw absolute disasters, three people in an illegal loft in DUMBO looking for a roommate and none of us spoke the same language. I'm thirty-two and just the idea of roommates whom I wasn't sleeping with— well, I couldn't cope with it and I wanted to live by myself really bad. He lowered the rent from the last tenant. I pay $700. She paid $850 but she never slept with him. It's very amiable so far.

Here comes your landlord now.

[ERIC] I could easily get $1,200 a month for the apartment. I should, but that's life. [SARAH] Of course, my rent went up $100 a month. When I lived *with* Eric, I only paid $600.

It gets even more complex because Eric, your landlord, is also your employee.

I'm opening a new business, massage therapy, two blocks from here and Eric is doing construction. [ERIC] She's paying me $20 an hour for my handyman work. Anyone else I'd charge $30. Also, I'm paying off her loans. I had credit card debt from construction on the house. Sarah had debt from living beyond her means. I combined our debts into a home equity loan and that's a fifteen-year loan, so part of her rent money is going toward paying off the loan.

This situation is like a Celtic knot. How far back does it go? Wait, you both have the same blue eyes!

[SARAH] We're both of Polish descent. We went to school together fifteen years ago, painting, in Indiana. I grew up in Bloomington. My mother raised me herself. Eric is from Ohio. He and I moved to New York in '88. We were living in Williamsburg. [ERIC] The FBI came to the door one night. They said, "*FBI, we're comin' in!*" The guy downstairs was a counterfeiter. I heard he was doing twenties. He was an old guy. He used to play the TV really, really loud because of the presses, to hide the sound. [SARAH] Then later, our landlord went into foreclosure. Eventually

You got that uncanny feeling one gets from the unexplained repetition, didn't you?
Yes! So *unheimlich*, as Freud would say.

Your bedroom door goes right out to the garden in back, which is full of herbs, since you study herbalism in the Greenwitch tradition. Then there are the deer skulls, the turtle shell in the cabinet. There's an LP record on the mantel of a woman in a steamy Hawaiian motif.
That's from my grandfather's house in Mishawaka, Indiana. In the forties, he sent away for a mail-order house for $300, Montgomery Ward. He packed it with Hawaiian things.

You seem to have inherited his fiery island palette—orange sheepskin rug, orange furniture.
When I lived upstairs with Eric, it was more orange and red up there. [ERIC] While we were breaking up, it went from red to gray. It changed over months of denial. [SARAH] It was cooling off, just cooling off.

October 17, 2000

we moved. [ERIC] I bought this brownstone in '94. I had down-payment help from my parents, twenty grand. My father's a personal-injury lawyer. I used to be an art mover. Now I play golf in between construction jobs. [SARAH] Another thing—the week before we went shopping for the house, I got a tattoo on my arm. I went in the house, in this apartment—there was this lighting fixture on the ceiling that looks like my tattoo.

MICHAEL SOFRONSKI

THE ROAD NORTH

LOCATION

New Rochelle, Westchester County

RENT

$1,150 (market)

SQUARE FEET

900 (renovated pumping station)

OCCUPANT

Ron Berler (editor, *NBA Inside Stuff*;
writer; Little League coach; lead
singer, Del Crustaceans)

Why are you, a single man with a glamorous Manhattan publishing job, commuting every day on the Metro-North with the beige molded interiors—where Meryl Streep and Robert De Niro fell in love in that movie but it was torturous because they were married to other people—to a suburb full of mostly families, and, in your own words, the most exciting thing that happens on a weekend is a Cadillac pulling out of a driveway?

When I came to New York for my job three years ago—I'd been living outside Chicago since college—I was staying with my parents in Westport, which was driving me crazy. People told me the only way I could find space was to get a loft. I saw one for $800 in the paper, but it was in Staten Island. So one night I got on a train, a boat, and a bus and I arrived on this corner in Staten Island and looked around. You know what I did?

I crossed the street and got on the next bus back.

So much for Staten Island.

Then I see an ad for a large one-bedroom for $1500 in Midtown near where I used to work. I meet the agent at this sooty dowager of a building. I thought, well, it's just the outside. We get on the elevator with what seemed to be a bag lady and I said, "Do you live here?" She said, "Yes, and if I had the money, I'd leave today." We got off. The carpeting looked like somebody had taken a razor to it. The agent opened the door. I looked at him and said, "This is a dump." He said, "What do you expect for $1500?" At that point I decided I would never live in Manhattan. So I got in a car and started driving north. I'm on the Hutchinson River Parkway. On a whim, I get off at this exit—I didn't know it was New Rochelle—and I just followed this road until I saw a real-estate office. It was called King David Realty. I knew I found home. I said I wanted a little house. They had just the place—a renovated red brick pumping station that used to regulate New Rochelle's water flow. After that, it was owned by the brother of Walter Lantz, who drew Woody Woodpecker, one of my cultural heroes.

It's so dramatic! One huge white room with a twenty-five-foot ceiling, a skylight, and your bedroom upstairs. But isn't it lonely living so far from everybody in New York?

I discovered I lived three blocks from a long lost aunt and uncle. They invite me over for Chanukah. Basically, my neighborhood is one of Orthodox Jews. At times in their lives, Jay Leno and Willie Mays lived here. And Doctorow's family—he wrote *Ragtime* about New Rochelle. Ossie Davis and his wife Ruby Dee live here now—and Robert Merrill. He sings the anthem at Yankee Stadium.

I have a sneaking suspicion you couldn't help moving to a suburb because you are driven to coach Little League.

Well, I am the Casey Stengel of Little League managers. I've been managing teams for twenty years. If I could spend my life coaching Little League teams, I'd quit my editing job today. But then I couldn't even afford to live in New Rochelle.

April 28, 1998

THE GRANT

LOCATION
New Brighton, Staten Island

PRICE
$305,000 in 2005

SQUARE FEET
6,800 (two-family house)

OCCUPANTS
Ann Marie Selzer (producer),
Wilder Selzer (performer)

Is this the woman you bought the house from?
[ANN MARIE] This is Mary. [MARY] I've been here seventy-one years. I lived with my parents up here. When I married, we moved downstairs.

Good-bye. [*Mary leaves.*] Your dining-room table looks like it's for dividing up the money. What did Mary's husband do?
[WILDER] He was a car mechanic. A lot of his tools are still down in the basement. There's a pinup of Mae West. Back in the day, the neighborhood was Italian, Polish, Jewish. Mary tells me these tantalizing stories: "I had my own butcher who would set aside cuts of meat for me." [ANN MARIE] The house reminds me of my grandmother's. I loved it. We closed on April Fools' Day.

Where did you get the money?
We got a first-time homebuyer's grant from Neighborhood Housing Services—a grant for being poor people.

How did you know about it?
Through the Staten Island Economic Development Corporation. We knew grants were available. [WILDER] One of us had to take a class. It turned out to be her. [ANN MARIE] How to talk to mortgage and real-estate brokers, get your insurance. [WILDER] She came out feeling pretty good. [ANN MARIE] The people taking the class were... [WILDER] A Costco clerk. She was making $13,000. For one person, you have to make under $40,000 a year. We did it just under Wilder's name. When I first called, the woman said, "Do you have a job?" I said, "No." She said, "Fine. Does your husband make under $40,000? Yes? Excellent. How's his credit?" I said, "He doesn't have any." [WILDER] I only have my father's credit card for renting movies. [ANN MARIE] They gave us the down payment and closing costs, $30,000. They helped us get twenty percent down, hooked us up with a 4.62 percent mortgage. I want to do it again, own more, right away.

You'd lived in that mansion for two years near the ferry with the dust, taxidermy, young men lying around, where Andy Milligan made the movie *Carnage*.
[WILDER] Yeah. [ANN MARIE] It was an SRO. We'd moved there after 9-11. I got to be good friends with the owner, a guy who bought it in the seventies for $30,000.

Were there moldings?
[WILDER] There were aspects that were

SHIGEMI IYOTA

exciting, an overgrown garden. There were twelve others when we moved in. [ANN MARIE] We got run out.

All these Staten Island streets near the ferry are named after people. One's even named after two people.
[WILDER] A lot of police and firemen live here. They got hit on 9-11.

Your neighborhood's so higgledy-piggledy: cracked concrete steps, sort of a seventies Laurel Canyon feel, but much more, ah, rough...
[*Ann Marie rolls her eyes.*] This is New Brighton, which to Staten Island is the projects. [WILDER] St. George is where the Victorian homes are. [ANN MARIE] Did you tell her about the cult? [WILDER] We don't say "cult." We say "intentional community." [ANN MARIE] They own the houses across the street, up the hill. [WILDER] They're called "Ganas." They were founded in San Francisco in the early seventies, moved to Staten Island in the late seventies. They own these thrift stores here—called Every Thing Goes.

How would you describe them?
[*Ann Marie is quiet.*] [WILDER] There's definitely a hippie edge—a puppy-dog friendliness.

Are they married to each other?
Some say they have open relationships. They have the core inner circle, six people...[ANN MARIE] You don't know this for sure. Check the Web site. Their antique store is gorgeous. It is so well run. [WILDER] Let's show you the garden. [*We go out back.*] See the snake.

It's crawling up the cement. Are there a lot of snakes in Staten Island?
[ANN MARIE] They're all over.

Are they just in the gardens?
No. The kids collect the snakes and put them out on the sidewalks in the sun to dry up.

July 20, 2005

DADDY

LOCATION
Greenwich Village, Manhattan

RENT
$2,500 (market)

SQUARE FEET
300 (studio apartment in
prewar building)

OCCUPANT
Smith Watkins (eighth-grade
math teacher)

You just wrote a check for $59,000.
To live in the most highly threatened city in
the world and make it my home! Can you
believe it? I'm buying a one-bedroom co-op,
not in this building, but in another prewar
nearby. The $59,000 check is ten percent of
the purchase price—the biggest check I ever
wrote. I didn't know—do I write five nine
thousand or fifty-nine?

You look a little flushed.
I was just coming back in the cab from
the lawyer and I thought, "I'm officially a
resident of New York for the next *ten* years."
I'm going to get a fifteen-year mortgage, but
to get the return on my investment, I have
to wait ten years. I found the apartment last
Monday. I walked in and the lady showed it
to me, 850 square feet. With the economy
the way it is, I decided it would be best to
invest in real estate, which turns out to be
what everybody's doing now. Because people
are afraid of the stock market, real-estate
prices have gone through the roof.

**You've been paying a lot for this tiny
room—$2,500.**
Before, I *was* paying $3,000. In January
I renegotiated the lease. I tried to go in
at $2,100 and the owner came back at
me with $2,500. I told her I rented the
apartment at a really high time, October
2000, and now rents are lower. The owner's
Molly Shannon. She was on *Saturday
Night Live*. She lives in L.A. now. I always
wanted to live in the Village. I came to
New York in May 2000. I stayed at my
cousin's, Eighth and Sixth, near Gray's
Papaya. I used to be a computer technology
consultant, designing the front end of
business software applications—things like,
is there a drop down or a scroll down?
When you click "submit," what database
do you hit? They shut down their New
York office in mid February. Then I was
spending every day in the apartment. It
was driving me crazy. I started to run like
Forrest Gump along the Hudson. Then I'd
walk a little. Then there'd be no reason to
go home. Then I'd start running again.
I'd be up to eight miles a day, and there
are only so many résumés a day you can
send out.

**This is one of the Bing & Bing buildings,
which they say are among the city's
finest prewar properties. I sound like a
real-estate agent or something. But I
read that Alexander Bing was one of the
great socially conscious developers. He
created Sunnyside in Queens, modeled
on an English garden city. Profits from
his Manhattan buildings subsidized
the experimental communities. Now,
are you in the mood to say, how, at**

twenty-eight, you can afford to buy an apartment with your current teacher's salary?

My family helped me. My father and his brother have a company, Watkins Trucking. My grandfather started it in Thomasville, Georgia.

With a pickup truck delivering chickens during the Depression.

Yes! Now he ships Gap, Sony, Clinique. I'm the only family member, out of seventeen, who could work in the company who doesn't. I'm the only one who lives above the Mason-Dixon Line. I grew up in Tampa, where the headquarters are. My dad has a farm in Thomasville. He raises pointers. My boyfriend's getting one from my dad. [*Her boyfriend, Rob, lives on Avenue A, is a digital retoucher, used to be a bartender, and met Smith in late September. He arrived later with a bag of pork chops and Coca-Cola.*] My dad raises the pointers for hunting. The farm used to be owned by the Whitneys. My dad's a wonderful businessman. Yes, he advises me. He told me that when you buy an apartment, you can write off a percentage of—wait, I'm not sure. I'll call him. [*She dials.*] Hey Dad, how's it going? Is the interest expense write-off the incentive for home ownership? Yes, OK. I wrote the $59,000 check today. Dad, you're going to

MICHAEL KAMBER

be proud of me. Last night I went to feed the homeless on the Upper East Side. I'm going into overdrive here. I'm going to be a math teacher, feed the homeless. I made fifty pounds of mashed potatoes. We served it with chicken and corn. Daddy, I love you. Thank you for all your help with everything. [*She hangs up the phone.*]

June 18, 2002

The retriever is proud, his blond hair flowing. The bulldog is drooling. Now come five on a leash, all pulling madly. The schnauzer especially. Their dog walker is making a living. I heard about another dog walker's long afternoons alone with the terrier in Patrick's apartment. Patrick lives in a white glove building.

In the mornings, the dogs and cats of the city wave goodbye with their paws.

Oh wait, where is this dog going? He is so long and low. What does he think of the Time Warner building, so high, or the glassy blue Gwathmey?

What are you doing?

Wait, you're the one I've been seeing lately, near the bakery with the marzipan eggplants. Your keeper always wears linen or the color of linen. Today, she is unlocking the community garden gate on LaGuardia Street near the statue of the former chubby mayor, his toe turned out.

Your head is going this way and that.

Look at you, taking in the morning.

But, dear dog, you are not the only animal in town.

ZOO

MOMMALA

LOCATION
Windsor Terrace, Brooklyn

RENT
$717 (rent stabilized)

SQUARE FEET
725 (one-bedroom apartment in 1961
elevator building)

OCCUPANT
Francie Albert (transition
coordinator/guidance counselor
for alternative high schools in
Manhattan)

**You walked in and she was on the
table naked.**
They groomed her and her hair was so
short. [*To dog*] Yes, you're like a little dream,
mommy's little dream. Oooh, yes. [*To me*]
I really don't want to say the O-word.
She likes to go [*Whispers*] out for walks, to
restaurants.

She has her little teeth around my pen.
No one turns her away—Le Zinc, Plumeria.
They're all in TriBeCa. We go to the small
dog run in Tompkins Square Park. They
used to be together with all these big punk
dogs. You just couldn't take a small dog.

But why not nearby Prospect Park?
No enclosed dog area. She has issues. She
never barks, but she's fearless and outgoing.
[*To dog*] Oooh, mommy-waammy. [*To me*] I
got her in a pet store in Bay Ridge. There
was another dog, really peppy. He was

starting to bite my shoes. He was too much
for my lifestyle.

**You're near Connecticut Muffin, the
park entrance with the high stone
columns with carved leaves—someone
was playing "Oh, Don-na/oh, Don-na"—
and the 1930s bar Farrell's with the
men standing in the brown gloom. Do
you go to restaurants around here?**
Aych! A few opened but nothing good.

**You moved into your 1961 LeFrak
building eight years ago. You said
you grew up in a late-1940s LeFrak
in Gravesend. A disinterested party
told me that LeFrak buildings are
always nicely built. Later, Mr. Cortese,
the LeFrak PR person, said that Sam
LeFrak's grandfather Aaron started
the company in 1901. He came from
France but, "They were somewhere
before that." Then there was the
Second World War, and thus "the
impetus for the company to enjoy its
enormous success, and it has built more
than 200,000 apartments, including
the 5,000-unit LeFrak City in Corona,
Queens. We name the buildings
after trees, presidents, colleges. But
we're running out of names—trees,
presidents, colleges." LeFrak buildings,
he said, are "typically six-story red-
brick with indoor garages, a bench in
back with a little play area for moms to
sit on." That's where they trained war
babies. By the way, the white balconies
outside, the empty green hallway, the
pink glass perfume bottles on your
dresser—it all looks kind of Hitchcock,**

JAY MUHLIN

like someone could get murdered here and a record would be stuck playing over and over. Do you have one of the balconies?

No, but this one-bedroom is bigger than the ones with the balconies. I got my pink glass from abroad, Czechoslovakia. I traveled with a friend…

Your ex-boyfriend you mentioned?

Not the ex. My life can get confusing. [*To dog*] No biting! Be nice, mommy, mommy—*no!* [*To me*] Sometimes she tears up her wee-wee pad when I go to work. [*To dog*] Yes, yes, you mommala.

I guess this isn't very Hitchcock. Do your parents still live in their LeFrak building?

They moved to Penn South in Chelsea. They were on the list fourteen years. My father worked twenty years in Phil Donahue's building on Fifth Avenue as an elevator operator. They went to Penn South because it's centrally located. I'm from Gravesend, *Saturday Night Fever*, Avenue X. I lived that life—DAs, gold heels. My hair, it still looks the same 'cause I'm into the retro. I've progressed from the moment. I always had it in my mind to leave.

Like John Travolta in the movie?

Right, they're sitting near the water. My ex was a local yokel. He was in fashion. Now he's a personal trainer. We lived in Brighton Beach. The story of my life is that I can't get out of Brooklyn. My parents got out. They wear black.

Will you move to Penn South?

I'm on some lists—Independence Plaza on North Moore. These huge buildings with below-market rents, subsidized. Now people won't be moving out at all after 9-11. People downtown are getting financial incentives to stay. It's backing up the list. [*To dog*] Oooh, you, mommy-mommy.

September 18, 2002

BIG AS PENCILS

LOCATION
Greenwich Village, Manhattan

RENT
$1,950 (market)

SQUARE FEET
1,500 (two-story apartment in 1841 building)

OCCUPANTS
Dug McDowell (coproducer, Pork at the Lure; live-act producer, Black Party), Kate Wagner (chef)

We are examining a miniature scale model of your apartment that you made after you were in the slammer.

[DUG] Yes, I started working on it the minute I got out of jail. I was just in for two weeks. See, last year this guy was staying with me. My roommate Kate said, "Gee, he seems to have a lot of guests." One night I was sleeping and eight storm troopers kicked the door open with two SWAT guys in black masks. While I was napping, this houseguest had brought five friends over and I guess there were things on the dining room table. If drugs are in plain view, everybody on the premises is charged equally with possession. In the end, the guy took the rap. The lawyer wanted a plan of the apartment so he could show my bedroom was back here and drugs were not in plain view of me. See, I used little flat wire for the models of my Barcelona chairs. I still can't get the Wassily

chair right. I've lived in this apartment almost twelve years. They've never raised the rent. The person who owned the building died. I've been on month-to-month since '98.

In the dining room, hidden under Indian blankets—a few feet from the baked ham and lavish dinner that Kate has prepared—are glass cages with an eight-foot boa constrictor and his partner, a four-and-a-half-foot python who I wish would drop dead. Just thinking about them sliding around in their cases with their horrible round selves makes me want to jump out the window.

There, there. I've had the snakes eight years, since they were as big as pencils. I've always taken in strays. I grew up on a horse ranch in central California. You *have* to feed the snakes *live* food. Of course, they only eat two days a month—they are all about efficiency. One eats two live rats, the other eats just one...

I can't believe we're having this conversation.

Well, this marine I knew who was a security guard for FBI headquarters—there's like penthouse housing for marines over the FBI building—he was breeding boas, green opalescent. They glistened like CDs. He could get $400 a snake. One year he made $16,000, bought himself a Jeep.

How could the marines let him breed snakes in New York?

These men are *assassins*. They don't want them to have hobbies like *knitting*. So he brought me one snake as a gift and told me to watch the other. He's never been back. I've had fifteen roommates. They've all been crazy. One installed a washer and dryer. I had no interest in a washer and dryer. Our living room is the color of makeup and dessert—pumpkin custard. I used my piercing jewelry to make tassels for the curtains. Here are some barbed-wire snakes on the wall. Don't think of them as snakes, think of them as sperm and egg. I like conceptual levels, physics. Kate—who's from Hawaii—she lives in the tower with the silver walls, that's on the second level. You can go out on the roof. That's where we watch the Halloween parade.

Is this cage with the metal chains and the rings for the snakes?
[KATE] That's for humans.

As a producer of Pork at the Lure on Wednesday nights, you helped invent a favorite "Shelter" concept, "Sadist in a Shack."
[DUG] My former roommate Peter and I designed it. We went from a two- to a four-wall construction—put in a porch, dirty mattress, beer cans all over the place. Peter's the sadist and he goes inside and tortures people and then guests watch through the slits.

Now what's *this* room in your apartment—*more* metal rings and the chains?
It used to be the dungeon. Then we painted it lavender and rented it to people on holiday. This house is like the center of the universe, like Grandma's house. It's the only place in the Village where our friends can drop by and go to the bathroom. We call it stop and plop.

May 15, 2001

THEY'LL NEVER BREAK SKIN

LOCATION
Prospect Heights, Brooklyn

RENT
$950 (market)

SQUARE FEET
900 (duplex in 1987 walk-up)

OCCUPANT
Ntozake Lundy (owner, the Chocolate Monkey and Muddy Waters Tea & Espresso)

Don't call off the dogs.
They are *so* bad.

Are they related?
No. I found Sylvester on the street. Phoebe I got in Tinton Falls. They're pointers. [*To Sylvester*] Right, big boy? You're going to stay with Mommy forever.

You have a double water trough for them.
[DOGS] Slurp, slurp, slurp. [NTOZAKE] That's Mama's baby boy.

Such big bones lying around. [*Sylvester scratches himself with his paw. I take off my sweater.*] It's warm in here. It must be the dogs. Now, your apartment history— so epic.
It was a nightmare. Last year alone, I moved three times. The first apartment was great. I loved the landlord, right near my cafe in Prospect Heights. Rent was $650. Then he had to put it on the market. I decided to leave early. He gave me back some rent though he still owed me half a month. I let it go because I'd often paid late and he never freaked out. Well, his ex-wife, who bought the apartment with him in college, came to pick up the keys to show it. My boyfriend, Anthony, and I had cleaned the place spotless because we wanted to get my security deposit back. She hated the color I had painted the place and went around to Muddy Waters and went ballistic on the barista working the counter and demanded that she help her tidy up the apartment. I wish I were exaggerating but when I got to work, Amy was in tears and all our cleaning supplies were gone. The landlord called and said he was sorry about his ex-wife. He gave me twice my refund back. I was so astounded but this was nothing in comparison to the ordeal of my next place. [*We stop to kiss Sylvester.*] My baby boy wakes me up in the morning with kisses, with kisses. Anthony and I had decided to shack up since he was always at my place anyway. I found a two-bedroom in Sunset Park for $1,150. The landlord must have called me fifty times to find out when he could come pick up the two months' rent and security. I should have understood that's a sign someone is desperate for cash. Three thousand dollars?! When Anthony came over to see the apartment, he noticed, as men will, so many structural issues. We asked the landlord if he could fix what appeared to be a leak in the bedroom and we noticed the carpet was brown, which might indicate a radiator leak. He told us

he was not fixing anything. If we didn't like it we could leave without our money. Anthony talked him into doing some things. That day Anthony did not go to work at his job at Home Depot. The landlord never came. I refused to pay rent but we'd already given him three months'. [*Sylvester walks over.*] What are you so happy about, precious? I'd come home. There was never any heat. My dogs were freezing all the time. I was on the phone with HPD every day. A few months later I got a notice to appear at a rent hearing. The judge informed me that unless I have all the back rent, I'd be removed by the marshal. A friend said I should call her landlords. I did. I love them. I moved here. The other thing isn't over. There's a hearing in a few weeks.

How much has this cost you?
It eventually cost $15,000 in lawyer's fees and back rent. [*Growling begins. Sylvester*

jumps on top of Phoebe and opens his jaws around her head.]

It's getting rough in here.
I'm so sorry.

It's exciting. So primal, in the middle of the afternoon.
[*She says something.*]

I can't hear you with all the roaring.
[*Yells.*] I said, they'll never break skin.

Look at those teeth. I guess it's so if they have to pick up a partridge.
It's this wrestling thing they do. I want him to have an active life. He's my baby.

December 1, 2004

SHIHO FUKADA

COCK OF THE WALK

LOCATION
Greenpoint, Brooklyn

RENT
$930 (no lease)

SQUARE FEET
334 (one-bedroom apartment in tenement building)

OCCUPANT
Kimberly Lane
(property controller, Christie's)

This rooster business…
I moved into this apartment in February. At first I was a little hesitant. It was the first time I'd lived alone. The first night, I go to bed, I freak. There was this sound…

Wait, I just heard a sound…
That's different, the people downstairs have a, I don't know what it is.

It's whimpering.
Anyway, it was 4:30 in the morning. I can't even describe it, like a loud animal. Oh my God, what's that noise? Then it was like—OK, I have a rooster in the backyard. I didn't think anything of it. The next night and the next, it kept waking me. So then I tried to file a complaint with the city to get the rooster removed. It belongs to the man in the next building. I asked the guy in the apartment next to me. He's an architect. I saw him at the Pencil Factory. I said,

"What's going on with the rooster." [*Regis and Kelly are on the television in the background.*] He said, "What rooster?" His apartment faces the front so I guess he didn't hear. So then I tried to file a complaint, I think it was with Animal Care and Control. I called ASPCA also. I went back and forth. They said, "We don't do it, we don't do it." Whoever said I needed to know the name of the owner of the pet. The first step is that they send a letter. I had to first see if his name was on the mailbox—no.

The mailboxes are a little informal in this row of buildings. The front door's open.
It always is. I called the community board. They had a list of everybody in all the buildings. I got the name of the person on the first floor. I called back. They said, "OK, we're going to send out a letter."

Did anything happen?
No. I finally got used to the rooster and started sleeping through.

The woman on TV is talking about how she had a guinea pig as a pet. I just heard more whimpering downstairs.
Last spring, then summer, the rooster would start going off later and later. When I first moved in, it was four, 4:30 in the morning. Now he goes off at 6:30.

The time's changing. He'll be on his early schedule again.
Yeah.

Then you said for a few months, you didn't hear him.

Yeah, I thought my problem was solved. I was calling everyone, my parents: "Oh, the rooster's gone." Everyone was, like, "Oh, what happened?" Everyone was, like, "Maybe he raises it for cockfights, uses it for voodoo."

What's that sound?
That's the clucking, hens and stuff.

Hens too? Hens sound like they're laughing. I feel like I'm in some children's story but an urban one. Hello, Mr. Rooster. Well hello there, Mrs. Hen. Did you lay an egg? No, not yet, Mr. Rooster. Here's hoping. Cluck, cluck, good luck. And so forth. Then later in the book one or the other would feel excluded and there would be class distinctions but in the end they would realize that all that mattered in life was being a good hen and/or rooster. [We look out the window.] There's the rooster, black with a red crown. It's such a mess down there, all the garbage. There's the hen. There's another bird. It looks like a partridge. Is that a rabbit sitting on top of the garbage?
He has a brown bunny and a black one. Oh, there's a black-and-white bunny. I have friends who stay over. They hear the noise. I say, "Oh, it's just my rooster, don't mind."

Who's your landlord?
He's Polish. He lives in New Jersey.

Why don't you have a lease?
When I asked for a lease, he said, "Do you have one?" I said, "No, don't you?"

November 3, 2004

HELP ME KILL THE BUG

LOCATION
Hell's Kitchen, Manhattan

RENT
$750 (rent stabilized)

SQUARE FEET
270 (one-bedroom apartment in
tenement building)

OCCUPANTS
Keith Rizza (freelance photographer),
Carl Ferrero (graphic designer,
Penguin Putnam)

The two of you are on the edge of the sofa with your hands folded.
[BOTH] We just quit smoking.

The jitters! Your sofa is a brown, black, and beige weave. In fact, everything in here is woven or it's a storage basket or a bundle of birch branches.
[KEITH] I'm used to a warm kind of house.
[CARL] I'm a big fan of wood.

Is incense burning?
[KEITH] It's probably my cologne—
Shiseido, Feminite du Bois.

You know, a smell is a whole place in itself. It can be a room with furniture. In the case of your cologne, perhaps a room in Asia in the early sixties. As Gaston Bachelard mentioned in his *The Poetics of Space*, when he was writing about raisins...
That's kind of what I'm going for, kind of Asia.

Let's get into something meatier. So how did you find this place?
Actually, five years ago I saw an apartment in this same building through my friend's sister. At the time I said, "No way on God's green earth am I going to live in Hell's Kitchen." The neighborhood was boring and depressing and had no character. When I first came to New York, I thought it would really be nice to live in the West Village, SoHo. They were all out of my price range. I'd come to go to school at Pratt. Then I moved in with my first boyfriend, who had a beautiful apartment in Chelsea. But then I broke up with him. I had to start doing roommate situations. I lived with insane people constantly. At one point I was sleeping where the front door was literally two feet from my bed. My roommates would come home at three in the morning with friends. Years passed. I heard about another apartment in this building and I didn't have to think twice. I'd learned that living in New York is about getting a good space at a good price. Meanwhile, the neighborhood has been changing. A lot more people my age and with the same taste as me are starting to move in. It looks like more tax dollars are going to fix the sidewalks and streets. Nicer stores are opening up. Of course, when I moved into this apartment, it was not a pretty sight. It was really dirty and infested with bugs. I talked to different people about

what to do. A lot had success with Combat roach bait. I had professionals come in, bomb three times. I'm petrified of roaches. I start crying when I see one. When I saw the first one, I flipped out so much that I had to call someone on the phone to help me kill the bug. They had to talk me through it. I was in hysterics. I sealed up every crack in the apartment. This place is always clean— clean behind places you wouldn't even know. I think the people who lived here must have been absolute animals. I found condoms behind the stove.

Did they toss them over when they went to make coffee? So what are your favorite cleaning supplies?
Comet, Windex, bleach, ammonia, and Murphy's oil soap. Anything that sterilizes.

Carl, before you moved in with Keith three months ago you had a problem with pigeons.

[CARL] I used to live on Pitt Street. The building I lived in was one step from being condemned. It was covered with pigeons. They never went away. They were just crawling all over, nesting everywhere. [KEITH] You couldn't even see outside some of his windows, there was so much poop.

Keith, did you start cleaning Carl's place?
He didn't have tilt-out windows, so you couldn't reach the outside. But Carl is a *very* clean person. Though he has a cat. It's kind of hairy. And now the cat is here. I vacuum twice a week.

Keith must be a joy to live with. He's so tidy.
[CARL] Tell me about it.

February 23, 1999

SANDRA-LEE PHIPPS

A LOT OF HOMICIDE

LOCATION
Lower East Side, Manhattan

RENT
$2,000 (market)

SQUARE FEET
1,200 (four-bedroom apartment over store)

OCCUPANTS
John Christian Huebert (real-estate agent), Nathan Azhderian (art student, Cooper Union), Adrian Salonga (assistant media planner, Communications Media), Fritz Vidanes (intern, Ford Models)

What I saw on the way! I passed through Chinatown—mushrooms, cashews, lavender underwear—then Mendel Goldberg Fabrics with a palmetto print in the window, Gertel's Bakery, Bialystoker Place where a man was on a bench with his stomach sticking out and he was saying, "Oh, that guy was fired." Then, the modernist Henrietta Szold School of Nursing and, of course, Rheba Liebowitz Square, and the store on the corner with the bananas.
[JOHN] That's us.

So, everyone's in their early twenties and sitting upright. Fritz, what a great name you have.
[FRITZ] I hate my name. It sounds like a butler. I'm from Atlanta. I needed to move because it got really boring and I had to do the New York thing. I moved to New Jersey first. I wasn't a fan of Jersey. I looked for an apartment for a month. I was stressing. I came here to see this and I had to take it on the spot. [JOHN] Oh, man. [FRITZ] There was a girl looking at the same room I was looking at. She wanted to see something else. I said, "I want it now." I felt bad. She had just come from Israel. [JOHN] I found it first through our office in Manhattan, Best Apartments. We got this weird listing on our computer. We've got like forty agents in a room. Everybody said, 1,200 feet—what's with this? I went down and showed it to two girls. They said, "We'd never live here." It was a real dump. Then my family came up and helped. We just sort of threw on stuff to make the floors more level. We made the market value a lot higher. No, none of us knew each other before. I moved in September 1. [NATHAN] I used to share a twelve-by-eight room on 14th Street, $525. At the end, it was bad news. I'm from Sonoma County, California. I'm kind of adjusting to the city. [JOHN] I'm from Williamsport, Pennsylvania—Little League World Series. [FRITZ] When your mom came here, she was walking around in her T-shirt. [JOHN] "I Got Squished." She got the T-shirt on Rosie O'Donnell. [ADRIAN] Fritz said, "What's that?"

So.
There's a lot of homicide here. We kill mice and rats. [JOHN] Adrian went all the way up to the Upper East Side. [ADRIAN] I got traps. Some people here free them.

Who is the humane one? Oh, John, the salesman! How interesting.
Oh yeah, there was the Tin Cat, a mousetrap that can fit about eight mice. It electrocutes. You can smell the burning flesh. The guy said, "I don't normally sell that to people because they'd forget." He didn't realize that I'd check it every morning. [JOHN] We used the dry vac on one of them. *Foonnk.* [ADRIAN] It suffocated.

Nice, gray, wraparound leather couch.
[JOHN] Yeah, that's me. All this was bought at bargain prices. We probably look richer than we actually are. [ADRIAN] He's a big-time hitter like Donald Trump. [JOHN] The business has its ups and downs. If I work alone, I get a forty percent cut of the fee. The boss was generous enough not to charge me a fee here. This guy's got a motorcycle. [ADRIAN] A Ducati Monster.

Fritz, what are you thinking about right now?
[FRITZ] Nothing.

Do you have a romantic life, other than the mice?

[ADRIAN] Groan. [NATHAN] My girlfriend's in California. [JOHN] I just got out of a relationship, a couple of days ago.

I bet you always have girlfriends.
After I rent to clients, we go and make out in empty apartments. [ADRIAN] Waive the fee. [JOHN] Increase the fee. [ADRIAN] This is my room, the boom-boom room. That's the new Outkast album.

Who are your neighbors?
[JOHN] Four girls upstairs. [ADRIAN] I think they're socially repressed. [NATHAN] You only met one of them. [ADRIAN] Stop writing. Take away her pen. Fritz is the beating heart of the apartment. [FRITZ] Everyone thinks I have a life. But if you knock on my door, I'm sleeping.

October 22, 2003

CLOVEN HOOVES

LOCATION
Fort Greene, Brooklyn

RENT
$1,300 (market)

SQUARE FEET
600 (studio apartment in tenement building)

OCCUPANTS
Kelli Miller (master's student in architecture), Jason Loewenstein (musician)

Well, a pig.
[PIG] Snork, grunt. [JASON] Come on, Bub. [*He goes to his water bowl.*]

That's a big one.
[KELLI] One hundred and five pounds. When we found him, he very easily fit on your lap. It was on the streets in Louisville. He was just in the gutter.

Lying there.
He was standing up nosing through the leaves. We found him two homes. They returned him each time. [JASON] Within a day. [KELLI] At that age, he required a lot of attention.

What kind?
He pees for a very long time. [JASON] We're talking minutes, five at least.

Is he housebroken?
[KELLI] Yes. [*She smiles.*] When he lived with the dogs, they didn't let him mess up. They taught him the ropes. When we moved here, they all slept together. When the dogs died, he slept with us for quite some time. That was three years ago. [JASON] For farm pigs, he's well over the offing point. [KELLI] He's not a farm pig. [JASON] The Jamaicans up the road totally want him. At first it was a joke. Now it's relentless. They'll be chopping a coconut: "Come here, pig." [KELLI] They don't even eat meat.

What is he thinking about mostly?
He talks to us all the time. He just stands in front of us and yells—urrrg, urrrg, urrrg, urrrg.

How long does he go on?
A long time.

Do you have to clean him?
I bathe him once every month and a half—in the bathtub. He doesn't have an odor of his own.

Like an actor.
He picks up the odor of dryer sheets, whatever the blanket smells like. He's a little territorial about the apartment. [*She shrugs.*] He kind of doesn't like people.

Right now he's in his cage snoozing but what would he do?
He'd kind of lunge. It's just sudden—as soon as you cross our door. Outside, he's very sweet. Little kids surround him at the

park. He has two sets of tusks. We have to have them cut every month.

Do you know others who have pigs?
[KELLI, *to Jason*] You know one in DUMBO. [JASON] Just rumored.

Let's get him off his blanket. [*He works his way over and lies at Kelli's feet, eye open.*] I don't understand why pigs are so fat. I'm not saying that your pig is fat or anything.
[KELLI] He only eats a cup and a half of kibble a day. They have young formula, adult, and mature. [JASON] His favorite fruit is pears. [KELLI] He won't eat the florets of broccoli. The Jamaicans on the corner give him mangoes. [JASON] Sometimes he'll run off with them like a dog.

The pigs were the organizers in *Animal Farm*.
[KELLI] He's such a higher thinker. We got the crate in June. Before, if we weren't here, he'd open the refrigerator and take what he wanted. He'd get very angry at us. Once we walked in on him. [JASON] He had built a ladder and he was climbing on it. [KELLI] He'd wedged a chair and the gate to where he could get up on the table where we kept his food. If we don't pay attention to him, he'll take CDs out of the cabinet.

How long does it take him to get up the stairs, with that big bottom of his?
He's just like lightning when he wants to be. [JASON] Three flights in five minutes.

Was he ever a father?
[KELLI] I had him neutered the day after I found him. The smell!

Can I pet him?
Yes. [PIG] Arrrugh. [KELLI] He's always moody. The first three years were really hard. I'll call it the terrible twos. He was angry all the time. I even looked for a pig psychologist. There's one in Texas. [JASON] The thing about it was he was so far away.

September 21, 2005

CARY CONOVER

75

HER

LOCATION
Jackson Heights, Queens
PRICE
$19,500 in 1929
SQUARE FEET
3,000 (three-story 1929 brick row house)
OCCUPANTS
Mary Ferrera (retired fashion designer's assistant), Richard Saja (art director, DCA Advertising)

You live together! You're not like Harold and Maude or anything?

[RICHARD] No! Mary's my grandfather's first cousin. Technically she's my third cousin, but I call her my aunt. I'm thirty-five. [MARY] I'm eighty-eight.

The eave over the door looks like it's made out of gingerbread. The pink-and-green flowered sofa is lovely.

These are the summer slipcovers. [RICHARD] We haven't changed over for winter yet. [MARY] See that planter... [RICHARD] It's a jardinière. [MARY] My father made it. He was a woodworker. [RICHARD] From Italy. [MARY] All the Europeans brought culture with them. They had a... [RICHARD] A craft! [MARY] I've lived here ever since the house was built, 1929. It was all country around here. A man was in business with bees down the street. He had honeycombs. We'd do our homework under the trees.

Alice in Wonderland!

Gradually, everything changed. There were Quonset homes on Northern Boulevard. Then it became a business area, apartment houses. My friends are gone now. Seventy-fourth became an Indian neighborhood. I more or less snubbed it. Now I've changed my mind. [RICHARD] I think I had something to do with that. [MARY] These people are immigrants. My people were considered immigrants ninety years ago.

The hall upstairs is red.

[RICHARD] Her mother wanted walls that looked like roses. [MARY] Don't look in my room. We had a flood. [RICHARD] She has a tenant upstairs who's in her nineties. She's been here fifty years. The tenant was watching the Olympics and left the water running in the bathroom sink for three days. [MARY] I was so stressed. Look in the guest room. This is the desk my father made us when we were children. I had beautiful parents. [RICHARD] This is my room. I'd say I have 3,000 CDs. And *Nest* magazine, the complete set. [MARY] My sister died ten years ago. She lived here with me. Neither one of us married. Both of us intended to get married at one time. It just didn't turn out. We were happy with what we had. We didn't turn out to be bitter old maids. [RICHARD] Not at all. Mary's very busy. She just went to Atlantic City. She used to be a designer's assistant. [MARY] They gave me the sketches, I draped the fabric. I worked with Pat Sandler, Frank Massandrea. The boys are all dead now, AIDS. We worked on Seventh. Once I worked for Elsa Schiaparelli. I had to run after the models and hold up their gowns.

When did Richard come?

Three years ago. I was crossing the street. A taxi ran right into me. They made me a knee out of my hip. [RICHARD] It was just the time I was moving out of a house. It seemed ideal—I could come and help her with things. It just settled into a more permanent relationship. I was born in Point Pleasant, New Jersey. I came to New York in 1983. [MARY] He lived with us part of the summer as a child. My sister and he were pals. She took him everywhere. [RICHARD] The Guggenheim, the Marvel Comics office. I brought my little portfolio.

How do you get along?

[MARY] We manage to have dinners together every night. [RICHARD] Well, when I'm home. I have a pretty active social life. A lot of my friends come here to stay when they're in town. Sometimes back-to-back. [MARY] I think he's comfortable. I don't interfere with his life. [RICHARD] She tells me, "The weather is cool, put on a coat." [MARY] Once in a while he doesn't listen. As a rule, we don't get into one another's hair. But if I need Richard, I think he'll be there. There's one thing about us. We both love that thing that's on the floor. [RICHARD] Her. [MARY] The cat.

November 21, 2000

THE CHIHUAHUA AND THE ECHIDNA

LOCATION
Grand Concourse District, Bronx

PRICE
$20,000 in 2000 ($277 maintenance)

SQUARE FEET
550 (one-bedroom co-op in six-story 1920s building)

OCCUPANT
Jim Comeau (freelance photographer; program assistant, Advantage Testing)

What is your Chihuahua doing?
He's humping the echidna.

What's an echidna?
It's an Australian animal. This is a toy.

The Chihuahua won't stop.
I've had him five years and he never did it with the other animals. When I went to Australia, I got him some others but it wasn't the same. This one I bought in Brooklyn, on Bedford. Within a matter of hours, he was humping it.

He might have a medical condition.
He'll bite it for two hours sometimes. He had a Cabbage Patch Doll but nothing

happened. And he's fixed. I had a birthday party a few months ago. Of course, he got excited and was humping the echidna. His lipstick got a little too far out. It took a while to get it back in.

We've really got to get onto the Finnish topic. So this co-op, Varma Cooperative Homes, was started by a Finnish community in 1925 and everybody was Finnish. Then I read that the first nonprofit or limited-dividend co-op was a Finnish one, the Alku in Sunset Park, in 1916. That inspired others like this and inspired the acceptance of the cooperative movement throughout the United States. In 1900, the city had 9,845 Finns, according to the census. In 1930 there were 20,043. In 1970, there were only 6,954.
The buildings were owned by Jewish people originally. In the 1980s things changed hands a bit here, and now it's primarily Asian. When we have co-op meetings, sometimes they have interpreters who speak Mandarin.

He's still doing it. I'm going to lift the echidna in the air. He goes right with it. He's just trembling.
He likes it rough, too.

Why is there a single wooden chair painted white on each floor?
I don't know, a Finnish touch.

You are just one block from Yankee Stadium. It looks all silver on top, from the lights. I heard people on the train coming here. This one woman kept

saying—though you could tell she would probably rather be home reading—"Oh, I'm so psyched." Everyone walking on the street has a single purpose—the game! Their eyes look like they are in a cult. There was a man with all gold teeth. People are crawling around outside your building, jumping up, hitting signs. There is a lot of banging. It wears on me a bit. Look, I can see the bleachers from my bathroom. You know the Yankees lost when they have Liza Minnelli singing "New York, New York." When they win, it's Frank Sinatra.

Liza's pathos.
A neighbor told me that Leonard Bernstein's personal assistant lived in my apartment. [*Jeannine Comeau, Jim's sister, comes in. She also has an apartment in the building.*] [JEANNINE] I work on *Law & Order*. I started as a stand-in. I'm the D.A.'s secretary. [JIM] We both moved to New York at the same time. [JEANNINE] We lived together five and a half years. [JIM] She's a slob. We were on 23rd Street. I slept in the hallway. She slept in the living room. The place was a dump. Steve Croman was our landlord. The *Voice* voted him one of the ten worst landlords a few years ago. [JEANNINE] One of my friends used to live on the Grand Concourse. I saw the sign advertising this. [JIM] Within two weeks, we bought our places. We grew up in Woburn, Massachusetts. We're very close. People think we're twins. We just vacationed in Florida. We went to Ireland last summer.

What are these miniature metal swords? Each one is in a holder.
My mom got them in the fifties. [JEANNINE] They're olive picks. Our mother died three years ago. I took her to the hospital on a Monday. She died the following Monday. She had lymphoma. [JIM] We were very close to her.

It's lucky you have each other.
Yes. Once at 4 a.m., I went to her apartment and just broke down.

That Chihuahua's going to collapse.

May 12, 2004

SHIHO FUKADA

A CUP OF TEA

LOCATION
Red Hook, Brooklyn

RENT
$650 (market)

SQUARE FEET
800 (two-story 1800s wooden back house)

OCCUPANTS
Sister Olivia Clifford,
Sister Dorothy Flaum

I like the rabbit welcome sign on the gate outside. There's another: "Sursum Corda."
[DOROTHY] It's Latin for "Lift up your hearts." Come in out of the rain. Catherine McAuley said, "Whenever you welcome a guest, offer them a comfortable cup of tea."

I read that she was the founder of your order, the Sisters of Mercy—ever hear of the band, kind of Goth? Anyway, she established the first house in Ireland in 1827 to serve women and children from the Dublin slums. The Sisters of Mercy were called "walking nuns," the first to circulate among the poor. They nursed victims of cholera, earthquakes, and floods. It's so cozy in your kitchen, with the ruffled curtains with sunflowers on them and the teapot. I feel like I'm in County Cork near the sea, though we're only in Brooklyn—but Red Hook has

that salty quality. You've lived together twenty-five years! What's up this tiny staircase, so old?
[OLIVIA] We have a chapel up here. We have mass. [DOROTHY] Sometimes it's just us, sometimes other people come.

Here's your videotape collection: Victor Borge, Meet Me in St. Louis, Lassie's Great Adventure. But you do most of your living on the first floor. Didn't one of you have two knee replacements?
Yes, but I'm able to get upstairs. I was just at Dancing in the Streets' Dance Swap. It was in that new club, Red Hook Blue.

Who were your partners?
[OLIVIA] Somebody might grab you and say, "Do this." [DOROTHY] The MC would announce: the Bump. The place was packed.

You're both from Flatbush. Did you want to be nuns early on?
It was Deanna Durbin's era, so I wanted to be an opera singer. Simply because I could hold a tune. But being in a very practically minded family... [OLIVIA] I was the *great* actress, of course. Vilma Banky—I could act just like she could. [DOROTHY] You're still good at it. You do good impersonations. [*Olivia blushes.*] We spent our novitiate in Syosset, Long Island—six months in long black dresses, widow's weeds. Then a black habit, white veil. We were assigned to St. Mary's Children and Family Services for dependent and neglected delinquent boys. That's where we met. In 1978, we moved to Red Hook and opened a residence for

developmentally disabled teenagers. We lived right there with them, across from Visitation Church. [OLIVIA] Now we're retired, or recycled, we call it. We found we were not only working with residents but with the people in the parish. So we looked for a place here. [DOROTHY] The Seaman Center had an apartment available. [OLIVIA] It belonged to the Port Authority and people thought it might not be a safe place for us. Then we looked at an apartment over a coffee shop. You had to enter by fire escape. The rent was too high. Then a realtor took us here. We told him right off, we can't afford the rent. He called the owner. He said, "You're not going to like the rent but you're going to like the people." The owner was delighted. He did come down in the rent. He's never raised it since. That was 1991. He's Bud Fisher, who had a bar near here years ago, Bud & Packy's. When we moved in, people said, "Oh, Rose Fisher's garden was never without people." [DOROTHY] We decided we're about people and witnessing to people and we would do as Rose did and entertain in the yard. We have a Welcome to Spring party and Farewell to Summer. We have some butterfly bushes out there. They attract butterflies. And we have azaleas, tulips, lilies. The dog is buried out there. [OLIVIA] Don't say that; it's not legal. [DOROTHY] The vet said we could as long as the grave is down far enough. He has a fitting headstone: "Brownie 1984–1998." [OLIVIA] We picked him up on the street. He was beautiful. [DOROTHY] Handsome! And so smart.

Are you going to be in the Earth and Surf Parade May 18? That's the day Red Hook comes alive!
Of course. Last year, I rode in a convertible.

May 21, 2002

MICHAEL KAMBER

I was waiting for a clipper ship to come in with gold, cardamom, and maybe some carpets. The black four-masted Peking with the gold letters has been parked here for years, rocking against the dock, but it never goes anywhere. Who will bring the Indian tea, the cotton from Alabama?

The water is empty. Here comes the Circle Line with the cargo now. Everybody is getting off in their shorts. They are going to have Mai Tais.

The South Street Seaport was one of the most important ports in the world until the late 1800s, when boats got too large and moved to the deeper waters of the Hudson. Then Marlon Brando worked there, and when someone tried to flatter him, he said, "Enough of the birdseed." Now shipping is in container ports in New Jersey. The fish market is moving up to the Bronx. Iceberg Tommy and Shrimp Sammy will be leaving. Will Shopping Bag Annie go along?

The East River is so narrow and has such tidal fluctuation and depth changes that it could suck a person into darkness and no return. In the 1800s, some brothels, they say, had trap doors that rolled the customers into the water. Then there was a bookie who was found floating one day, shot four times, with his feet bound. Not to mention the British frigate Hussar that sank near Hell Gate during the Revolutionary War and was full of prisoners chained below deck. It is as if the East River has a black gloved hand, a long glove to the elbow. It is reaching up to get you. You have to be careful of that river.

New Yorkers have always had a hands-holding-head conflict between land and sea—steak or lobster. Even though the city began as a great port and its money came from trade, the rich never wanted to live near all the sailors because they might get scurvy or become opium addicts. They preferred to live on the earthy middle of Fifth Avenue. Today, water is all the rage. People are moving to DUMBO, Red Hook, and the West Side Highway. You can hear the steel drums of island life as you skirt the deep where the sirens call, God is mad at Odysseus, and mermaids comb their hair with seashells. There is a sound of blows, a scuffle. Oh matey, the treasure lies beneath in a sunken ship.

WATER

THE SEA IS HIS MISTRESS

LOCATION
Hudson River, across from the World Trade Center, Manhattan

PRICE
$20,000 in 2000 ($750 dockage fee)

SQUARE FEET
34 (1972 sailboat)

OCCUPANT
Colin Stanfield (production manager, Independent Feature Project; saxophone player)

Hey sailor, got a match? Who would have thought that to board your apartment, I mean, boat, one would have to pass through white marble halls with clapping tourists, 5,000 gift shops—the World Trade Center—and then move outside to the vast stone plaza of the North Cove and get on the water taxi to your marina, where all you can hear is the lonely creaking of the boats in the gray soup of a fog. You've been living on the water, with the sea as your mistress, for almost a year. Is this a real-estate alternative?

It's not really cheaper than living in an apartment. You have to *buy* the boat. I have a mortgage. Dockage fees can run to $5500 a season. I'm at Liberty Landing now. Chelsea Piers is more expensive—I

was there in the summer, but they close in winter. I'll be back at Chelsea April 15. One guy there, an actuary, has quite a livable boat—real couch, refrigerator. I moved to New York from Canada two years ago. I was sharing an apartment with a friend in Chelsea. I'd always toyed with getting a boat. I had friends living on boats in other cities. I bought one, took my stuff right down 22nd Street, most painless move ever. I just threw all my furniture in the garbage, which is where I got some of it in the first place.

It's pretty intimate in your cabin, with its two-foot passageway. We're squashed in the bunk with six portable heaters cooking. Do you, ah, have a girlfriend?
Yes, I do.

Oh.
This cabin is like a really small studio. I wouldn't advocate it for a lot of people. I did a seven-day trip with three friends to the East Hampton Film Festival. There's so much work keeping an old boat together. It's a commitment to becoming a handyman, which is exacerbated by living aboard. You become keenly aware of everything you'd like to fix.

It's hard.
Also, some marinas don't encourage people to live aboard—there are all these issues, pro and con, about people living on the water. I participate in discussion groups online. The amount of information-sharing going on is extraordinary.

MICHAEL KAMBER

I skimmed through the live-aboard Web site. There were ninety-nine entries under suggestions for upgrading the AC circuitry and thirteen on the matter of installing tiles on a wooden boat. A man named Larry wrote in wondering why silicon adhesive didn't work. I got so dozy. I thought people on boats would be talking about the soft wind off Woona Woona. You have a Domino sugar package in the kitchen, some dish detergent. Let's turn our heads around and look at the ship's library. *The Water In Between* by Kevin Patterson. There he is on the book jacket with his beard.

He felt sorry for himself after he broke up with his girlfriend, and he sailed across the Atlantic by himself.

Seeking ruin and catastrophe! You have a book on Edie Sedgwick.

My mom gave me that. I grew up on a farm, hippie commune, Prince Edward Island.

Is that where you get your love for the sea?

From a very young age I considered myself a surfer guy. I used to teach windsurfing at a resort. I was in a band.

You must have been very popular with the guests.

I thought you'd be asking me more about the pros and cons of living on boats. You know, what's dangerous is they sink from time to time. There are all these holes in boats. Now if water gets in and freezes, it can crack, and in spring, when it thaws, there's a hole.

Can't we just cut loose and go to South America?

January 23, 2001

SEA OF LOVE

LOCATION
Sag Harbor, Suffolk County

RENT
$225 per weekend

SQUARE FEET
(two-story, six-and-a-half bedroom,
mid-nineteenth-century whaling
captain's house)

OCCUPANTS
Eight or nine people each weekend
(bankers, lawyers, insurance
underwriters, real-estate agents,
computer salespeople, etc.)

So Tony—you with the Monkey Bar hat and the golf club—you got here last night?
[TONY] Yeah, and boy were we howling. We were being, like, ma-has.

You were drinking Mai Tais?
No, ma-has, being like, you know, a maharajah. We were smoking cigars, having our cocktails at the American Hotel…

The white hotel with the red and blue bunting?
Yeah, then we went to Murfs, the dive bar behind the cop station. I'm just a guest at the house—I know a couple of the girls.

Debby, you've been renting a share here for five years?
[DEBBY] I take twelve out of seventeen weekends. We can come out during any

of the weekdays if we rent one weekend or more.

So, do you hang out mostly in one of the two living rooms with the wing chairs and the hunting-dog lithographs or in the kitchen with all the white semigloss enamel and the harpoon?
We're mainly on the porch or at the beach.

A race car driving show is on the television in the den.
ESPN is just always on. [TONY] I put it on 'cause I was feeling mopey.

Don't be mopey. Oh Tony! You're reading *Moby Dick*! Sag Harbor used to have a bustling whaling industry.
[TONY] I've been reading this book for two years. I'm struggling with it like Ahab struggled with the whale.

You said nine people are staying here this weekend and there are only six and a half bedrooms.
[DEBBY] One bedroom is called the Sea of Love Room. It got its name because it used to have a seafoam-green headboard. There's the Red Rum. [TONY] Murder spelled backwards like in *The Shining*. [DEBBY] I think Larry and Jean were in there last night. I don't know—it wasn't my turn to watch! [TONY] I stayed in the Voodoo Lounge, which is what we call the cottage out back. [DEBBY] I was in the room with the twin beds. It's not my favorite.

Steve, the volunteer house manager, said he changes room assignments every

week so early arrivals won't always get the best ones.
[TONY] Last night I could have slept on a slab. [DEBBY] It was extreme. [TONY] We were all decompressing. When you work as hard as we do, it's like a champagne bottle being uncorked.

Steve said more women rent summer shares because the men are busy in Manhattan dating younger women.
[SARAH] Whaaat! That's not true! [JEAN] Absolutely not. [SARAH] And anyway, I know so many women involved with younger men.

Since you all live alone in the city, wouldn't it be cozier to live together like this all the time?
[DEBBY] We talk about it sometimes. [SARAH] Coming out here is like being in high school, all the gossiping.

Maybe you could get a ski house?
[TONY] A ski house wouldn't be the same at all. You can't just lie around. You gotta get up and go whooossh.

August 12, 1997

GREG MILLER

EARLY MAN

LOCATION
Inwood, Manhattan

RENT
$1,002.60 (rent stabilized)

SQUARE FEET
700 (four-room apartment in 1907
building)

OCCUPANT
Captain Max Patterson (woodworker,
marine and terrestrial)

You have a captain's certificate: "Master of Steam, Motor, or Auxiliary Sail Vessels of Not More Than 100 Gross Tons Upon Inland Waters." What about the ocean?
I can go on the ocean but it's very complicated.

Atlantic or Pacific?
In the last five years, I sailed across the Gulf of Mexico four times. In '99, I sailed from Salvador, Brazil, to Ghana.

The PBS special *Middle Passage Voyage*! With your love for the sea, why are you in Inwood?
It's part of my quirky lifestyle. I love New York. When I moved into this neighborhood about eleven years ago, it was the last decent deal in Manhattan, my first real adult home. I didn't have to have a roommate.

If you lived in Titusville, Florida, where you grew up, would you be partly on land?
No, I have my urban lifestyle and my more far-flung life. Variety is the spice of life. A lot of my sea adventures happen in winter. I was on my sailboat during 9-11. I was behind the Statue of Liberty in Liberty Marina, in New Jersey. The night before, it had rained really hard; I was in my boat bailing out water. May I demonstrate something? [*He comes over, put his hands on my shoulders, and…*]

Oof.
I felt the percussion from the first airplane hit. It felt like somebody pushing—like I pushed you. The sound went right across the water. We hopped in a launch to see what we could do. All these people charred and covered with ash were going across the river. That afternoon, there was nobody around North Cove—a few loose dogs. My boat is now out on City Island. I have a great photo of her.

Where do you go in her?
I'm going to take her to Martha's Vineyard this summer.

Where did you get all the scabbards?
Samurai swords—I found them. I found the musket in a trash can.

I'm feeling an era here but I'm not sure what. What haven't you seen?
[*He shakes his finger.*] No television, no computer. I make these wooden vases. I turn them on a lathe. I just spent several years working on the Maritime Hotel, the Matsuri restaurant. It's quite a spectacle. I did all the walnut work.

Walnut...

is a European/American wood. It's very somber, very soothing. It's dark and deep. It is extremely hard—that's why they use it for gun stocks and pipes. Real hardwood trees take years to grow. When they grow slowly and under the right conditions, they produce a very stable wood.

I wonder if that applies to human intelligence.

Pine grows very fast. People buy pine futons and they're out in the trash in a year.

You work on luxurious apartments.

Last week I built an African mahogany deck on Barrow Street. It's a very rare wood. It's got fire in it. The owner saw another deck just like it and wanted one. I started doing woodwork when I was on boats. Sailors are called *jacks*. That's where *jack-of-all-trades* comes from. Sailors have to be very stable people because what they're on is constantly moving.

You just showed me an old bag with ropes and string.

I like to do fancy knot work at sea. It's a sailor's ditty bag. That's a Turk's head and that's a crown sennit. [*He puts a small object on the table.*]

A wooden seashell, how transgressive!

I model them after real shells. Shells are all one line, interior and exterior.

Like the Guggenheim...sort of.

Remember the Möbius strip? It's never ending.

Is the animal born first or are they born inside the shell?

I think mollusks grow their shell, but there are other animals who adapt to recycled shells. Hermit crabs do that.

August 10, 2005

STEVEN SUNSHINE

How can you _possibly_ go to work when you can hop around in the sand, ride the Scooter, have an ear of corn or something, and stare at the seagulls that fly to "There You'll Be" playing at the refreshment stand where the men with tan stomachs sit on white plastic chairs screaming at each other, "I don't want shit"? Then there's the old Shore Hotel with the laundry out front. This place is compelling.

[G8S] We don't go to work until the graveyard shift. [DENNIS] So in the mornings, we can sleep on the beach for hours. [G8S] It's low key around here. You can walk out in your bathing suit, hair a mess. I got the apartment over two years ago. I was living in Park Slope, but I was down here taking photos. I thought it would be nice to live here. I couldn't find a real-estate agency. The woman at the deli said

most buildings are owned by government agencies, seventeen blocks of projects. She'd heard of a landlord who was remodeling a building. All of us came to New York a few years ago from Kalamazoo College in Michigan.

You're the boys of summer. I was just looking at a book of Bruce Davidson's photos from '59, kids from Prospect Park going to Coney Island, boys in T-shirts, with long arms, big hands, tattoos, who spent their days smoking cigarettes and kissing their girlfriends on blankets under the boardwalk, and then the famous photo of the blond girl combing her hair in the mirror of a cigarette machine. She was very beautiful. Then I read, "She was always sad, always fixing her hair," and when she grew up she "put a shotgun in her mouth and blew her head off."

Like in _Requiem for a Dream_, which took place around here. [PATRICK] Our neighborhood—we're just west of the water—is mostly Dominican and Puerto Rican, though a Russian laundry just opened. [G8S] It's all mixed. I eat a lot at La Frontera, a Mexican restaurant near the subway. It's across from Carolina's, where you see old Italians come on weekends. [PATRICK] There's a lot of action in the Little Mermaid Bagel Shop. [G8S] One of the bagel ladies manages Astroland in the summer. [PATRICK] She looks very tired sometimes.

This apartment is so old looking, stucco ceiling, crumbly sash windows, like where someone would be in a T-shirt in

the forties hoping he'd get the dough to put on the feedbag.

[DENNIS] I do feel like I'm being pulled back in time. [G8S] The light here is so amazing. It bounces around through the space all day long. [PATRICK] We like to sit in the kitchen and look out the window at the restaurant across the street. Everybody's always out in front, like twenty people. [G8S] They have roosters in back. [PATRICK] People think I'm insane when I say roosters are keeping me up. [G8S] Then I'll be on the phone and my mother will say, "What's that?" "Oh, that's just the Cyclone."

Are you going to be here forever with calliope music in your brain?

The winters are hard. It's so cold near the ocean. There's a lot more blue in the light. It's very empty. [PATRICK] It's hard to get friends to visit. I'd say gentrification

begins and ends with us. [G8S] It's an hour commute. [DENNIS] I probably pay twice as much on car service as I do on rent. My roommates make fun of me. The car service pulls up. I don't even have to tell them where I'm going.

They *know*—Cafeteria in Chelsea for your waiter job. You get out, flashbulbs popping.

Oh, sure. Sometimes we all go to Manhattan together for dinners, parties. We'll be all punked out. There was a period where we all dyed our hair primary colors.

You're like the celebrities of Coney Island.

The neighborhood has names for us. G8s is Chino. Patrick is Blanquito. I don't know if I want to know what mine is.

July 17, 2001

CALL ME ISHMAEL

LOCATION
East Village, Manhattan

RENT
$0

SQUARE FEET
500 (three-room apartment in church)

OCCUPANT
Edward Bordas (executive director, Shelter and Food for the Homeless, Trinity Lower East Side Lutheran Parish)

It seems we should begin speaking of your destiny, since you've already run into it. As we sit near your 175 editions of *Moby Dick*—more on that later—please begin.

I was living in Williamsburg a few years ago. A friend at work asked if I'd build him some bookshelves in his new apartment in Brooklyn. I said, "Sure." A few days later, I said, "Serge, can I have the cheap apartment that you're vacating on 9th Street?" This isn't the one I'm in now, though it's on the same street. Serge said, "A lot of people have expressed interest, but I'll keep you in mind." I forgot about it. A few months later, he said, "The apartment's yours." It was just over $400, significantly cheaper than Williamsburg, which was $600. The morning I got the apartment, I called my mother at work in Massachusetts. I

was raised in New Bedford. I said, "Mom, I'm moving to Ninth Street." She said, "Between what and what?" I said, "B and C." She said, "Get out of here." I said, "It's a safe neighborhood." She said, "I *know* it is. Do you know who lived there?" I said, "Who, Frank O'Hara?" She said, "*No, your father!* We met on that block, three doors away."

Tell about your father, the Catholic priest.

He was ordained in '67. In '69 he came to New York from Iowa with a group of priests and seminarians to work in a poor neighborhood. The seven of them rented an apartment at 644 East Ninth. My mother's good friend from high school lived on the block. When my mother was moving down to 13th and First, her friend said, "I know a bunch of young, strong guys." So he got all the priests to help her move—well, except my father; he came later to the party she had to thank the priests.

Was it love at first sight?

I don't know, but my mother said to my father, "You *can't* be a priest; you're too short." Then it sort of blossomed from there. He decided to leave the priesthood. This was a time when so many were leaving. My mother's friend next door on Ninth Street was a parole officer and got a job in New Bedford. My parents went, too, and got jobs as supervisors at a halfway house for mentally retarded men. We lived in the house. I remember one guy, Uncle Bernie. He never knew what day it was, but he had social skills. He'd take us to the dog pound—a wonderful guy, a sweetheart.

I went to Brandeis. After college, '94, I commuted to Boston from New Bedford, three hours each way—I couldn't afford an apartment on my salary—and worked in Boston for City Year, an urban peace corps. Then I was at a VA hospital in Maryland, a Red Cross Disaster Relief Center—there was some flooding in Washington State— the Community Service Society of New York, the Family Center...

Now you run a soup kitchen where homeless people come to eat.
I always wanted to do this kind of work. I feel I have an obligation to help other people. It's just the values my parents instilled in me.

But you do get to live in the church's cheerfully renovated apartment that comes along with your job, which you got by accident online over a year ago, after you lost that other apartment. We don't have room to discuss your

girlfriend in Hell's Kitchen—you met her when she was working at the Museum of Jewish Heritage and you said to your friend Josh, "Who's the one in the brown cords?"—but how do the 175 editions of *Moby Dick* fit in the picture?
When I was in AmeriCorps in Maryland, I had a friend on my team, and we'd hit all the used-book stores. I began seeing different editions. I said, "I'm going to start a collection." You see, New Bedford suffers from a terrible inferiority complex. It fell on hard times like a lot of smaller cities in the Northeast. *Moby Dick* celebrates New Bedford as *the* wealthy whaling port of the nineteenth century. So the greatest American novel begins in New Bedford. Though, wait, *Moby Dick* actually starts in Manhattan.

The same fate may be thine.

April 16, 2002

THE BATHS

LOCATION

Brighton Beach, Brooklyn

RENT

$236.80 (government subsidized)

SQUARE FEET

450 (one-bedroom apartment
in 1960s Mitchell-Lama
regulated high rise)

OCCUPANT

Etta Sherez (retired hatmaker; retired
supervising clerk, Department of
Water Supply, Gas and Electricity)

You're going away from here soon, from your apartment on the boardwalk where the Russian couples walk arm in arm and the air comes in from the sea. I notice you have an avocado velveteen couch, gold vertical blinds, and a framed photo of Einstein. When did you move here?
I'm here about nineteen years in this building. I'm from the Lower East Side, then Williamsburg. I came to visit in the twenties. My family always went to the baths.

The Brighton Baths opened in 1907— swimming pool, knish-eating contests, mah-jongg. In later years, Milton Berle, Herman's Hermits. Those were the days!
I took a locker. I was always here. My sister Minnie came with me. She said, "This is no-man's-land. It's all women." She was a big hit with the men. She married three

times. My father went to yeshiva in Europe, Austria. He didn't have a trade. In the yeshiva they told the boys they should go to the new country. He left my mother. She was angry. She came here to get a divorce but she decided not to. My father was a very handsome man and she thought she'd have attractive children. I have two beautiful sisters who look like my father. I look like my mother. If it weren't for Poppa coming here, we'd have been in Auschwitz. At first, he slept in the back of a shop. He didn't have an apartment. He bought a house in Williamsburg. He said it was beneath him to live in somebody else's house. Peter Luger's was a few blocks from our house. I've never eaten there. Who comes to a neighborhood like that and pays those prices? We had this mortgage on the house. So I only went to school to 9-B. I took typing. It was the Depression.

You got a job in millinery?
Arlé Hats, with embroidery, very expensive. I lived at home all the time. The others got married. I lost my mother in '55. I moved out, to the Belleclaire, 77th and Broadway. My friends from millinery were there. These gals were like sisters to me. I hated the Belleclaire. My two girlfriends had a three-room apartment they shared. I had a room. I couldn't live like that. My brother-in-law walked in and said, "This place is going to be a hot box in the summer." I moved to Crown Heights in Brooklyn 'cause my brother lived there. Crown Heights changed. I moved to Flatbush, Garfield's Cafeteria. Wherever I lived, I went to the Brighton Baths. When I worked for the city, I'd get off at four, ride to the baths instead

MICHAEL SOFRONSKI

of going home. Of course then I'd jump in the ocean and swim.

Did you always know you'd move to Brighton Beach?

I was going to move to Kings Highway. I said, "What am I doing? I'll move here." One of the girls in millinery, her cousin lived here, in this building, which is for senior citizens. It's only a block from the baths. On the building's twenty-fifth anniversary they made a beautiful party— unlimited liquor. There's nothing here anymore. The baths closed. Only Russian restaurants. I can't go in the ocean—I get ear infections. I look out. I cry. I see them jump in the water. I can't take one step on that sand. The sand shifts. I'm arthritic. I'm ninety. I won't be here very long. I don't kid myself. I just want my last years to be comfortable. Where I'm going, they include one meal a day.

Seabrook in New Jersey—one of the new senior "campus style" communities. They have a lovely pool, classes. I'll take computer. It's $148,000 down for one bedroom but you get it back if you move, or it goes into your estate. Rent's $1,290 a month. For dinner they have a very nice restaurant.

There's a photo in the Seabrook brochure of all these men wearing yachting caps and working on model sailboats.

The thing is, you don't have to worry about the weather. You don't have to worry is it raining or snowing. You never have to go out.

September 7, 1999

The city can be so dark during the day. The tall buildings of Wall Street, the black eyes of the garment district, the buildings where money is made. But in the night, the earth and brick move into the shadow. Night Town turns liquid, all white and gold. More than 300,000 street lights go on, mercury green, sodium pumpkin. There is the street of chandeliers on the Bowery, the Empire State Building all colored on top for holidays, the nocturnal purple of where bats live at the zoo.

Rooms appear and disappear as lights go on and off. There's a reading light all by itself.

I never wrote a "Shelter" column in the moonlight—most are white and blue, the light of people in the day or at sunset— though one time, way past midnight, a man showed me Jupiter light in a telescope.

I never went to Times Square in the mad neon night where new worlds await. Here it is now: the Madame Tussauds sign in orange—the "u" is out. "JVC" in white under a big globe, a video of a giant lizard, a shocking pink for NASDAQ.

The sky is a dark and blueless gray.

Wait, it's turning yellow—a storm is coming. Got to go.

LIGHT

BLINDING LIGHT

LOCATION
Greenwich Village, Manhattan

PRICE
$425,000 in 1997 ($2,065.43 maintenance)

SQUARE FEET
1,400 (renovated loft apartment with two-hundred-square-foot terrace in 1899 former spice factory)

OCCUPANT
Fred Hanson (theater director)

Your view of the Hudson River is like a 1930s movie set, boats moving left and right on the wavy blue water.
It's like being in a stateroom in an ocean liner in this apartment, except for the shore of New Jersey. The apartment was previously owned by Lanford Wilson, the playwright. Though he wasn't living here when I bought it.

You see the sun come up. You see the sun go down.
I don't often see it come up.

You may not see it forever.
No.

I heard developers are tearing down the factory in front of your building and putting up an almost two-hundred-foot-tall condo that will block your view.

Aren't you frightened?
We always knew we were vulnerable because the building in front is the last manufacturing building in this residential neighborhood.

The Superior Ink Factory—where I was sure that the squid came up from the docks to deliver their ink, wobbling in on all their legs.
I haven't seen any walking squid.

It turns out Superior does not use squid ink, just tree resins. Their three-story building on the West Side Highway has two hundred-foot smokestacks and it used to be the National Biscuit Company in 1919. Superior is consolidating its operations in New Jersey. Look, you can see the back of the factory—all that chipped green paint from when there were chipped biscuits maybe.
A developer has either bought the site or rights to the site.

The Related Companies! The same people that put up the building at Astor Place that Gwathmey designed and it's all blue and I bet people inside are going to wear blue glasses so it will always be blue for them. Apartments costs millions. Related is trying to get a zoning variance here so they can build even bigger. They have to prove that that's the only way they can get a return on their money. They are crying hardship. The Greenwich Village Society for Historic Preservation director Andrew Berman said that Related has

a portfolio worth over $10 billion. So where is the hardship? Then if Related succeeds, all developers will be sobbing because of their own hardship. I heard the building is going to be twenty-some stories. So your view will go...

It's not just views. It's a question of light and air for some apartments.

CARY CONOVER

They call the West Side Highway the new Gold Coast, Miami Beach. It began with the Richard Meier condo buildings, which are so sea-green glass and perfect in the spirit of the greatest of glass, like Mies buildings, Bunshaft's Lever House...

The *Meier* buildings are what prompted the community to take action and get the city to reconsider the zoning and extend the Village landmark district. The city only cherry picked certain buildings for landmarking—Superior was not one.

What are you going to do if they build in front of your windows.

If I lose all four, I would have to consider moving.

How could you sell the apartment without a view?

Others have sold since the word is out. Somehow the market takes that into account. But it will put a cloud over it.

Did you ever have a water view before?

I grew up in the Midwest, Downers Grove. We had a pond across the way.

You also have an apartment in Brazil.

Yes, the apartment in Rio, I share with a friend. It looks out on Sugar Loaf. The side faces a garden that used to be the presidential palace.

The colors are green and yellow there.

We wanted color. In Brazil, class and elegance in home design equal white. It's very hard to find things that aren't white.

The water here turns almost blond when the sun is going down. What was the last show you directed?

Oh what was that? *Oklahoma* based on the 2002 Broadway production. It was touring all over the place.

What happens in the show? Oh, I know. She has a dream. There are bentwood chairs, lots of vice, crooked signs.

August 24, 2005

VERMEER LIGHT

LOCATION
Red Hook, Brooklyn

PRICE
$90,000 in 1996

SQUARE FEET
1,200 (two-story hundred-year-old wooden house)

OCCUPANT
Tina Olsen (creative arts therapist, South Beach Psychiatric Center; artist)

Go ahead, feed the birds. We're standing on your back deck, not far from the sea.
This is a wonderful bird area because it's not as populated around here. Fewer people live at the end of the road. There are a lot of vacant lots where wild things grow. A purple finch just came over. This garden out back is very fertile because they dumped cotton bolls here. Ships brought cotton up from the South. The ones that got wet and rotten down in the hold, they'd throw them in these yards, partly to fill it up because it was a swamp. A lot of these houses are built on semifill.

That music in the air sounds Scottish.
No, it's Pentecostal, from the church. I moved here in 1996. Look at that gorgeous light. It's like Vermeer light because it's low. Most of these old houses were used as rooming houses for people who worked on the piers. The beam in the living-room ceiling was put in to hold everything up. These beams got washed up by the sea. The first artist in Red Hook, 1980, used this house as a studio. Now she lives in Nyack, where she's a therapist and healer. I met her at a peace demonstration there. My boyfriend knows her ex-boyfriend because they were working in a tofu factory where my boyfriend was one of the first tofu makers in the seventies—he's Sam Weinreb, one of the original hippies. He had a loft on the Bowery. Got disillusioned with the art scene and said, "Fuck it, I'm going to make tofu." He delivered to the Park Slope Food Coop, the Ananda Ashram in upstate New York. He lives in Nyack now. I just met him four years ago dancing at the Duane Hall in the Village. It's mostly all old hippies who do this old English dancing. Sam and I have the same values.

I've been married a couple of times, two children—they grew up with me in Washington Square Village. Their father is Persian, a professor at NYU. This is kind of amazing. When I came here to look at the house, the man living here was the brother of my best friend from SoHo. That was sort of a good omen. My best friend, our children went to P.S. 3, one of the first alternative public schools in the country, open classrooms, no grades. We imported kids from Harlem because we wanted it to be mixed. The kids made puppets. The whole population of the Village was different then. Those people were pioneers. Some parents were in Mexico doing mushrooms and the kids were going to P.S. 3 on their own. *No*, of course not everyone. Most parents were hardworking, very involved.

This photograph of a farmhouse...
Was my father's family's. Mennonites. They
came over at the invitation of William Penn
to farm in Lancaster. Mennonites were
being murdered in Germany because they
were pacifists.

**Does your boyfriend have a country
house?**
Not exactly. He got into this subsidized
old people's housing. Nyack is kind of an
arts community. They take care of their
old people. Did you see my front door? All
peeling. Actually, it was a new door. It took
me a lot of time to get it that way.

**The scale of houses by the sea, they're
always small, little doors.**

I like that it's no bigger than I need. You
can see one side to the other. I like that it's
quiet. Because there are no street lights, the
light at night is kind of majestic, like what
you get in Maine. I go to Maine whenever
I can. I like that isolation. I like houses that
were inhabited by many people passing
through, all ghosts. I really feel the ghosts,
in the fallen-down buildings by the water.
The deserted quality of industrialization,
the half-sunken ship. Like dreams that have
crumbled. It's sort of past, so it doesn't have
to intimidate you anymore—the grandiosity
is finished, it's over, like Western civilization
falling into the sea.

February 12, 2003

WHEN THE WORLD TURNS PINK

LOCATION
Greenpoint, Brooklyn

RENT
$1,350 (market)

SQUARE FEET
800 (railroad apartment in three-story house)

OCCUPANTS
Susanne Bellinghausen (architect and interactive spatial designer), Stephen Kovats (architect and media theoretician)

[*Door crashes open.*] **Whew, just in time for the sunset. The L train didn't come for an hour. People were ten deep on the platform, getting to know each other. This man with a diamond ring on every finger said we should "just calm down" because "New York works pretty well, considering." Anyway, you'd told me about your sunsets, and I was so excited to talk about them, but I realized, after thinking for a week, that I don't have much to say about sunsets. When something is beautiful and happy, what's to say? Once a friend came back from a sublime sailboat ride. I said, "Well?" He was speechless. Oh, but wait, I do have some thoughts: old people watching**

sunsets, sitting in Adirondack chairs, having lived their lives as twosomes, now waiting for the end to come. Sunsets do make us feel larger than we are. You know how people toddle to their jobs every day and then they go on vacation and they're watching the waves crash in and they start thinking big thoughts: Oh, how small the sand is and how big the moon!

[STEPHEN] When I first moved here, I was so fascinated with the sunsets, I'd stand by the window every day. I thought I was going a little bit crazy. It makes the whole apartment change—whitish blue to deep orange. Look at the light on her face. [SUSANNE] You're so good with words.

So here we are in Greenpoint with your landlord's wood-grain wallpaper in the building's hallway and the red-brick, retrofitted former warehouse across the street with small one- and two-bedrooms renting for $1600 to $2500. The landlord over there said, "I want to attract those midtown Manhattanites, and not artists." [STEPHEN] We moved from Berlin in '99. I'm originally from Ottawa. My parents are Hungarian, my father a '56er—one of the ones who left after the revolution. After college, I went to work in East Germany for ten years, dealing with unification as a teacher, architect. [SUSANNE] I met Stephen at the Bauhaus in Dessau in '91. [STEPHEN] The Bauhaus finished as a school in Chicago after the war. It's just the building now in Dessau. There's a foundation dealing with international issues of the urban realm.

What about that time in Addis Ababa?
One day, we got a call from the foundation
director. He said, "We have a problem
in Ethiopia, and it's next week." We flew
there and did an exhibit on proposals
for redeveloping the city's master plan.
[SUSANNE] The plan was ten years
old and never applicable, politically.
[STEPHEN] Master plans are basically
political processes that are then imposed on
a city and space to make them conform to
an ideology. There was a Marxist regime in
Ethiopia until the early nineties, and they
produced a model of an Eastern European
socialist town plan. When the regime fell
apart in '92, '93, there was a big push to
quickly develop Ababa as a free-market city.

**Now for another topic: You got married
on the Arctic Circle. Yellowknife. I know
about Canada because the *National
Lampoon* used to have a column called
"Canadian Corner." There was a picture
of a Mounty in his hat.**

Yellowknife's the gateway to the Northwest
Territories, the last frontier in North
America—75,000 people, and it's half the
size of the United States. [SUSANNE] Steve
was there doing a television documentary.
[STEPHEN] Things tend to be easier in
Canada than Germany. To get married,
it takes twenty-five minutes. Then we
ended up on the front page of the paper—
"Wildcat Wedding." The documentary was
about this thousand-mile-long river system
that goes from where the Chippewas live,
where there are trees, to where the Inuits
live on the tundra. But for the Chippewa,
the edge of the forest was the edge of the
world, the end of life. The Inuits didn't
want to go to the forest because it's dark.
Every now and then, they'd meet at the tree
line and think, "Oh my God, the people
on the other side are the devil." And they
would kill each other.

April 9, 2002

MICHAEL KAMBER

BEFORE SHABBOS

LOCATION
Crown Heights, Brooklyn

RENT
$856.69 (rent stabilized)

SQUARE FEET
900 (one-bedroom in 1926
six-story building)

OCCUPANT
Shaunya Hartley (fashion stylist)

Look at those great ink drawings.
My father gave them to me as soon as
he found out I was moving. He put them
up for me. My uncle polyurethaned the
floor. I grew up a block away, on Empire
Boulevard. My dad grew up a block away
from there, where my grandparents have a
house. He's a computer engineer.

How did you get such a big TV?
My mom bought it. I moved here last year.
I just turned twenty-four. My really good
friend is a fashion stylist. She's in Clinton
Hill. She's the one who pushed me into
moving out of my parents' house. I wanted
to stay in Brooklyn. I can't relate to the sort
of Manhattan-centered, elitist-liberal lifestyle.
Though I went to school in Manhattan—
FIT, then City College.

**You have to pay rent by money order
here, you said.**

Quite a few buildings in the neighborhood
won't accept personal checks.

**How would describe your immediate
neighborhood?**
There is a Hasidic Jewish influence.

**I didn't see that. I got off the subway
at Sterling and Nostrand. I saw Smell
so Sweet, "Department Store Within,"
then a school playground. The children
were all screaming at the same decibel
level—the scream of being tickled.
There were some Tudorlike houses.**
Most of those are owned by Hasidic Jews.
Crown Heights is like: Hasidic, Hasidic, and
then a West Indian restaurant—primarily
black and Hasidic. A lot of Hasidic shops
are on Kingston Avenue.

**Are you friends with your Hasidic
neighbors?**
You do say hello to some. You're supposed
to say hello to neighbors. Before the
Sabbath, you walk down the street. They'll
say, "Excuse me, lady, could you help me
cut the light off or turn off my stove?"

**Right! They need a gentile to do the
work because on Shabbos, beginning
at sunset, a Jew is not supposed to
sow, plow, reap, bind sheaves, beat
wool, slaughter, salt meat, kindle a fire.
It goes on, but with the modern age
comes the complication of electricity,
which is associated with work. So you
even have to unscrew the bulb in the
refrigerator. You go in their houses...**
You just do it. I have a very trusting face.

They explain. Usually they'll send children or a woman to ask another woman on the street. Hardly do they ever ask a man or does a man ask.

If you needed help, could you ask someone Hasidic?
When I lived on Empire with my parents, sometimes if I had a heavy suitcase, some man would say, "Do you need me to get that?" [*I decide I have to explore Kingston Avenue. I call her later after she's finished watching her favorite cooking show,* Barefoot Contessa, *and report back.*]

The Young Timers store had long rose-colored gowns for children in the window. So old European—not like the baby at the Skyscraper Museum opening the other week who had miniature motorcycle boots on.
All those cute clothes make you think of Communion or Easter. My mother used to buy my dress shoes from one of those stores.

Then there was Hamafitz Stam, importers and distributors of *Esrogim* and *Lulavim* from Israel and Italy, with silver candelabras and deep-blue velvet cloths embroidered with gold. Signs were on the street. "It is worth emphasizing...that girls and women (who wear non *tzniinsdik*) garments and thereby call attention to themselves *disgrace themselves* by 'proclaiming' that they possess no intrinsic qualities for which they should garner attention and according to which they should be evaluated (and their sole worth is) only through a manner of conduct that is the opposite of *tznius*...all women and girls, whether living here or visiting, adhere at all times to laws of modesty...(collarbone should remain covered) elbows..."
Calves should never be shown.

February 9, 2005

CARY CONOVER

CAMERA OBSCURA

LOCATION
Fort Greene, Brooklyn
PRICE
$330,000 in 1998
SQUARE FEET
2,400 (four-story 1860s brick townhouse)
OCCUPANT
Nicholas Evans-Cato (painter; teacher, the Maryland Institute College of Art)

You paid for your house from a car accident?

I was a seven-year-old asleep in the back of a car. A drunk driver of an eighteen-wheeler killed my father instantly, broke eighteen bones including both my legs, and I almost bled to death and spent the next ten years in and out of hospitals. My mother was away on vacation. My father was a painter and teacher at Brooklyn College. This was 1980. The insurance settlement was the down payment on this house. Interest rates were what they were in '98. A cutout cardboard model was the invitation to my housewarming. I have two tenants. I can't move my painting studio here because I need the rental income to pay the mortgage. I've had a studio in Vinegar Hill since '95.

Let's discuss why we're really here. The living room windows are blocked out with cardboard. Only one has a pinhole. You've turned the room into a camera obscura, a darkened chamber that collects the inverted image made by light rays passing through a pinhole, the most ancient form of projection, which Mo-Tzu—you know, the fifth-century B.C. Chinese philosopher—called a "locked treasure room."

Shall we begin? Let your eyes adjust as I turn down the lights...more...and more...

Look, there's a car on the ceiling, a house on your wall. There goes a person, and another car, a red one. The whole thing is in color...

Pretty neat, huh? What we're seeing is across the street but upside down, backward, and out of focus.

Like a little movie...

No! People have tried to compare the camera obscura to movies and photography. A better analogy might be a live broadcast of whatever happens to be in front of you.

Ernie Gehr made a video of the giant camera obscura's mirrored reflection at San Francisco's Cliff House. Sometimes the ocean waves were on their sides. You need a bright sunny day outside to see all this.

Are you sad when night falls that it's gone?

No! At night what you see are the brake lights.

So, if we look at the house across the street on your wall, it's like being a spy upside down.

No! It's no more like being a spy than looking out the window.

I'm just trying to get some footing here. That water tower on a rooftop is my favorite part. Water towers are always so hopeful, with their pointed heads, standing proudly on four legs. Now as soon as you hold up that illustration board to capture the image, it's like a little painting.

No! It's not like a painting. The clouds are moving. You can say it's like a painting because this image has a poetic quality in and of itself. There's something ineffable about it. There's nothing too dark or too bright, something very calm and silent. My living room's just been this way for three weeks. I have my students making cardboard camera obscuras as drawing tools.

Landscape painting—your field, though you do strictly industrial scenes—has its origins in the power politics of property, you said.

It's about who owns the view, what's being viewed, where the artist stands. I prefer painting standing on the sidewalk than from a rooftop. There's something more democratic about it. Pissarro did a beautiful series of paintings looking down from his windows in Paris. But there's something agoraphobic about them. Why didn't he go outside and paint them? I don't like the idea of looking down.

Why are you living on the top floor?

I chose this apartment for life, not for art.

Did you spend a lot of time as a child recovering in the hospital?

No! I spent a lot of time at home looking out the window. That's probably one of the reasons I do like to paint outside.

November 6, 2002

JAY MUHLIN

INNER LIGHT

LOCATION

Chelsea, Manhattan

RENT

$688 (rent stabilized)

SQUARE FEET

420 (studio apartment in prewar building)

OCCUPANT

Dawn Suvino (computer technology instructor for the blind and visually impaired, The Lighthouse)

You say you're happy your apartment faces the backs of four buildings.

Of course! It's quiet. I'm off the street. I don't care if the view is shitty. Blind people don't care about the view. It's not exactly a selling point.

It's cozy.

I moved up from Thompson and Bleecker about six years ago. I couldn't afford downtown anymore. I was a little bummed. I never wanted to live above 14th Street. I'd always lived in the Village. I did my graduate work at NYU. In 1984 I lived in Paris. I had a great place, a tiny room in the best possible neighborhood.

You said you're going to renovate this summer. That's risky for a renter.

I figured, if I stay here for five more years, why not! I'm going to have the place

repainted. I took out a loan. People said, "You're nuts."

How's your landlord?

He's okay. It's his family's management company that tried to evict me three years ago. My refrigerator wasn't working and I refused to pay the rent. They put eviction papers on the door. I threw away the papers. I told them, "I'm blind, what do I know?" Well, I knew damn well what the papers were. Anyway, two days before the court date, the landlord showed up with a new refrigerator. He's an old Italian guy, so sweet.

What are your renovation plans?

The carpet's going to feel great—something kind of plush. For me, it's comfort that's important. I'm getting tile for the kitchen floor area instead of wood. I love to hear the sound of the dog's little nails clicking on tile. And I'm getting a sleeper sofa. The bed takes up too much room. This is not a hell of a lot of space for a blind person and a seventy-pound dog to run around. Then there's the computer, the scanner, the reading machine, and all these books—1,500 audiotapes. They're overrunning my life, drawers and drawers of them.

You mentioned a new kitchen set.

I want to get a retro sixties one. The Formica should be white with a gold and purple boomerang pattern.

What do you know about purple?

I was fully sighted until I went blind from spinal meningitis in one week when I was fifteen. I have complete visual recall. So,

GREG MILLER

think about all your memories until the time you were fifteen. I love to watch *I Love Lucy* reruns because I remember the facial expressions she's making. I remember Lucy's living room. In the same way, I remember what gold and purple are. If I don't like gold and purple after a while—I just change it in my mind. I'll decide the kitchen set is turquoise and pink. Its reality is the color I decide it is.

A triplex. There'd be a playroom for the dog and voice recognition systems all over the place. Everything would be computerized. I'd need a few million. But you know, when I ask any blind person what they'd rather have—ten million or their eyesight—they all say, "Are you insane? I'll take the money!"

April 29, 1997

And what would you decide is the ultimate apartment?

KODACHROME

LOCATION
Little Italy, Manhattan

RENT
$501.72 (rent stabilized)

SQUARE FEET
295 (ground-floor studio apartment
in tenement building)

OCCUPANTS
Guy Stricherz and Irene Malli (fine-
art photographic printers, CVI),
Matilda (two and a half years old),
Guy Emil (one month old)

Four of you live in one room.
[GUY] It makes life rather simple. We've got
a chair, sofa, TV, and a kitchen. At night,
this becomes a bedroom. Three of us sleep
on the foldout.

**First, let's discuss your *Americans in
Kodachrome* book, which is impossible to
stop looking at.**
We sent a release to community papers
saying we wanted old Kodachrome slides
of family and friends for a portrait of the
American people in the postwar era. We
looked at about 75,000. When we selected
the images, we made these dye-transfer
prints and sent them back their slides.

**The little girl on the cover, her hair
in that golden Kodachrome light, the
light at the end of the day, the end of
the summer. The photos look as if they
were made from gold and partly from**

**that miraculous Kodachrome purpley
blue, as in your own family photo—
Enumclaw, Washington, 1952. It makes
me think that everybody in Enumclaw
lives in an indigo light—your father,
coach of the high school Hornets, all
his sons, your mother, that smile. The
couple in the living room at Christmas,
Anniston, Alabama, 1947—again the
golden light. The woman is in a perfect
black dress, sparkling sequin appliqué.
He is so handsome, his arm on the back
of the couch. Does he have a secret life?**
Doc and Helen Bagley. I like the
understated quality of their tree.

**The man and woman dancing in the
kitchen in Preston, Connecticut, 1955,
the black curtain with cream and red
roses. He's holding her tight, Irish love
in his eyes. Though maybe he's not
even Irish.**
That wasn't his wife. She was holding the
camera.

**Then, the older man on the back of a
motor boat, laughing in Carancahua
Bay, Texas, 1956, his arm around a
woman, another to his right with silver
hair, everybody loving to be with each
other and the white and bubbly foamy
wake behind them.**
The confidence of the era.

**You wrote that two classical musicians
named Leopold saw a color movie in
1917 and got so inspired that they
invented what became Kodachrome in
the bathroom of a New York apartment,
and America lived on inside that film.**

CARY CONOVER

One of the Leopolds was the brother-in-law of George Gershwin. From 1945 to 1965, the largest record of America was on Kodachrome. Other color films from the era have faded. [*He sings to Matilda, "Mama, don't take my Kodachrome, mama don't take my Kodachrome awaaaay…"*] Modern processes are much more limited, not as complex. Kodachrome, dye transfer, and Technicolor, like *The Wizard of Oz*—they all have a similar, complex palette of colors.

You've had a lab around the corner for twenty-two years. You worked on the book seventeen. You've lived here over twenty-six. You do everything for a long time!
I hitchhiked to New York from Washington in 1977. It was the blackout, summer of Sam, Elvis died. I lived in a couple of fleabag hotels, nine dollars a night. I wanted to work in the photographic industry. I didn't know anyone. I found this apartment in the paper. You'd get the *Voice* on Wednesday mornings in Sheridan Square. Scorsese grew up near here, above Albanese

Meats. Remember Carmen Galante, the Laundromat was his headquarters. [IRENE] It was a dry cleaner. [GUY] It was a dry cleaner. Sorry.

How did you meet?
I ran an ad. [IRENE] I had graduated from Cooper Union. [GUY] I hired her. [IRENE] We got along really well. [GUY] Six months later I married her, in 1989.

Irene grew up in a Sears, Roebuck house that came in a kit.
The kit for the house came inside the garage.

The book's last photo is Irene's father lying on a couch. A baby and two boys are behind him. One looks like he's going to torture someone with his Slinky.
[IRENE] I'm the baby. You know, my father told us he quit smoking before we were born. But you can see a pack of Kools in his pocket.

December 17, 2003

The thing about journeys is that one never knows how they are going to end. They are linear, like movies. A person is deeply in one moment without knowing the next...well, except for when the car is coming down the road.

I am thinking about this while I am writing a book that I never would have imagined writing in a two-room apartment that I never would have thought I'd be living in thirteen years ago.

How would I know that I would spend a night in an ice storm in a Holiday Inn in Pennsylvania, stay in a loft with paper bag sculptures by a woman who liked Joseph Beuys, and have to pour kerosene into a funnel into a fiery space heater?

How would I know that I would eat most unusually shaped eggs in an Ecuadorian restaurant, walk on Greenpoint Avenue at frosty holiday time with all the candy boxes with photographs of roses, and then lie down under an old cruise ship blanket from Canal Street Jeans and wonder if I would ever see someone I knew?

How would I know when I moved to the old horse stable that a local ice cream store was the place to buy crack, a man would stand outside the bar in the morning sun wearing a wig, and I would take a walk on Easter morning and see a man holding his girlfriend's hand in his left and, in his right, a black and orange snake?

How would I know when I moved to the building in SoHo that there would be a fire two floors below, a neighbor would want to buy everybody a drink the day the landlord died, and one September morning hundreds of people, covered in ash, would be running up Sixth Avenue. And years after that I would open a cookie at Ollie's Noodles and the fortune would read, "A thrilling time is in your future"?

JOURNEY

MISS LUTSKY CALLED

LOCATION
Upper East Side, Manhattan

RENT
$703.34 (rent stabilized)

SQUARE FEET
237 (studio in prewar 1939 building)

OCCUPANT
Linda Emond (actress)

Do Broadway actresses have apartment problems?

Oh, please. I moved here two years ago from Oregon. I was staying on the Lower East Side and my boyfriend and I were apartment hunting. It became clearer each day that we shouldn't be, and one morning I left. I ended up with a friend in Hoboken for a week and then on 105th, but during that period I was shooting some TV series, and I got a day on a movie, and in two weeks I was beginning rehearsals for a workshop at Lincoln Center, and I had no place to live.

But your career was going well.

It's hard for people who've been in New York to remember how disorienting it is. I didn't come here with a bank account. I came from the Oregon Shakespeare Festival playing Lady Macbeth for five months.

Lady Macbeth is like a trainer for New York.

So someone told me about this guide to no-fee apartments. I called fifteen. All the recordings said, "The apartment's still available, leave your number." No one ever called back. I called one place five times and said, "This is a scam and if somebody doesn't call back I'll..."

No one ever calls back unless it's about a job or sex. Now enter the apartment fairies.

Oh, them! So there was this horrible day. I saw this studio in Hell's Kitchen—unbearable stench, windows beyond filthy. Meanwhile I'd seen an ad for something with great light but I thought, Upper East Side, $679, it must be a dump. I called assuming no one would call back. But Angela Lutsky did! I was stunned—clean hallways, big window, normal-size bathroom. Then I walked out and saw these lovely grocery stores.

I thought around Lexington there're just women in white buildings who have lounge coats from Alexander's.

There's a big cross-section. Anyway, I got the place but I had no furniture. A friend steered me to the Ikea bus. Now, in two days I was going into rehearsal to play the poet Anne Sexton.

She carried "kill-me-pills" in her purse.

It wasn't exactly stabilizing. Onstage I wore a short zebra dress, a cigarette in one hand, a drink in the other. Anyway, I ended up in Ikea for eight hours. For seventy-nine bucks they deliver everything. I got a sofa, desk, tables. Now I must tell you about my bed. While I was in Hoboken I went shopping

GREG MILLER

at a well-known mattress store, which at the time was a little expensive for me. But a few doors down there was this mattress wrapped in plastic standing up on the sidewalk, advertising another place. I went in their warehouse and a man named Happy, who was very large with food stains on his shirt, was eating a sandwich. He proceeded to drag the mattress in from outside to sell it to me. I remember I was lying on top of the plastic and I kept thinking, "If I give money to this man, will I ever see the mattress again?" Then I thought, "How can I not trust Happy from Hoboken?" You know what was waiting for me the day I moved into my apartment?

The sandwich?

No, the mattress.

February 17, 1998

NINETY-EIGHT APARTMENTS

LOCATION
Long Island City, Queens

RENT
$1,200 (market)

SQUARE FEET
1,000 (two-bedroom converted loft in factory building)

OCCUPANTS
Tom Aulino (actor),
Robert I. Rubinsky (writer; producer; personal trainer)

You're so pleased now that you're living in a great big loft.
[TOM] We finally have enough kitchen counter space for our Ron Popeil rotisserie chicken maker.

Though I must say it is a little industrial. The factory stairway is so fierce. There are water puddles in front of the doors in the hall. Your neighbors are all auto transmission installers.
I *knew* you didn't like the apartment when you walked in.

I do, I do. It's so nicely renovated. But I have some thoughts about all this living in places that were not designed for intimate domestic life. In the 1970s, people would be so excited: "Oh, we live in a converted bowling alley," or, "This used to be a Laundromat and we sleep where the dryers used to be." It's not easy in New York, but it would be nice to live in a place made for a human. In your case, you're sort of grateful. Especially since before this, you and Robert had to move every year. Why are you showing me a black-and-white photo of a woman in a chiffon garden hat cutting a wedding cake?
That's Joanna, who married a rich pig farmer from England. If she hadn't fucked it up with the real-estate agent in 1990, Robert and I would still be in this great apartment in an ex-convent in Chelsea, but Joanna was the leaseholder's girlfriend and she moved in for a while, and everybody lost the apartment. So then we moved into what's-his-name's house, who was on the road with *Les Miz*. He used to call all the time for his phone messages. It was so intrusive. I put the answering machine in a drawer and it blew up because it overheated. Then Robert and I looked at *ninety-eight* apartments, no exaggeration, before we found the perfect one, 103rd and Riverside, a co-op. The owner said, "I'll rent to you for a long time, though when my mother dies, I'll have to sell." So we begin keeping track of the mother's health. We hear she's going to the dentist. We think, "Oh great, you don't go to the dentist if you're on your last legs." She lives. The guy decides to sell it anyway. Then Amsterdam and 101st, which I liked but Robert didn't—the gunshots at five in the morning. We never agree on anything. I can't remember where we went after that.

What about the dumpy Midtown place?
Yes, the dumpy one rented by Robert's ex,

who got it in the seventies and was living elsewhere but wanted to hold on to the lease. The rent was $230. The place was so small you could make breakfast, scrub the bathroom, vacuum the entire apartment, and never get out of bed. That apartment drove us to California.

But the minute you move, then you get the part in a Broadway play.

Wouldn't you know it. So Robert stays, house-sits for people in every California hill and canyon. I'm back here. Then both of us are back in the dumpy apartment. But we have no furniture. Our friend says, "Don't *buy* chairs. I've got two Billy Baldwins. They're at an upholsterer's in Long Island City. Go get them." Well, we think this neighborhood is interesting. We see this apartment advertised. There were twelve

people competing but we go to Kinko's at midnight, fax the papers, and we get it.

You're from New Jersey. Robert, who was in the cast of *Hair* in 1968 and whose father was Mr. Miami Beach in *Annie Hall*, is from Brooklyn. Here's Robert now. He just rushed in the door, breathless.

[ROBERT] I just heard you can get grants for a Harlem brownstone. [TOM] Then there's always Forest Hills...

But you're so happy here. A rolling stone gathers no moss!

After you've looked at ninety-eight apartments, you're *always* looking. Even if you don't want to move.

July 11, 2000

SANDRA-LEE PHIPPS

THIRTY YEARS

LOCATION
East Village, Manhattan

PRICE
$330 in 1981 ($650 maintenance)

SQUARE FEET
1,600 (limited-equity co-op in
eight-unit 1872 building)

OCCUPANTS
Sally Heckel (independent
filmmaker), Smokey Forester
(filmmaker; executive producer,
American Museum of
Natural History)

You'd been living here thirteen years before Smokey moved in with his coriander from the East. But let's go back to 1969 when...
[SALLY] I drove here in a BMW—BMWs then were only $200 more than a Volkswagen Bug. I had an avocado tree in the back. I came to go to the NYU graduate film program and live with my boyfriend, Josh, who had moved to New York first. He was in some cousin's apartment in Washington Heights, giant buildings, derelict parks. We were paying $66 a month. Then I met Mark...

What happened to Josh?
We split up. Mark fixed cars on Seventh Street, where I was going to school. He was very active at the Metropolitan Council on

Housing. They had a storefront. People came in with their problems. By then I was living at 70th and Central Park West, $125 a month—I've always paid very little rent in New York—and I moved into Mark's teeny apartment on 11th near Second, $53 a month. Mark had been there since the mid sixties. I was also renting a space at 41 Union Square to make my films. A lot of artists had studios there for $80. So I was paying a total of a hundred something for a work space and a home. Then in the late seventies, Mark and I moved to a former Civil War tent factory. It's that loft building on Bleecker and Elizabeth, 2,500 square feet, eighteen windows facing east, south, and west. The windows were really leaky. But we were paying $167 a month.

Someone should have put an implant in you and tracked you over the past thirty years. You're a historical specimen—all that low-cost housing.
I wanted to live so I could make my films. We were in the tent factory three or four years. We went on rent strike for a couple of years because there was no water. But then a neighbor saw an abandoned building near First Avenue. She said, "Let's get permission from the city to renovate it." People were doing that back then. The city had acquired thousands of abandoned buildings.

Yes—4,907 by '81. They wanted to keep them viable, on the tax rolls. You had to show you were of modest income. The city put in a boiler, you did the rest. You bought your floor for $330. It was the Urban Homesteading

SYLVIA PLACHY

Program—382 units were homesteaded citywide until '96, when the program was discontinued.

I've realized it's not really a solution for low-income people. We figured it cost $75,000 per floor to renovate, bring the building up to code. All that was left from 1872 were brick walls, pine sub-flooring—no pipes. We had to rewire everything, lay out sleepers. We had to get every piece of wood shimmed. For hours and hours, I was crying, "I can't do this." Mark was working for the sanitation department. He was a great mechanic, carpenter. The ceilings had curved. He totally leveled everything. While we worked on the apartment, we lived with dear friends for two years, and we're still friends. They were cab drivers because they wanted a job where they could spend more time raising their children. We moved in in '83…

Now Smokey lives here. What happened to Mark?

He moved upstate, became a veterinarian—large animals.

Smokey comes from Corpus Christi, Texas, by way of Indonesia and Morocco and all the places he made documentaries about, and then he lived for five years in that building in the West Village that looks like the one near Versailles where Marie Antoinette played milkmaid, but it's where Walt Disney reportedly lived as a young man—there are cartoons of dolphins on the wall. Errol Flynn, they say, used to practice rope moves on the top floor.

I'd forgotten it was dolphins.

August 7, 2001

THE GRAY AREA

LOCATION

SoHo, Manhattan

RENT

$1,000 (sublet of a rent-regulated apartment)

SQUARE FEET

220 (tub 'n' kitchen in tenement building)

OCCUPANTS

Joshua John (general contractor); Vlada (clothing designer; owner of Vlada)

How does this sublet work?

[JOSHUA] I pay $1,000. The guy I pay pays $264. Scandalous! He sits in Portugal. I'm sort of his retirement fund. The Portuguese have a tremendous presence in the neighborhood—the M & O grocery on Thompson. Living on the top floor of my building, the sixth, everyone complains. My father has never visited. I'm thirty-three. Dora down the hall, who's got to be close to ninety, can barely move up and down the stairs. It takes her a half hour either way. I got this apartment before September 11. It hadn't been touched in thirty years. There was a greasy stand-up shower, couple of valves. Floors, ceilings had rotted. I tore everything out, clandestinely. Then I spent September 11 down at the Trade Center. I spent a week digging with the fire and police

departments. Then I went back to work, and renovated my apartment at night.

You made the tub 'n' kitchen concept modern—it's all concrete.

It was the only way to stop the roaches. See those little recessed cavities in the shower? I was really irritated by the lack of space in the apartment. I actually hollowed out spaces between the studs. If I were to take my finger and run it against the surface, it would go into the neighbor's apartment.

I've never lived in a legal situation my entire time in New York—fifteen years. First I was on Mercer. I paid $170 for a 1,200-square-foot loft, which I built from materials I found on the street. They were all gray, illegal situations. I grew up in Riverdale, a small house. During the late seventies, when we were getting beat up everyday, my parents decided to move to Westchester. My brother and I were ostracized for our Led Zeppelin T-shirts and hair down to our shoulders. My father is director of brain research labs at NYU. My mother's a psychologist.

Fifteen years ago, I moved back from living in Europe. I worked in a law firm for a couple of months. I hated it. It was a music law firm. My boss told me the goal was to screw the artist. At some point I realized I was the artist. I had a friend in architecture school. He'd grab me late nights to build his models. I was his slave. He was at Cooper Union. They are so passionate there. It's very hard to get in. They give you a home test. It's really merit based.

The questions are really diabolical: Draw the inside of a line on a plane.

CARY CONOVER

Document the one object in your home that represents your life. Then I went to architecture school at Columbia and there was a professor going on, with these run-on sentences about Wittgenstein. I couldn't stand that elitism. I was also working full-time. I had to make a choice. Somebody offered me the opportunity to design a five-story building on Mercer Street.

Then I had to sleep on the floor of some office when I was evicted from one of my buildings. My girlfriend at the time didn't enjoy it very much. We probably don't want to mention the old one. I met Vlada in a bar. I had spent the day running around with friends giving them the ins and outs of real estate. They were wealthy, uptown kids who were going to impulse-buy an apartment for $1.3 million, a year and a half ago. I spent the day giving my opinion on all these places. At the end, we went out to dinner at Lombardi's on Spring. The bill came, my friend's husband started coughing. Why? He was cheap. I ended up picking up the check and I was pissed about it and I ended up going to meet a few friends in a bar and I got there and I was talking to this woman. I was very unfriendly. By the end, we were happy.

Vlada, where are you from?
[VLADA] Azerbaijan.

December 10, 2003

NO LOCKS, NO CEILINGS

LOCATION
Greenwich Village, Manhattan

PRICE
Under $5,000 in 1972 ($693.75 maintenance)

SQUARE FEET
950 (five-room co-op in 1905 tenement building

OCCUPANT
Susan Hoover (guitarist, poet)

I met you last summer near a bowl of Wheat Chex on a bar in a roadhouse across from the Full Moon Hotel in Oliveria, New York, where they say at the desk, "Welcome to the Moon, *man!*" Hippie talk. Anyway, you promised you'd be in a "Shelter" column and talk about your cabin in the Catskills and your Village apartment. Now you say you can't deal with anything but thinking about the tragedy and terrorist attacks, but I'm forcing you to. So let's have a refreshing country getaway and talk about the cabin.

It was spring 1980. I felt like getting out of the city one weekend and riding my motorcycle insanely. It's a white vintage BMW, and I was all in white. I always wear high heels. I was visiting a chiropractor and his wife in Woodstock, and I arrived covered in oil. But it was a great, great weekend.

When I was ready to leave, I don't know what made me say this, but I said, "If *somebody*"—I put this in the third person as if I were getting information for somebody else—"if *somebody* wanted to try to buy a house here, what would they do?" My friends immediately called this real-estate agent, and I said to her, "I'm not looking for anything, and even if I were, I would *only* want something on top of a mountain and totally isolated, and I don't care if it has electricity or running water." I had lived like this when I graduated University of Colorado in the sixties, but I only said all this to fend her off. But then she said, "I have *just* the thing." She whipped over, and when we got there, I remember standing at the top of the driveway. Every cell in my body knew I was going to have this place. It's a hand-built cabin with logs from the land. It's small, on three levels. It's just totally charming, bluestone floor. At the end of the driveway, there's a gigantic stone circle commemorating an Indian tepee. Two hippie people built it and had two babies there.

What were the hippie couple like?
They were getting divorced. So, anyway, you could be in the Wild West up there. No sense of anything human, so kind of primitive, gorgeous. I've had bears standing on their rear legs and sniffing at my windows. I have no running water. I buy an Empire State Park pass and pump water out of a well. I take showers there, too— five minutes for a quarter. Most people think I'm crazy to do this. I'm there June through mid September. This year,

I had this legal matter about my car and I chose a hearing date in Manhattan on September 11. Oh, God.

Let's back up a minute. You said you were born in Montreal. Then your family moved to Vermont after your father invented the hydraulic variable-pitch propeller that was on all warplanes, but then the government appropriated the invention and your father signed away all his rights, and it's a long story.

We lived in Vermont on top of a mountain. I remember snowshoeing down to go to a one-room schoolhouse. My mother said she would divorce my father if she had to stay on the mountain any longer. So we moved to Williamstown, Massachusetts. By 1966, I was in New York, in an apartment in the building next to the one I'm in now. The rent was, like, $91. The story was that the girl who'd lived there had a dog. She'd been up on the roof playing with the dog and a

ball, and the dog went sailing off the roof after the ball. There were no locks on the front door; garbage pickup had stopped. I got pissed off and decided to sue. It took two years, but I won rent reduction for everybody in the building. We had a pretty strong tenants' advocacy group. We went to the city and kept hammering to buy that building or the one I'm in now. We had to get financing because none of us had any money. We lived with our bags packed. The landlord could have evicted us at any moment. Finally, everything was a go. We got the building next door. We had twenty-four hours to get out. The buildings are connected. I moved across the roof in the night. When I got here, all the ceilings were gone. Everything had to be redone—wiring, plumbing. I bought the apartment sight unseen. I picked the top floor.

November 20, 2001

JAY MUHLIN

STRIPPERS AND CULTS

LOCATION

Astoria, Queens

RENT

$1,020 (rent stabilized)

SQUARE FEET

500 (two-bedroom apartment in
prewar brick building)

OCCUPANTS

Derek Scott Graves (publicist),
Jeremy Paskell (photographer)

You moved into this apartment in one of the hundreds of gloomy brick buildings in Queens with halls the color of the bottom of a lagoon because you said you couldn't take it anymore. You used to live with ten people.

[JEREMY] That was in Chelsea, a one and a half bedroom. The rent was $1,895. It was my friend's idea. We'd only pay a few hundred each if we could bring in a lot of models. We had two on the loft bed, two below on the futon, three in the living room. [DEREK] I'd rent out half my futon for $450. I became friends with these people because we were forced to sleep next to each other. Though some were sleeping with each other when they shouldn't have been. [JEREMY] Like if somebody from the upper bunk wanted to sleep with someone from the lower bunk, they couldn't do it because they

weren't really paying for that. [DEREK] People had to take showers together to save time. Then I went to the Lower East Side and had a sublet above the Pink Pony. I wondered why my rent was only $750 when others on Ludlow were paying $1,600. I said to this girl, "The building's not owned by that guy who tried to kill his tenants?" The girl didn't laugh.

Mark Glass. Now he's in the big house.
Yeah. Then I lived in the converted truck factory on South Fifth in Brooklyn, where all the burned-out buildings are. It wasn't a happy experience. My friend Kamia lived there. She likes to wear high heels and fur coats and she didn't really blend in with the neighborhood.

So Derek, you, and another roommate—now gone—got this apartment, which you painted red and purple with pretend cheetah skins for lounging on.
The roommate went to a broker against my will. I have a thing against brokers. This guy in Astoria said, "OK, $1,000 for the broker's fee and $700 to pay off the listings person." The listings person was just some girl at a desk. Jeremy moved in a few months ago.

Jeremy is putting on white nail polish now while we listen to hard trance music on the radio playing from the laptop. You two met when Jeremy was working in a health food store in West Hollywood in 1997. Jeremy moved to New York two years ago, lived on Staten Island with a couple of strippers,

then back and forth to L.A. and San
Francisco, then that apartment with ten
people, then a 6,000-square-foot loft in
Bushwick with not much heat. Moving
around isn't a new development for you.
You said you lived in four states before
you were nine. It's not because your
father worked for an oil company or
something.

[JEREMY] No, we were in a religious cult.
We traveled around a lot to avoid police
activity. It was the Sherman Tabernacle.
My mother left us when I was four. My
dad was a carpenter. He worked odd jobs
in places like Piggly Wiggly. When I was
nine, 1984, the FBI came and broke up the
whole cult. All the kids in the cult went to
foster homes for a few years. When I was
eleven, my dad and stepmother and sisters
and I moved to a house in Massachusetts. It
was the first time I lived anywhere normal.
When we lived in Texas we were in a
big former retirement home, a hundred
bedrooms. In Oregon, it was a compound,
all fenced off. [DEREK] This has been
pretty stable here in this apartment. I'm
from the San Gabriel Valley, West Covina,
California—one hundred fifty people with
two malls and a toxic dump. My family was
in a cult, too—Soldiers for Mary, a Catholic
fundamentalist militant offshoot. But we
didn't have to live with them. We just had
to go out in the desert on weekends and sit
on folding chairs.

June 27, 2000

THOSE GRIFTERS

LOCATION
Upper West Side, Manhattan

RENT
$750 (rent stabilized)

SQUARE FEET
355 (studio apartment in nineteenth-century graystone)

OCCUPANT
Rachel Kerr (theater director; voice professor, Long Island University and CUNY)

We have been talking two hours and here is what we know. One day last June you came to live on the top of this gray stone building where there is a famous documentary filmmaker's office downstairs, a screenwriter neighbor who plays his guitar on the roof, and your studio so spare with your embroidered pillowcase, a large gold picture frame without a picture, and cool air that comes through the windows.

You came here after moving sixteen times since you left San Francisco in 1994. Your first New York apartment was the one with the lobby that looked like it was in *Double Indemnity* with stucco walls and black iron curtain rods, and then came the one you sublet from the dancer in Hell's Kitchen with the candles and rocks, and the place on Convent Avenue and 145th that was beautiful but there was a leak in the ceiling that ruined your bedclothes and an insane woman in the hall shaking herself into a trance.

Your last ten moves were in one year after you fell in love with, uh, we'll call him "X," as they do in French novels, but then the relationship did not work, and you said it was the oldest story in the book because it was his apartment and you had to move out, and you started subletting because you were not yet in a financial position to get your own place but you could not bear living with other people's smells, other people's things.

The most memorable sublet was the East Village one—that was during the time you were "conned out of $1,000" by professionals on the street, the wallet scam, which you said the police told you is the oldest story in the book, and your friends could not understand how it happened because you are no dunderhead, but you said the woman who approached you looked like women you knew in Berkeley, and you were so vulnerable from all the moving. Then you sublet more places, lived with your Aunt Johanna in New Jersey, and one day a man who, oh, we'll just call him "Y," told you his sister, who is an actress in a famous sitcom, was giving up her charming studio, and he would like you to have it. So, for the first time, you had an empty apartment to fill, though you did not have much because you had been living like such an ascetic, and you told me how exhausting it was to always be saying, "I cannot buy that

SANDRA-LEE PHIPPS

because I do not have room for it, I cannot carry it, I have to save my money to get another place" though in San Francisco you used to have a very big apartment.

Now that you're finally here in one place, you have become very homebound and are happier, though I told you about this psychiatrist, who I sat next to at a film dinner, who said New York is about going out. People who stay home get depressed. But you disagreed and said New York is also about artists who stay home to work. Then we discussed your stolen bed, and how one morning you decided that you absolutely had to have an iron bed, and you found one in an antique store, and during your sublet travels the bed ended up on the set of a play in a loft building on Hudson and 14th Street. After the play closed, the bed mysteriously disappeared. Your good friend had also

bought an iron bed, only she thought yours was cooler, so you thought she had taken yours out of spite because you had had a problem over the summer when she was directing you in the play, which was called *Betrayal*. Then months later someone tipped you off that a woman in the tango studio downstairs in the loft building had taken the bed and put it on her fire escape to grow plants. Just last week your good friend went with you to pick up the bed. You are speaking to each other again, and you decided that you are going to do a show together on the roof with the two iron beds. It will be a play about jealousy between two women. One last thing, it seems there is no room left for you to talk as I've stolen your voice.

The oldest story in the book.

December 8, 1998

CHILD JOURNEY

LOCATION
Sunnyside, Queens

RENT
$560 (rent stabilized)

SQUARE FEET
550 (two-bedroom apartment in prewar building)

OCCUPANTS
Pat Connelly (social worker, director of Jewish Care Services, Rego Park), Leandra Jimenez (fashion marketing major, New York City Technical College)

Here we are in Sunnyside, where I bet it never rains. The living room is cool celadon green. The prewar building has mainly Romanian and Armenian residents, though it used to be German and Irish like all of Sunnyside. It's not far from the 1920s garden-housing community where Lewis Mumford and Perry Como once lived. Pat, you came here twenty-two years ago to stay with your mother after your father died. He was a Queens midtown bridge and tunnel officer. Then your mother died. Leandra, you arrived two and a half years ago when you were fifteen. You have a huge bedroom with stuffed animals and perfume bottles. How did you get here?
[LEANDRA] My mother kicked me out of the house when I was thirteen. We had

a fight. She decided she didn't want me to live with her. This was in Washington Heights. I went to stay at a friend's, but she started hiding my clothes so I had to move. I went to another friend. I slept under her bed so her mother couldn't find me. I had nowhere to go. I stayed in a hospital and pretended to be waiting for a patient. I was attending Seward Park High School. I went to my aunt's house for two weeks, my mother's friend's for three months, then my cousin's in New Jersey. She found these St. Joseph's nuns in Queens. They set up a meeting with my mother. My mother was very enthused about me living with them. I stayed four months with three nuns, a senile old lady, and four dogs. They enrolled me in St. Joseph High School. I was doing very well, but I had an asthma attack for the first time in a long time. I went to the hospital.

A social worker thought you should go into the foster care system.
The first home was in the projects in East New York. I was the only light-skinned little girl walking around there. The woman I lived with was loud and obnoxious. She put a lock on the refrigerator so I couldn't take her food. The elevator was filthy. During all the moving, a lot of my clothes were stolen. I only had like two pairs of pants, a comb, some gel. Then I lived in a two-family house, a brownstone. It was decent, homey. But this lady was the biggest blabbermouth. She bragged about being a foster mother. Then she started getting mad at her husband, saying he was too nice to me, bringing me fruit all the time. I don't think he meant anything. Once again I was

ANDRE SOUROUJON

kicked out. The agency found this lady in Harlem. I was the only Hispanic. She had four foster care children, five of us in one room. By then I'd saved enough money. I was working in a pizza place forty hours a week, going to school forty hours, tuition cost $280. I rented a studio, Washington Heights, $425 a month. It had this crusty little cot. It was a drug spot. One night guys came banging on my door. I left and slept on the streets until I found a room for $380.

The agency sent an investigator.
I said, "I'll only go back to foster care if I can meet a person I can live with." [PAT] So she could screen them. [LEANDRA] I just didn't want to be thrown in any house, like a North Shore animal kitty. I'd moved over sixteen times. My counselor spoke to an old friend of Pat's... [PAT] Who I told I'd recently lost my mother. I was having

a difficult time living alone. She asked if I'd be interested. I'd never thought about being a foster parent in my entire life. I'd always wanted to have lots of children. It just didn't happen. So we set up a meeting. [LEANDRA] I fell in love with Pat. [PAT] She also said I talked too much. [LEANDRA] She was a chatterbox. [PAT] I wanted her to know everything about me. So the next day the super said a young girl came by and left her things in the basement. I became an official foster parent, six weeks of training. [LEANDRA] I got the big bedroom because Pat doesn't like big spaces. [PAT] Yes I do. I just wanted her to have the bigger room. [LEANDRA] Would you rather have the big room? [PAT] No, no, where would you put all your clothes? [LEANDRA] You're right.

August 10, 1999

FIRE, BETRAYAL, AND MURDER

LOCATION
Park Slope, Brooklyn

RENT
$708 (rent stabilized)

SQUARE FEET
500 (five-room apartment in tenement building)

OCCUPANTS
Yvonne Derrick (scheduler for council member Angel Rodriguez; sales, Almars Cards & Gifts), Kyle (junior, Lincoln High School), Wyatt (seventh grader, M.S. 51)

I'm torn. I don't know whether to ask if you're stockpiling antibiotics in your closet or talk about what happened in 1977 in San Antonio when you said a man soaked the roof of your parents' house with gasoline and lit a match.
[YVONNE] Let's go with the latter. It was like the first house my parents ever bought. We were the first Mexicans in an all-white neighborhood, and we were pretty much ridiculed. One day, some guy broke in and stole my mother's ring. He was arrested, and he and his friends retaliated by setting the house on fire. We got out, but we lost everything. My mother found us another house, but by then my father had gone off and married my best friend in high school, the blond beauty every boy wanted. I just got up one day in 1978 and went to Hollywood to be a comedienne. I was eighteen, working as an usher in a lot of these famous theaters.

It was the Aquarius that changed everything for me. *Ain't Misbehavin'* was there. I formed a friendship with Nell Carter. I lived with her awhile. When she went to New York in 1980, she said, "Come, too." And that's how I met Frank, the show's drummer. He'd been Cab Calloway's last drummer. We were together sixteen years. We have two boys and a daughter, Rheanna, who's eighteen. She stays with her boyfriend in Staten Island. Frank and I moved here in '83. But first we lived in the President Hotel when he was on Broadway and raking in the bucks. Later in Hempstead, to take care of his cousin, also a musician, whose wife was murdered. My sister Margaret was murdered four years ago in Laredo. The man she lived with for ten years was indicted, but he fled the country. Me, my mom, and my dad went on a mission for justice. He was missing for years. No one helped us—not the cops, not the FBI, not Governor Bush. Only the editor of the *Laredo Morning Times* helped. We finally got the monster in Mexico. They put him in a cell. Later that night, he hung himself. Then we had to fight the Mexicans to do an autopsy to make sure it was him. That was last year.

All your individual terrors in the midst of this monster horror of bombs and powder and never a moment's rest!

We all have a poisonous gas in our family. I look at my life in the last four years—losing my sister, the relationship with Frank disbanding.

Everything happened in this apartment. Do you have indelible images of the past here?
Not really. When Frank left, I got a brand new bed. But I still have all the little things he used to bring me from traveling—a piece from the Berlin Wall, a small Colosseum from Rome, a stone from Morocco, a little gondola.

The world is in your living room! Miniature is always a more perfectly realized universe.
When we first moved here, we lived in a smaller apartment upstairs. This one is better but I always say, "I *want* to move," but I can't.

It's as though no one's allowed forward motion now—economically or any way.

Also, if I did get something I want right now, I would feel a sense of guilt. Who am I? I think about the 100,000 who lost jobs at airlines.

Where is the card shop you work at?
Fifth Avenue and 11th. I'm there weekends, Valentine's Day. I used to have four jobs; now I just have two. The card shop's my connection to the community. I was also PTA president and a board member for twelve years at P.S. 124. That school is my heart. I used to schlep up and down the street to get donations from merchants, fans for the school. When my sister died, the teachers raised enough money for me and my kids to fly home. I've also been vice president of CATS, Care About the Slope. In the past, we've talked about the neighborhood post office and complained—how it takes forever to get a stamp, a lot of things we thought mattered.

November 6, 2001

SIX FIRES

LOCATION

Williamsbridge, Bronx

RENT

$1,487 (Section 8 subsidized housing;
tenant pays $86)

SQUARE FEET

1,050 (floor of two-family house)

OCCUPANTS

Stephanie Brown (parent mentor,
Good Shepherd Services),
Shana Brown (19, student, BMCC),
Walter Brown III (18, student,
Manhattan Career Center),
Stefon Bland (student, C.S. 134)

You have been in six apartment fires.
[STEPHANIE] We got burned out June 25,
in the South Bronx, the Southview area.
I was living there for six years. Everyone
was out. I was at work. My grandson was
at a doctor's appointment. What didn't get
destroyed by fire got destroyed by soot and
water. It was an electrical fire. That's all
we know. The landlord was very rude and
snotty to us. He didn't even come to see if
anybody got hurt. You have landlords and
you have slumlords.

I was in previous fires when I was little.
I remember all of them. I was four years
old, living in Bed-Stuy, Lexington Avenue.
Kids were playing with a match. They threw
it into an electrical socket, burned the whole
building down. We got out just in time, four
families. Then they fixed the building and
there was another fire. The third was when

I was eight, also in Brooklyn. Oh God,
what do they call them? I think something
happened in the vents. Nobody got hurt.
A couple of apartments got destroyed.
The fourth was 150th Street in Harlem.
Somebody fell asleep with a cigarette. It
was the apartment right next to us. Three
families got burned out. A burning mattress
is no joke. It burns slow.

The fifth fire was in '91.
I'm a recovering addict. I have fourteen
years clean. I had two years clean then.
I was living at 127th in Harlem. It was
drug dealer infested. The whole building
got burned out, five floors, four families on
each floor. The addicts were getting high.
Who knows how it started. The building
was old. A hot match probably would
have set it off. I wasn't at home. I was at a
meeting. The kids weren't with me. They
were in care, kinship care. Three of my
friends were living with me, my father-in-
law. He got housing quickly because he
was a senior. I went with Red Cross. They
put you up for seven days, a hotel on 76th
and Amsterdam. Then they put me in this
shelter, 136th Street, for two months, until
I started raising hell. It was a lot of addicts,
unisex, had to use the same bathroom.
They wanted to put me into an all-women's
shelter. I just went off: I'm not having any
more shelters and I'm going to tear up your
place and I want my place. That's when
they put me into NYC public housing.

The latest fire.
I was coming from a friend of mine's
anniversary. My kids were outside. When
I went to get out of the car, they said,

"Mommy, Mommy, don't get upset." You know, I have a very bad temper. I saw the landlord on the stoop. I looked up, no windows, no lights, no nothing—flashlights searching around. It was disgusting. They sent me to HPD. They were going to put me in a shelter, emergency assistance unit. No way! I wasn't going in. I've got family and friends, thank God. I just got this place in October. It's nice but it's isolated, too quiet. All of us are bored here, even my grandson. The South Bronx, I loved it, I really wanted to stay. The apartments available there were dumps. Since I've had Section 8, I've never had dumpy apartments. I tried so hard to get in an apartment building. But most Section 8 apartments I saw were in houses. But I saw the kitchen here. I told the landlord, "Can I please, please have the apartment? Here's my packet."

I've got a fiancé. He's a security guard. We met in a Laundromat seven years ago. I was working in a Laundromat across from the PJs—the projects—Martin Luther King Towers. Yes, we'll get married. I want four bridesmaids, a matron of honor, a maid of honor, four groomsmen, two flower girls, two ring bearers, a junior bride, and groom. I told him, "No shorts!"

December 3, 2003

JULIE SOEFER

"Esta sala de espera sin esperanza
Estas pilas de un timbre que se secó
Este helado de fresa de la venganza
Esta empresa de mudanza
Con los muebles del amor"

Joaquin Sabina is singing about the strawberry ice cream of vengeance and a moving company hauling the furniture of love. I am looking up at a purple octopus on the ceiling. There are little paintings on the walls of sailboats on a blue sea and white houses with pink flowers. It must be the coast of Peru.

How can this half of a roasted chicken cost only $5? Is this Peruvian economics? I don't know about Peru. This is the first Peruvian restaurant in the East Village. The handsome waiter explains the chicken situation: "The more you make of something, the more you can offer it for less." The restaurant is owned by a Peruvian man and a Bangladeshi man who is backing him, he says. He brings over extra sauces, four kinds.

I am thinking about the Department of City Planning's latest book: *The Newest New Yorkers 2000*, and all the neighborhood statistics on immigrants: 248 from Nigeria in Bedford-Stuyvesant, 377 from Ireland in Inwood, 5 from France in Great Kills, 1,180 from Rumania in Astoria, 63,663 from the Dominican Republic in Washington Heights, 62 from Israel in the Theater District. The numbers are always changing. It is as if New York City is always being newly hatched out of an egg.

New York has more diversity in its immigrant population than any other city in the country. Foreign-born immigrants and their U.S.-born offspring account for approximately fifty-five percent of the city's population, according to the Department of City Planning. People are talking in more than 175 different languages, says demographer Joseph Salvo. In 1643, a Jesuit missionary, after escaping from Mohawk captivity, reported as many as eighteen languages in New York City, which was a lot considering he reported New Amsterdam's population as approximately one thousand. Today all the foreign-born diversity is in addition to the 100,000 or so who come to New York City from the fifty states every year.

The waiter and I listen a little more to Joaquin sing about a bell that lives in its bell tower, "the half that's split in half...." "*Esta campana mora en el campanario. Esta mitad partida por la mitad.*" He moves the glasses on the next table, lining up the napkins, making them perfect.

IMMIGRANTS

LA PÁGINA DE LOS NIÑOS

LOCATION
Elmhurst, Queens

RENT
$1,100 (market)

SQUARE FEET
575 (one-bedroom apartment
in house)

OCCUPANTS
Verónica Rosendo (publisher,
La Voz de México), Fernando Rosendo
(retired machinist; journalist),
América Rosendo
(third grader, P.S. 12)

Why did you name your daughter América?

[VERÓNICA] We were at the hospital. Her father says, "Well, we are here in America." So—América! She likes music like "God Bless America" because the song is for her. We've lived in this apartment two years. I came to New York about fifteen years ago from Veracruz. My husband was born in Guanajuato. He started reporting in Los Angeles in 1980.

Mexicans are the fastest-growing group in New York City, reports the Department of City Planning. The population more than tripled, from 55,700 in 1990 to 186,872 in 2000.

Mexicans are the third-largest Latino group here after Puerto Ricans and Dominicans.

I would say the total of documented and undocumented Mexicans here is a million. When we started the paper in 1992, there was only one Mexican restaurant in Queens. Now Roosevelt Avenue is all Mexican. Also, Fifth Avenue and Wyckoff in Brooklyn, Staten Island, the Bronx.

I also read that a big Mexican middle class is forming.

Still, most are poor people. They come from the mountains. They don't know how to read or write. [AMÉRICA] In Mexico, it is not that well. They only give you ten dollars a day. It's not fair in Mexico.

What are you working on, América? Your pencil is poised in the air.

[VERÓNICA] She has a column in *La Voz*. [*We look at the fifty-two-page September 23–29 issue.*]

"La Página de los Niños"! "Contemporary Mexico—the Reconstruction of the Country." You begin: "Although the constitution was proclaimed in 1917, the war continued in various regions of Mexico until 1920. By the time it finally ended, many things had changed.... Destruction was everywhere." Powerful! Soon you'll have a blog. The living room looks like a second newsroom.

Our office is in Astoria. I work both places. [AMÉRICA] I help them at 2:30 or something.

I was reading about the transnationalism concept—a population living between two countries transcends its geography— they visit, send back money. Mexicans sent an estimated $10 billion to their families in Mexico in 2002.

[VERÓNICA] Mostly those are the grocery store owners. They go back every two to six months, open new businesses. Over there, there are no businesses. Everybody's here. It's only all old people and little children there.

América, is your next column going to be about the elections?

[*She puts her arm around her mother.*] [AMÉRICA] I don't like George Bush because he only likes Americans.

Now you're wrestling with the cat on the floor.

No, I'm just bringing her down.

Does the paper have a stand on Bush or Kerry?

[VERÓNICA] Not yet. The Hispanic community doesn't care about Kerry or Bush. Kerry and Bush don't have anything for immigration, nothing concrete for the illegals. Mexicans are very important for the economy and the jobs. Did you see the film *A Day Without a Mexican*? All the restaurants and factories stand still. The Mexican community wants to work, pay the bills. There are lots of citizens but they don't vote. It's like in Florida. When Bush won, there was little controversy. Mexicans say it's the same thing in Mexico. They win because a rich person put them in.

Were you a reporter before you met your husband?

No. I worked in a beauty salon on Fifth Avenue. I did nails. My husband moved here in '88. He was a machinist. When we finished working, we'd go work on the small newspapers. They don't exist anymore. Now just *La Voz*. We did everything ourselves.

Do you go to all the restaurants?

My favorite is Colombian, because of the soup. I'm expecting a baby in March.

October 13, 2004

OKRA AND FOIE GRAS

LOCATION
East Fifties, Manhattan

RENT
$1,558 (rent stabilized)

SQUARE FEET
500 (one-bedroom apartment in tenement building)

OCCUPANT
Geetika Khanna (chef/co-owner, Kalustyan's Masala Café)

Scrabble in the morning!
I'll have my coffee and play five or six games on the Internet. There's a place where you can chat. Some people are mean. You can challenge them. There was someone from Israel. I said, "You should know how to spell that." He said, "Give me a break, I'm twelve."

This man in the photograph above your computer is so dashing—collar open, hands in his pockets, mustache.
That was my father. He died when I was nine. He sold tires. It sounds sad but he was very charismatic. Every man now has to look just like him. They have to be tall and handsome. I was born in Jaipur in '69. Then we went to Simla, then Delhi, then Lucknow. That's where he got ill. He told my mother, "Get out of here—don't live in this country." My mother was twenty-eight. In India, in those days, one of the only

options for survival was to get remarried. She had a sister in London. We went. My mother was studying to be an aesthetician. [*Phone rings. "When you see Aziz, ask him for the chicken guy's number. Oh please, I finished the okra. We have crabs sitting upstairs." Then her mother calls. Then her cousin.*] My cousin is on both sides. Two sisters married two brothers. He's very attractive, and if he wasn't my cousin....So my mother asked me, "Do you like it in London?" I said no. I was watching all those Indian movies with stepfathers and stepmothers. If my mother married again, it could be horrible. She sent me back to her sister in Delhi. My mother came to America. Why? I don't know. England has a whole thing with Indians. You're never really equal. She became a hostess. She met my dad. He works at 21. He's a bartender. My mother doesn't like to go and see him in uniform. I lived with them off and on. My parents live near here. They have a beautiful apartment, large building—sturdy, as opposed to mine, which has Sheetrock everywhere. I moved back with them at the end of '97. I got my master's. I had worked with developmentally disabled kids, which was very depressing. I quit.

So my cousin was getting married in India. My mother said, "You're just sitting around—go." I had this epiphany there. I wanted to do something related to India. I thought, I'll sell jewelry or artifacts. My relatives said, "You're not some business mind." I'm home watching the Food Channel for two weeks straight, me in a La-Z-Boy in my pajamas. My mom said, "Take a shower." As I'm watching, I knew I had to get a job cooking. My dad sent me to the chef of Café des Artistes. He said, How old are you? I said twenty-eight. He said, "That's old. I started when I was fourteen." I thought, "That's your problem." I've lived a whole life. I can be a little cocky. He said, "All right." He gave me a whole box of foie gras to clean the veins out of.

A friend said that living in another country is like being an actor, having to pretend, take on the role, the language. Yes, you know, I love to live in New York but I'm very Indian. But I don't feel at home in India. I'm in love with my vision of India. When I was growing up we were middle class. India is very classist. We lived in a very simple apartment.

Everybody drove motorcycles—not for fun. That's how they traveled then. Now my generation there has moved to upper middle class—they have a house, yard, two cars. When I go back home, it's as if the whole neighborhood moved from the East Village to the Upper East Side. It makes me very uncomfortable. Everything is very materialistic. What used to be farms, rich people are buying but they are not working the farms. My cousin said, "We're going through what America went through in the 1950s." The simple life has gone. We never used to lock our doors. Of course, here, if I'm not expecting you and you ring the door, I won't answer.

March 10, 2004

JAY MUHLIN

CHOPIN, BORSCHT

LOCATION
Yorkville, Manhattan

RENT
$1,009 (rent stabilized)

SQUARE FEET
335 (studio in tenement building)

OCCUPANT
Katya Grineva (concert pianist)

Your piano is half your apartment.
For a while I had two pianos here. I had another Steinway. It was white. It was kind of a gift. But the people wanted it back. I play Chopin, Mozart. I invite people here before I play big concerts at Lincoln Center. I'm playing November 30. They sit on the floor. It's everybody's favorite thing. I make borscht, something creative. I have a special sponsor, Bellefon. I play a lot in France. It's a kind of French champagne.

Champagne and borscht.
No, *caviar*. I will play for you Chopin, "Fantasie-Impromptu." It's the piece I play for the encore of every concert. I give you my encore. [*She plays.*]

There's really not much to say. [*Pause*] But then there is. When you play, the walls disappear and the sound takes you away, beyond the room into a music dream, a huge rolling space, a musical infinity.

It's true! I'm playing also "Andante Spianato," so uplifting and full of life and it takes you to a completely different realm. You know when you experience ecstasy and freedom. That's what people want to feel all the time but it's difficult. Before Carnegie Hall last year, I invited fifteen people over and they said they actually felt they had been on a trip to the Pacific.

Do your neighbors mind that you practice or are they happy?
Most people work. I always practice in the morning. My apartment faces the garden. I have squirrels in the backyard. There is this big tree. Very often I see tons of birds sitting on the branch. I wonder if it's the music that attracts them.

They feel the emotion.
I used to be in the front of the building. My friends Lily and John, they loved it. They used to invite friends over for cocktails. We would open the doors. We were always joking that we would break down the wall. They moved to Guam and that's why I go to play concerts there. It's a big American base. People are from all over the world. I won an award in Guam, all because of my neighbors.

When did you come from Russia?
I came here fifteen years ago. I was living here for five years with an American family who kind of adopted me. By accident I met this lady who invited me for dinner. At the time, I thought I should move. I said, "I wish I could live here and be your neighbor." She called me the next morning and said someone in the building

CARY CONOVER

was moving out. I've been here a long time. It's a charming neighborhood. I come home and my landlord will always come out and give me a kiss and say, "Are you making money? Are you making money?" I am away and they fix my bathroom. The landlord does a better job than any doorman. He's an Italian guy from Sicily. He holds packages for me in the barber shop. His brother came to my Carnegie Hall concert last year.

I was just thinking about the puce-, ah, mushroom-colored walls in the hallway here, not unlike the hallways of thousands of people and artists in tenements in the city—such a contrast to the glamorous concert halls. You have a stuffed Dalmatian. [*We pat its head.*]

My father brought it for me after my dog died. My parents visit twice a year. I studied piano by accident. It was because of my neighbors. They were taking their children to register in the music school. They asked my mother if she would let me go for the walk. I went along. They accepted me into the music school. My parents bought for me a German upright. I loved that instrument. There was something so mysterious about it. My mother said, "Now, don't worry, if you decide you don't want to play, we'll sell it." I played all the time. I didn't want them to sell it.

November 24, 2004

AU PAIR

LOCATION

Upper West Side, Manhattan

RENT

$0 (in exchange for work)

SQUARE FEET

130 (room and bath in condominium
in prewar building)

OCCUPANT

Miriam Ruth Anna Marie Schleser
(au pair; artist)

This is the building they show at the beginning of the *Seinfeld* show, you said! Sort of ivy covered, with rosy pink flowers on the trees. The birds are chirping madly. [*First we visit Miri's employer, Barbara Nair, who has lived here for twenty years. The lovely apartment is being renovated. A golden retriever is tied to a pole while a cleaning lady is tidying up. Barbara is at a computer in her daughter Priya's room. The bed has a hundred stuffed animals, mainly dogs with floppy ears, and a pillow that reads "Princess Priya."*]

[BARBARA] Miriam is a wonderful au pair. I've had twelve. She is one of the few who has been able to get into the family. I have two older boys. They either like the au pairs or they can't stand them. One is studying at Wesleyan. [*We go to Miri's room.*]

What color pink is this? It's like being inside a seashell.

[MIRI] Bubble Bath. I went to the three hardware stores to pick this one. Colors, art are my life. Since I have to work forty-two

hours a week, my only free time I spend doing my art. I do a lot of little sculptures that are very fragile. I like things that float in the air. Everything is sparkle. See, I put sparkles on the walls.

What is your schedule?

I wake up at six. I do Priya's washing, her clothing, then her breakfast, and I bring her to the bus. Balan, her father, he's from Malaysia. He works on Wall Street. He's ten years younger than Barbara. Priya and I fight every morning. She tries to copy me but on the other hand she's independent and wants to choose herself what to wear, what is cool. I have the biggest sticker collection. She is very jealous of my collection. Here's Hello Kitty. I started it in Germany. Teddy bears and clowns. Eight o'clock, I am at the Art Students League. I help monitor, set up. I'm at school until one. Then I come back and work for the art center from one to three. [*Barbara Nair has started an art center in Killingworth, Connecticut, near her country house.*] I go up on weekends to teach the other people.

My father died when I was five. My mother left for Spain. I was living alone with my grandma. Then my grandmother died. I moved to Spain when I was eleven. [*She brings out a blue glass music box.*] The engine for the music is broken and I'm so sad. Somebody told me years ago that because there weren't people, I had to focus on things. I never watch TV. They said I should have a TV in my room here. So I put it up on the wall. I did it myself. My mom had a boyfriend in Spain. We lived in a *finca*, a traditional old Spanish farmhouse. We had to install everything. My mom was

JENA CUMBO

always busy. He taught me how to get wires together, fix lamps.

You're leaving here in August.
Barbara wanted me to stay longer. I want to spend full time on my art, study for degrees. A friend, who's an au pair in New Jersey, we're looking for an apartment. We went to International English school in Spain together. She didn't know what to do with her future. I told her, come with me. She's my best friend. We love each other. We both had very confusing childhoods with lot of things happening. We've been looking in Williamsburg, Chelsea. We go to laundry services and look on the boards. Because we speak Spanish and German, we get papers in those languages. We look on the Internet, on traffic light poles, on bulletin boards in supermarkets.

We forgot the rest of your schedule.
I pick up Priya at three and from three to seven, we do everything together. She goes to ballet and I bring her there. We go and buy clothes. She wants to have everything I get. I have a Burberry jean jacket. I take her to Century 21. Lela, the cleaning lady, makes dinner every day. I make Priya her dessert. Then I'm free at seven or eight. I do some art work and go out partying, with some people I met on Halloween on the street. They are older, twenty-four. One is a lawyer, the other works on Wall Street. They take me everywhere. Sometimes, I sleep only three hours.

May 5, 2004

BASICALLY THE SAME

LOCATION

Bayside, Queens

RENT

$1,785 (market)

SQUARE FEET

2,000 (three-bedroom apartment
in 1970s townhouse)

OCCUPANTS

Dr. Reucar Quijada (pediatrician,
Pediatric 2000), Dr. Alba Pumarol
(family practice resident, Bronx
Lebanon Hospital), Paola Quijada
(first grader, Our Lady of the
Blessed Sacrament)

A bright, icy day, the wind pushing against houses and trees. We came off the Cross Island Expressway and there was all this slate-blue water with whitecaps. Then the streets. New York can become suburban so quickly. All the houses look the same: mid-1970s, two apartments each, two garages each, two kinds of shingles each—each home with two apartments, attached to another two. All these blocks of fours. Soon there will be four of you.

[ALBA] I'm expecting in January.

Look, a bassinet—white ruffles, pink, blue, and yellow dots. You came to the States in 1996, lived in Elmhurst, then Flushing, then...

I wanted a dishwasher, dryer, washing machine. People are telling me, "You are requesting a lot. You are in New York now." I said, "Well, but I want to pay for it." They said, "Why do you want a three-bedroom apartment if there are only three people?" We looked at like seven or eight houses. We even went to Astoria. For the same price as this, the apartments were so small. You have trash in the entrance of the buildings. My husband was not as demanding. [REUCAR] We got this through a pediatrician who lives in Bayside. The owner is from Korea. The area is very diverse, people from Colombia, Dominican Republic, a lot of Italian, Greek. [ALBA] Next door are Americans. [REUCAR] Chinese are in the front. African American all the way in front.

You like to play baseball. Is there a team around here?

The New York Mets!

I meant for you.

Oh. The Dominican League. I play every Sunday in warm weather, in Corona, 114th and 37th. I play first and third base.

You look so proud.

[ALBA] He is a frustrated major-league player. [REUCAR] My father had something else in his mind. [PAOLA] You could still make it. [REUCAR] I'm getting a little old. [ALBA] Reucar's father is a doctor. My father is a doctor. Paola said she will not be a doctor. [PAOLA] I want to be a singer and an actress.

W. C. Fields used to live in Bayside when they were making lots of movies in Astoria—*Sally of the Sawdust*, 1925—a fact that has nothing to do with your lives or mine or probably the reader's, just a floating scrap of history. Every day, both of you cross the Throgs Neck Bridge, which sounds like you're crossing through the neck of a frog. Reucar, you are in a special doctor's program?
[REUCAR] If you work in an underserved area for three years, you can get your green card and work anyplace. I work in Washington Heights. Most of our patients are from the Dominican Republic.

That's where you went to medical school, though you're from Venezuela.
[ALBA] Latin Americans everywhere, basically it's the same. I'm from the Dominican Republic. I was born in Mexico. My father went there to do his medical training. I'm the oldest, there's another girl, and triplets, brothers. That's incredible. When they were born, they had to bring

extra doctors to help. In my practice, I also do home visits. Mainly Hispanic, African-American patients. [REUCAR] Very old apartments and crowded. [ALBA] If you are just in a clinic, you don't know anything about the person. When you go to their home, you realize more. One lady was using a cane. She lives on the tenth floor!

You have a wall with little pottery houses, the red one...
Two balconies with flowers, typical Colombian. Here is Venezuelan. My mother has a collection. Every time she visits, she brings me one. I say, "No more."

And all these little paintings. Each one has a small house, with two black windows and a palm tree. Those lavender clouds above, island clouds, always moving, very hormonal. Did you have a house like this?
[REUCAR] This isn't anywhere we lived.

December 18, 2002

MY EARS ARE PAINTED ON

LOCATION
Greenpoint, Brooklyn

RENT
$900 (market)

SQUARE FEET
500 (floor of house)

OCCUPANT
David Latimer (magazine publisher:
The Thresher, RES, Fringe, etc.)

How is it living near Sharkey's Driving School?

More importantly, I'm living near the Slovakian Men's Club—$2 beer, but there's no one Slovakian. They all died. It's pretty much Irish. Annual membership is $10. I'm the youngest member, forty-six. You have to be sponsored. My sponsor was a guy at the end of the bar, home from Desert Storm. He said, "I'll sponsor 'im." Then I had to be approved by the president. He said, "No shenanigans." I moved to New York in '95 from San Francisco.

Where you were the owner of the famous Buster's Newsstand and founder of the hilarious *The Nose*. Everyone's still laughing at issue number three. Ha-ha.

We operated many magazines out of my apartment there, a converted grocery near the Fairmont Hotel. We had a trapeze. Why not—there was a fifteen-foot ceiling. When I came here, I got this place through a Polish real-estate agent for $600. They've raised the rent $100 a year. They never fix anything. That's why I don't have doorknobs.

How about that circus wagon you used to live in?

Circus trailers are well designed, like a yacht cabin. I was a producer for Circus Vargas when I was twenty-two. I ordered hay for the elephants, paid off the police. I knew Simone the Chimp Handler, Wally the Bear Handler. He wore a cossack outfit. Simone was a man from Argentina. He and Wally were lovers, though they were married to twin high-wire performers and had children. Nuns traveled with us, too. There's an order of the Catholic Church dedicated to ministering to the spiritual needs of circus performers—well, travelers—and the nuns ran the popcorn concession. They had their trailer and wore a modified sports habit. The circus years were after I came home from my mission in Japan. I was raised a Mormon in Montana. I lived with eight missionaries in different cities in Japan, small awful apartments, one with rats so bad. The apartments doubled as a church and English-language school. That's how we got people interested. We'd go door to door, which was very ineffective in Japan. You knock and they call through the door, "My ears are painted on." Or my favorite was, "No one is here." After Japan, I lived at my grandmother's house in Salt Lake City—a close-knit Mormon community, cottonwood trees, like a fairy-tale house. My grandpa chewed tobacco. He had to sleep in the garage. When they came to Utah—he was a teamster—he traded a lot of the land he owned for horses. My grandmother was furious.

So now you're sitting in this house with gray and pink siding near a park where you said the Salvadorans play volleyball, Colombians play baseball, a group of men from Poland drink, and young attractive couples lie around on top of their dogs. Don't you feel far away from all the places you've been?
I'm not really connected with this neighborhood. When I first moved, I was always in the East Village—bars, restaurants. There is an age difference in Williamsburg between myself and most of the young bar patrons. I haven't really connected the way I did in San Francisco.

Also, I work more here. I mean, where's the party? I bought a house recently. I'm fixing it up. It's in Spokane. I don't know anyone there. I got the house on the Internet. It's sort of weird, but like twenty years ago I was driving through Moses Lake, Washington, and I got this impression I should move there someday. Last year I went to Moses Lake, but I couldn't figure out what I was doing there. When I came back, I started looking on the Internet. This house in Spokane came up. I bought a house in Denver a few years ago, one in Utah, too, near my family.

Are you laundering money?
No! It's just that I can't afford a house in New York. The way I look at it, I'm going to Spokane so I can figure out what I'm supposed to be doing in Moses Lake.

July 24, 2001

I AM EVERYTHING THERE

LOCATION
East Village, Manhattan

RENT
$1,200 (commercial)

SQUARE FEET
600 (storefront)

OCCUPANT
Geova Rodrigues (fashion designer)

I think I'll sit down in this one chair you have. Well, it's a ninety-eight-degree day and we're in your twelve-foot-wide home and atelier with the wool carpet and the scraps of leather and fur floating around. Oh, the pincushion looks like a tomato. You used to be a painter and you are from Brazil. How long have you been here?

Two and a half years. My landlord, Mrs. Shirley, attends my shows. She gives me advice. I say, "Mrs. Shirley, I wish you be my mother," so I don't have to pay the rent. She love what I'm doing. She want me to do something commercial. She want me to make money. I pay my rent late but all the time I pay. I find this place from another painter. He discovered the space is very small for him. Mrs. Shirley's husband say to me, "You can afford?" I say, "Yes, sure."

Does Mrs. Shirley wear your clothes, like the bra made out of airline sleeping masks?

No, I like to do maybe a T-shirt for her. My clothes are too weird for her but she like, she watches *Sex and the City*, she says, "Geova, you have to be in *Sex and the City* because all the clothes look like that." My birthday was on August 2. Her birthday is the same day. I'm always using my home for everything, a garage for my bicycle, a showroom. No one helps me. I do every single thing. I have the ability to make ugly things beautiful. When I work, I have to be a mess. When I have the mess I get inspired. All my fabric is found on the street, the garbage. I was born in the northeast of Brazil, Barcelona, eight streets, very small. I am not from a rich family. Twelve brothers and sisters. My father, he was a farmer, cows, bulls, corn, beans. Here is a picture of my family's house, it looks like a train, one level, each house looks alike, eleven rooms. The last time I was there, eight years ago. The city wants to do something public for me. I am everything there. They watch me on TV in Brazil, MTV. I sent to them *Elle* magazine. I have a big article, May 2000. The immigration approved me today for a green card. Designer Jussara Lee is my sponsor. I've lived in good places and very worst. I live on 8th, 12th, 14th, 15th, 16th. I was very excited when I came to East Village. I love East Village. Once I live on 76th and Third. When I moved, I was depressed because I would be not part of East Village anymore. Next, I had a basement, a very teeny room in East Village. It was illegal. The landlord wanted to put all my stuff

ROBERT HALE

onto the street. I had fashion shows in the basement. I make a fashion movie there, documentary for European TV. Famous stylists were there. They love it. One day there is a London magazine journalist. A big *cucaracha* ran on the floor. Ha, ha, ha. She laughs. I say, "Don't worry, this is very New York." She says, "Of course." I've never have a formal job, I never finish high school. I went to Sao Paulo when I was sixteen and a half years old, 1980s. I was in Paris two years, painting. I met a friend and moved to Charlotte, North Carolina. Then I came to New York in 1990, the summer, I come to place of Keith Haring, Warhol, SoHo. I say, "Where is the beautiful city in the movies? This is ugly." I left after five days. I was very scared of New York. I couldn't speak English. I was not prepared to be in another city. I go back to Charlotte. My friend in Charlotte is like my family. I find a big loft, a beautiful house. I say, "I don't want to go to New York at

all." Then '92 is when I move here. When I left Barcelona, I say I know it is past. Sao Paulo, past. Paris, Charlotte, past. But maybe one day, I go back to...

No one leaves New York. You've entered hell—choose your sofa. Do you cook in that tiny kitchen that kind of merges into the bathroom in the back? Oh, you do. You make fish Wanda?
No, I said, I make *feijoada*. I sit, eat here near the window.

You sit next to the high-heeled shoes and the lace hoop-skirt dress in the storefront display. You have your plate next to the sewing machine. Do you ever feel claustrophobic?
No, because all the time, I watch the street.

August 28, 2002

YOU NEED SOMETHING BIG

LOCATION
Hell's Kitchen, Manhattan

RENT
$3,725 (rent stabilized)

SQUARE FEET
982 (two-bedroom apartment
in new high rise)

OCCUPANTS
T. J. Mitchell (assistant to the
president, major record company),
Lori Davis (hairdresser, the
FaceStation)

You're like two birds up here, looking down on New York.
[T. J.] Every time it snows, I'm so excited. *Whooo-ee.*

This building with concierge, "lobby as lounge," "rough-hewn concrete water wall," and Juilliard concerts, has a name that makes it sound like some factory from 1840. It wasn't built until 2001. The brochure has photographs of poor women sweeping tenement steps.
I came from L.A. for a job relocation interview in September 2001. This was the only place I looked at. Nobody had ever sat on my toilets before. *Whooo-ee!* I had to make forty-five to fifty times the rent to even qualify for the apartment. Lori and I had savings. The management said, "We don't care. We want to know what you're making." I said, "Great, I'll let you know when I'll give you my first-born." That was only my second time to New York. I was like a kid coming into a candy store. I love that I can get a cheeseburger delivered at four in the morning, *whooo-ee.* You come home, have a little hangover thing goin', you need something, *big.*

The two of you remind me of a TV show, I don't know what.
We are *Sex and the City*. I'm definitely Samantha. She's probably Charlotte. Samantha doesn't live by women's rules. Yes, we go to lots of parties. [LORI] Last fall, we went out five nights a week. [T. J.] On a normal night, we might go have a burger and a Bud and then we're hanging out with Gene Simmons and the prince of Saudi Arabia. I'll sit in bed at night and say, "Damn, we did that." We met President Clinton. No, he didn't hit on us. I saw him again a few weeks later and he said, "So nice to see you again." He squeezed my hand. We were backstage at Creed. Mark Tremonti is playing Ping-Pong with a six-year-old girl. I said, "So this is it?" [LORI] My mom owns a nightclub outside Dayton. She has these matchbooks. They say, "Our customers always come first at Bojangles." [T. J.] You open it up and it's a condom. We met in Houston, where I'm from. She was dating one of my best friends. Then I met a guy in L.A., moved there. Lori said, "Find me an apartment." [LORI] The weather was so perfect every

day—actually, so boring. [T. J.] I worked for ICM, Capitol Records, Oprah. I'm your typical Texas cheerleader. Oprah said, "I hired a beauty queen from Texas." My dad was a fireman.

Now you have the comas in common.
At twenty-one, I was in a nearly fatal car accident. I had eight surgeries. Before that I was a bathing-suit model. They cut me from the breast to the belly button. I said, "Oh God, I'll never put on a bikini again." [LORI] Mine was a motorcycle accident, '95. I broke my face. I was thirty-two. [T. J.] We have our bad days. Lori's got steel in her face. I have it in my neck.

No wonder you're always talking about the weather!
After I woke up from my coma, I'd argue with my grandpa. He'd say, "Who promised you tomorrow?" I'm kind of fly-by-the-seat-of-the-pants, see the sun, *whooo-hoo.* I just

went to Paris for my 36th birthday on the Concorde. [LORI] I was raised by a single mother. My whole life, I didn't spend my money. I had savings when I moved here. Now I've only got half. Do I have enough to cover my rent? No. When I moved, it was a bad time for building clients. Now I'm at my third salon, I'm happy. T. J.'s rubbed off on me. [T. J.] I'll never be homeless. We're both too smart, have too many friends. When I see Lori down, I feel responsible. [LORI] T. J.'s seeing someone. He's over a lot. No, it doesn't bother me because he's a really nice guy. It was a little tough around the holidays. I felt like everyone was in a couple except for me. My mother came in for New Year's Eve. She's my best friend. We sat here, drank champagne, ate lobster, and watched the ball drop.

January 29, 2003

ROBERT HALE

MIMOSAS

LOCATION
Washington Heights, Manhattan

PRICE
$80,000 in 1999 ($461 maintenance)

SQUARE FEET
790 (one-bedroom co-op apartment in postwar building)

OCCUPANTS
Radda Rusinova (PhD student, biophysics, Mount Sinai School of Medicine), Victor Prieto (jazz accordionist/composer)

How joyous to hear the sound of the crickets or some animal as you come out of the 190th Street subway and look beyond to the green forest of Fort Tryon Park.
[RADDA] We have lightning bugs here, too. [VICTOR] And snow snakes. In the winter, they come up to the door.

Outside of a lovely elevator building!
[RADDA] The doorman was putting down poison.

I always thought there was no slimy animal life in winter.
[*An interview with Bronx Zoo herpetologist Bill Holmstrom revealed that snakes are strictly summer animals. There are snow corn snakes but "snow" refers to their color, bred for the pet trade. Are area pet snakes reproducing in winter and jumping out windows?*] [VICTOR] Radda is the owner of this apartment. [RADDA] My parents

did everything for me to get it. They live a block away. I came with them from the Ukraine in '90. My father's a mortgage broker. He used to be a movie producer. My mom's a biophysicist.

You yourself work on ion channels.
They are like machines that enable the passage of charged particles into and out of the cells. They're important for signaling and communication between the cells.

You're an only child!
Yes. [VICTOR] The mimosa. In Spain, they call it when they give you a lot of love—only child or the youngest.

So glamorous to be the mimosa.
Ja, I'm the youngest in my family. Radda is coming with me to Spain for a month. It will be two years I haven't seen my family. Every week I call.

You're the mimosa! You left Spain in '98 to go to Berklee in Boston, then a ninety-square-foot room in Williamsburg.
Ja, like the closet.

Then you met Radda when she heard music coming from a club and she lost her will and was drawn inside. You were a prodigy at nine.
Ja, I made my first concert when I was twelve. The Principal Theater of Orense. It's like Lincoln Center but it's Orense, ja.

Usually it's not politically correct to spell out a person's accent, but for you, it's your personality, so musical.

Ja, it's my way. Even in Spanish, it's really funny the way I build the phrase. [*He eats an almond.*] Ja, ja. My eyes pressing in all ways. Ju know, New York's the most difficult in getting what you want. In my fifth month, I was playing like six nights a week.

There's more that you want?
Ja ja, the Victor Prieto Trio. [*Radda smiles.*] Once I came to New York, I realized how well I am on my instrument. I'm the best I've ever seen.

Why did you choose the accordion?
Because my mother love it, ju know. Next door, there was a blind gentleman. He was always waiting for me to practice. I used to play for my family at all the [*unintelligible*].

At all the mittens? Oh, meetings. What is your mother's favorite song?
"The Bird Dance." [*He whistles and flutters his hands.*] Ju know it? [*He brings out the accordion and plays.*] I play the other things, jazz. [*I request "Bésame Mucho." He trills a key a bit.*]

What do you think about when you play?
My girlfriend who I love a lot. [*Radda is thrilled. We look at family photos on the computer.*]

Your uncle's house is blue.
The whole family lived in Venezuela before. I was really a jam boy [young boy].

Radda must laugh all the time.
She's juiced to it. Here's my grandfather. He was really tough people, man. He was a fighter. [RADDA] Was he in a tank? [VICTOR] Foot soldier.

Your grandmother looks tough too.
Whew, whew, man. My grandfather and grandmother are really nervous because the photo is for me. That one is my moomy.

September 8, 2004

THE FIRST ON THE BLOCK

LOCATION
Mott Haven, Bronx

PRICE
$50,000 (1957–1975)

SQUARE FEET
5,000 (each lot)

OCCUPANTS
The Ortiz Family

[*The Ortiz family owns four houses on the same street. But not everybody lives in his own house. The discussion begins outside, where Luis Ortiz Jr., a restorer, is working on his mother Carmen's 1880 brownstone.*] **Hi, what are you doing?**
[LUIS] We're bringing it down to natural stone, putting acid on the bricks. Once we fix it, we don't want any more tenants. Six are furnished rooms. [*Luis's brother, Norberto, walks over.*] [NORBERTO] I'm a bellman at the Ritz, eight years. I make the big tips. Just put in, we're the Addams family. [*Aunt Minerva Gonzalez walks over.*] I was nine when we came from Puerto Rico, on a propeller plane. My father bought a house for us. He paid $29,000 in 1957. There were only Irish people here. That's why he paid so much. He was in the housekeeping department at Beth Israel for a long time. My sister, Luis's mother, got this house. [LUIS] $18,500 in 1961. [MINERVA] I got mine in 1975, $5,000. I won't give it

away for $250,000. In the fifties, we were the first Puerto Rican family on the block. They used to hit my brother. The Irish don't come here anymore. [LUIS] We were living here when it was a war zone. You couldn't walk around. You had to crawl. [NORBERTO] It was like a cowboy movie. [LUIS] Shootings on the roof. [MINERVA] That was in the eighties. [LUIS] Charlie, he had a deli, he shot a guy back in the days. [NORBERTO] Charlie was known for his ham and cheese sandwiches. [*We go to Luis's room in his grandfather's house.*] [LUIS] I live in my grandfather's house. My brother lives in my mother's house but he's back and forth. Though he now owns my grandfather's house. I own my mother's house.

It's so green in here. Well, maybe it's the green blinds.
I try to keep the sun out.

You have a big bowl of pink potpourri, purple candles. What's the big color photograph of a bride and groom—hand-painted backdrop, palm leaves, balustrades?
My mother and father. They met in the Bronx. They split apart. My father moved just a couple of blocks over. That was his hat, with the P on it—for Papi. He left a lot of land upstate near Woodstock, twenty acres, in Bloomsfield.

Is your brother Norberto working on this, his house?
My little brother doesn't know anything about fixing houses.

These photos?

That's when I was younger, I was into modeling. I didn't have the patience. Here's one of me and my brothers eating chicken. That's from Puerto Rico. My grandfather had properties there.

More property! You're all so handsome. What's this one? You're holding shotguns and suitcases full of cash.
That was in a Florida studio, they give you costumes. This one, don't ask, a good friend. He's doing life. He and this guy went to a party and killed everybody at the party. It was called the Prospect Massacre. They had tried to kill his brother. Then they went back for revenge. Eighty percent of my friends were on drugs, in jail. Me, I'm trying to forget the past.

Will you live here forever?
Norberto's moving to a house near White Plains. The only thing keeping me here is my mother. Someday I'll go to the Poconos, Florida. It's about time. I've been here all my life. [*We go to Aunt Minerva's house, sit on the porch swings and rock back and forth.*]

What's growing in the garden?
[MINERVA] Corn, tomatoes. That's a peach tree. My goddaughter is coming to live upstairs. She's going to be a veterinarian.

It looks like Connecticut in your house. Oak cabinets in the kitchen, captain's chairs at the breakfast bar.
Gaby—that's what we call Luis—did it all. I lived in Queens for seventeen years, Jackson Heights. I moved because I thought it would be safer. Hah. I was so scared. Over there, nobody knows if you scream. I moved back here three years ago. I just wanted to be close to the family. I was lonely in Queens.

August 13, 2002

MICHAEL KAMBER

HARRISON FORD

LOCATION
Roosevelt Island, Manhattan

RENT
$2,700 (market)

SQUARE FEET
950 (two-bedroom apartment in
Manhattan Park complex)

OCCUPANTS
James Mwangi (consultant, United
Nations Development Program),
Sharmi Surianarain (development
associate, the Learning Project),
roommate

Roosevelt Island is more complex than I thought. I was thinking about this while I was dangling 250 feet in the air over the East River and God knows how many bodies are down there but anyway I was on the tram, which makes living on Roosevelt Island like being in a cartoon or an amusement park. You get to go on the Wondo Ride every day and, oh, that dip when it takes off from the platform. I got a little sick riding in the front. Drawings of the future always have flying cars, and there's that thirties movie where they're at the cocktail party and then they're in the flying car. I read that the residential community on this two-mile-long, six-hundred-foot-wide island was this 1970s Big Idea—utopian master plan by Philip Johnson

and John Burgess, traffic-free, 20,000 people. Now, though, there are cars and trucks and the population's still only about 8,500, but more development's on the way: 2,000 units for Manhattan hospital employees. There's a sort of sporty feel here, like a big health club—tennis courts, swimming pools, big brick apartment buildings. On the other hand, it's very noir. So deathly quiet. But then, the whole place used to be all asylums and smallpox hospitals. It was called Blackwell's Island, then Welfare Island in 1921, before the first apartment dwellers came in 1975. You still see people being rolled around in wheelchairs on the green grass outside the hospitals, and then there's something that used to be called the Strecker Institute, which I'm sure was a wonderful place but it sounds like it's in some 1950s movie where they brainwashed people or made them think they were insane. I read that some thirty to forty percent in your 1,107-unit 1989 apartment complex are U.N. employees.

[JAMES] I looked here before I worked at the U.N., in 2000. I was with a friend from Harvard. He's Palestinian. The big selling point was that there was a big international community here. I have another roommate now who's from India. I grew up in Nairobi, in a fairly standard city row house, the predominant middle-class housing. I went to boarding school up-country. Why did I go to Harvard? Well, I was run out of town. Friends of mine, we wrote a political satire of things going on in Kenya. It was a what-if play. Unfortunately a few weeks after it was written, it happened. The government saw it as a quickly put-together criticism. The police got involved. The students had a bit of a riot. [SHARMI] I'm from India—Madras, suburban area. For six years we lived in Nigeria. My dad's a businessman. Nigeria was really hot for business in the early 1980s. James and I sort of knew each other at Harvard. He did African gumboot dancing. [JAMES] Not in Africa. I picked it up in college. We met again in New York. [SHARMI] It was late last September. I'd just moved to New Jersey September 10. The next day, I was going to the second day of my new job. I was walking up Broadway and Canal and... now I've moved here with James. I used to have a cat. [JAMES] Pets aren't allowed on Roosevelt Island. [SHARMI] My cat wasn't too happy with James. [JAMES] The cat was pretty ill tempered. [SHARMI] It

isn't as though James made me give her up. When I first met James, all he used to talk about was the tram and how fun it was. [JAMES] But then the tram was down for a few months for maintenance. You meet people. I met a guy who was originally from Cote d'Ivoire, no, wait, he was from Cameroon, a soldier who'd come to join U.N. ops, and he had just come from Kosovo, where he was one of their security honchos. There's a group, they're in our building, Botswanan guys who work at Goldman Sachs. I see Harrison Ford on the tram. [SHARMI] One morning James called to tell me, "Sharmi, I saw Harrison Ford on the tram." He was so excited. [JAMES] He was right there with a big diamond earring. It's really disconcerting. You see people you normally see and then there's Indiana Jones.

June 4, 2002

ROBERT HALE

RED
SHOES

LOCATION

Astoria, Queens

RENT

$948.53 (rent stabilized)

SQUARE FEET

435 (one bedroom in thirty-six-unit
prewar building)

OCCUPANT

Ali Gentles (yoga teacher)

You have a swimming pool in your living room. Well, it's a big, luminous, silvery black-and-white photograph of the Astoria pool. I just happened to stop there on my way over.
They were looking at the pool for the Olympics.

The Olympic swim tryout finals began there the day it opened, July 4, 1936. What a day. The pool was Robert Moses's biggest—330 by 165 feet. He built ten that year. *Fortune* called it the "year of the swimming pool."
Wow.

New York City was receiving one-seventh of the Works Progress Administration allotment for the whole country—all those grand, sweeping WPA projects, bringing joy to city children. At the opening, the underwater lights flicked on, the crowd gasped for breath. **In later years, the Aquazines did their swimming choreography with backdrops, props, dogs.**
Wow.

I see more images of swimming here. How did your swimming pool theme begin?
It really started with the shower curtain.

Don't you love how exciting water is? It can't stop moving, as opposed to earth, which just sits there. Swimming pools are all about freedom, but contained freedom, not like the hidden dangers of the ocean and possibility of disappearance and underwater monsters. Swimming pool water gets all mixed up with the sun. The splashes look like they are made from light. In the forties and fifties, swimming pool blue found its way into architecture, all those insets, blue tiles on the outsides of buildings.
Like when I painted my bathroom the color of the turquoise beaches of Greece.

Your neighborhood is so Greek: creamed custard, accountants, olive oil.
A lot of families live here. It's very quiet. I was married for six years almost, living up in Spanish Harlem. He wanted out of the marriage. He's a musician. I ended up renting a room from a man in the West Village. The man had lived in his space a long time. He got really upset that I kept frozen water for my cat in the freezer. He said, "I need the space because there might be a sale on meat." I lived there six months. I don't think I've ever had a more

difficult living experience. Except for when I came to New York and I was a nanny. This family was on the Upper East Side and every time they'd have a fight, the wife would say to her husband, "I could be with Robin Leach." She used to date him. When I lived with them, I really thought I was a piece of property. After that, I was an actress/waitress, a personal trainer, now yoga. After Perry Street, I was looking in Spanish Harlem, Inwood, Astoria. All three were in my price range.

From where did you move to New York?
Ohio.

You said it so sadly.
Well, Ottawa, the northwest part. I came to the city fifteen years ago.

You have lilacs.
In spring, I have to buy the lilacs and the peonies. Every fall, I have to buy dahlias.

Was your father a farmer?
My grandparents were. My grandfather died a year ago, in May. Two weeks after

he passed, this tornado went right through the barn.

You're wearing red shoes. Is New York like Emerald City?
My time in New York is starting to wear thin. All I know is I'd like to live...

With Auntie Em! Who is the stuffed black cat with red shoes?
I'd taken my cousin shopping. We went into Takashimaya, just for fun. I just fell in love with this cat. I thought the price said $35. I signed. I got home. I saw the receipt said $95. I returned it. But I thought about it. The months would go by. I'd been nursing my kitty Oscar, who was sick with kidney disease.

Yes?
So she passed on April 8. I was really alone. This cat with red shoes was calling me. It was Halloween weekend when I first bought it, April when I went back. It was up on this ladder. I brought it home and I sleep with it every night.

May 25, 2005

"Dear Diary, New York is so busy. Why is my mother the way she is?

I just found someone's diary at the café. I'll just take a quick, accidental look at the pages while I have my morning snack.

"I adore SoHo's cast-iron architecture. Some of it is oh so Palladian. I read that SoHo is a historic district and it used to be called Hell's Hundred Acres because there were all these fires in warehouses. The first artist moved here in 1950, the SoHo Alliance newsletter says.

"I went to the cheese shop on Sullivan with the big Auricchio hanging in the window, and the man said, "You can't come in." OK, fine. Who wants cheese this early any way? He's down the street from the store with the midnight blue velvet furniture and the silver martini shakers. What a place to set a play! A man is ironing at Sullivan Cleaner, with the pink cocktail dress near his head and the acrylic sweater in a plastic bag. He's listening to opera. "Hello," I said. They are making new exhaust pipes outside the West Lake Laundromat.

"My writing teacher says it is important to note these details. I saw a bunch of people going into the Shrine Church of St. Anthony of Padua which, by the way, was founded in 1866: 'Confessions 4 to 5. Devotions Tues 8 AM to 12:10 PM. SICK CALLS—ANY TIME. Baptism by appt.' There is a sign on the basement door one day: 'AA Meeting.' My friend told me how his mother used to have a few drinks at lunch but then she'd have to lie down in the afternoon.

"The deli today has pears, plums, and Holland pompoms. A man is painting the door blue of the bistro with the large gold-framed mirror. White cloths are on the tables. They are getting ready to serve the carré d'agneau, the lapin des garrigues, and nu and cru.

"I may buy E a present at The Question of Time. They have these old watches. But I don't want to get him one that's ticking. I don't want things to advance. The Koho School of Sumi-E is open mostly in the afternoons. It's so tiny inside. There are some old kitchen chairs, a circulating fan, and all the ink.

"A letter in the window reads, 'May 30, 1985. Ms. Koho Yamamoto....I've been terribly busy as you can guess and have not had time to write...and return...the examples of your Sumi-E....I found them beautiful and I wish you much progress....I will be back from Japan the latter part of July...and hope you may be in touch with me at that time....Best wishes, Isamu Noguchi.'"

NEIGHBORHOODS

GREEN THUMB

LOCATION
Williamsburg, Brooklyn

PRICE
$300,000 in 2001

SQUARE FEET
2,500 (two-story house and garage)

OCCUPANTS
Mike Ballou (artist; builder; director, Four Walls Projects and the Slide & Film Club), Kara Van Woerden (graphic designer)

An important thing happened. You, Mr. Williamsburg—in the neighborhood since 1983, living on the edge, in a garage, cold for eighteen years—have just bought a house and the first stove you've ever owned in your adult life! Now I hear your action has set off a buying frenzy among your Williamsburg colleagues in their forties—maybe six of them—who have been living similar, touch-and-go existences in commercial buildings.
[MIKE] I'd been thinking about buying for a while. I heard about this place last summer. You hear all these horror stories. But this was almost headache-free. Mary, the owner, had raised a family here, and she had a really reasonable price. My mortgage worked out to be cheaper than my old rent. Here's a picture of us at the closing: a group of people agreeing on something we all want.

You broke out in hives before the closing, you said.
That was before September 11. After—my closing date was September 12, but we postponed—I realized there are far worse things that can happen than losing everything you own. Everybody who buys a house fears this. Look, there's an arbor in the garden. The grapes are glorious, so sweet—red, white ones. It's like being in paradise. There's all this stuff from the Italian immigrants, people around here were mostly from Naples. There's a winepress in the basement, a fig tree. We're putting an herb garden here. [KARA] No, that's for the climbing vegetables. [MIKE, *inhaling his cigarette*] Another wonderful day on Maspeth. The garden is Kara's call. But I have a *very* green thumb. I'm going to widen the garage about eight feet, make it my studio.

Your house has yellow siding, like your video piece, a meditation on ninety-five kinds of siding.
Here's the Afro study room—orange walls, dark wood.

What's this Post-it note on the computer?
"I love you and will daydream of you today." That's from Kara.

Fortunately, being a big, tough builder, you know how to do renovation.
I'm working myself to death here. I'm convinced I'm cheating myself on the job.

You goofed up your kitchen counter.
The contractor's curse! Counter tops are

pretty expensive, so I thought I'd just make them out of yellow pine stair treads and laminate them. When the time came to cut, I fucked it up. You do really nice work for jobs, but when it comes to yours...

How did you and Kara meet?
Kara had bunion surgery. I saw her recuperating with crutches on her roof. This was last year. I waved. I said, "It looks like it hurts." Later that day, I was working on some scaffolding. It fell. I broke my foot. A week later, we ran into each other. We were both on crutches. The rest is a very happy life.

I came over thinking we'd be talking about how the Four Walls Gallery was always part of your house, how early on you became this prime force in an alternative world with one-day exhibits and art panels with hairdressers, priests, and psychiatrists in all those Williamsburg years when people carried knives to survive, and then that July day in '88—the barbecue by the river; two hundred came, you said. The streetwalkers were out and it was like groovy. You saw thunderclouds coming from New Jersey and you all thought, Nothing can hurt us. But then it rained. This was after you went to the Minneapolis School of Art and read Heidegger with a local plasterer and...
[KARA] Did you see the worms?

December 18, 2001

JAY MUHLIN

LEOPOLD AND LOEB

LOCATION
Fort Greene, Brooklyn

RENT
$2,700 (market)

SQUARE FEET
1,500 (renovated loft in former warehouse)

OCCUPANTS
Arthur Fournier (director of sales and marketing, Delano Greenidge Editions), Clayton Harper III (software designer), third roommate

What about the sperm in Williamsburg?
[CLAY] I made a very discrete decision not to live there. Ever see Williamsburg boys? They're like in *Peter Pan*, little city of lost boys. Everyone has their loft clubhouses with the action figures, guitars. They're in their work pants saying, "My band just put out a seven-inch." What do they do? Work at a restaurant! You say, "You're thirty-one. You're only going to be able to have a child for another seven and a half years." Williamsburg is a *self-selecting sterilization clinic!* [ARTHUR] Those chemicals in the water and the ground naturally decrease sperm motility, which also decreases with age. Now, this is all speculative. [CLAY] We're not the AMA.

Did the light go on when you slid open the sliding door to this bedroom?
No, it just looks that way. I made these doors to the bedrooms. Here's our third roommate's room. [ARTHUR] We can't talk about his whereabouts.

Envelopes are scattered on the floor.
[CLAY] He doesn't come to get his mail, pays his bills online. He doesn't have clothes.

I have chills from the mystery. Clay, you're such a man of the Web—not many possessions except a titanium laptop.
Everything's in the computer—six hundred albums.

Have you ever known any other kind of life? Though you are only twenty-five.
Yes. Not everything was in the computer. But then I was living in Texas at my parents'. It was relatively boring, so I bought computer parts and learned to work stuff.

What's the fake Gucci-print golf hat with the big black felt letters: "FAKE"? It looks so Japanese.
I made it. I wore it in Japan. They loved it.

Their culture has a celebration of the artificial.
No, simulacrum, any attempt to reproduce the real, is *despised*.

I didn't mean celebration of the word "fake." I meant reverence for the created as opposed to the organic.

Ahem. What's all the evenly cut grass on the window sills? It's like it's from a juice bar or the grass around that swirling wood reception desk at the Union Square W hotel.

It's fake, plastic. I got it from a gentleman in SoHo. I traded some watches from Japan that have faces on them which are bar graphs made of LED lights. There are five dots in a row. If it's on red, red is equal to a value of five in all the rows, and, well, I had to read the instructions. Trust me, I'm a lawyer. That's the only thing I can say in Japanese.

I don't know why, but you make me think of the Tony Matelli sculpture called *Lost and Sick*, with the Boy Scouts throwing up their s'mores. Now that I think of it, *he* lives in Williamsburg.

[ARTHUR] Clay and I were roommates in college. We lived above a pizza parlor in Hyde Park, in Chicago. After we graduated, I moved four doors east of Louis Farrakhan and his Nation of Islam. I was in a Frank Lloyd Wright coach house. I came to New York in July. I was hoping to go to Turkey to live on the second island in the chain of Princes Islands, in the Sea Marmara. But after September 11, I decided to stay on in New York. Clay's been in the city since '99. [CLAY] I got this through a broker in June. I like Brooklyn a lot better than New York. Fort Greene reminds me of Hyde Park. Lots of young people with babies, a lot of mixed-race couples. The thing about Fort Greene, people aren't afraid to grow up. They haven't fallen into the yuppie thing. Fort Greene is for practical, responsible, upright people.

What about the other roommate? Does he like Fort Greene?

You don't even know if he's really a person. Maybe we just made him up.

February 19, 2002

MOTHERS' COCKTAIL HOUR

LOCATION
Williamsburg, Brooklyn

RENT
$1,150 (market)

SQUARE FEET
730 (ground floor of two-story house)

OCCUPANTS
Kevin Smith (psychology researcher, Cornell), Jennifer Smith (archivist), Astrid Smith (four months old)

So the last apartment was pretty bad. [KEVIN] No sink in the bathroom. [JENNIFER] Tiny, dirty kitchen, $990, illegal sublet in South Williamsburg. [KEVIN] The landlord was a crazy drunk guy. Our electricity would go out and he'd come to the door. [JENNIFER] "Gimme a dollar, gimme a dollar." [KEVIN] For the fuse. I just gave him a dollar so he'd go away. We got this apartment nine months ago. [JENNIFER] I begged him to move into this. We'd gone to a broker. [KEVIN] I said, "Show us a loft." They said, "We have a perfect place. It has a nursery. The landlord wants someone with a baby." I said, "No, it's not a loft. It reminds me of my parents' house in the suburbs." It wasn't what I moved to New York for. [JENNIFER] The first night, I looked up at the ceilings and I thought, "We can't

live here." But it really grows on you. [KEVIN] The landlords have a grape arbor outside. They clean our house when we go on vacation. [JENNIFER] We're from Pittsburgh. That's where we met. He worked at the record store and I worked at the sunglass store. It was love at first sight. Excuse the mess in the house. It was clean before. When you're pregnant, you get this hormone that makes you want to clean. But then the hormone goes away. Look out the window—there's Mario, our landlord. He's taking out the garbage.

I hear him rumbling about. Listen, he just removed the top of the garbage can. Now, your low ceilings here... [KEVIN] Like a rec room.

Low ceilings. Let me explain. I should really bring a blackboard. There are different theories as to how high to make a ceiling, one being that ceiling height should be related to a room's length and breadth. Palladio believed height should be intermediate and, well, I don't know that your landlords took this into account during remodeling. There isn't time for a full discussion. But, under a high ceiling, people seem farther apart than they actually are. Note how public spaces have high ceilings—appropriate, considering one is stranger-to-stranger. Lower ceilings make for more intimacy, That's why those low basements were so perfect for steamy slow dancing to Johnny Mathis. A time of sex and Ping-Pong. We live in the room, but without the sexual overtones. All our friends come here, drink

JAY MUHLIN

beer. [JENNIFER] Especially friends with babies. All our friends have a baby.

I thought Williamsburg was about people living like wild dogs and band practice and throwing food on the linoleum floors of the homes of the Italian couples who are watching TV. So the thought of everybody being responsible parents and wagging their fingers, playing grown-up... On the way, I walked past Salerno Surgical Supplies. There's a plastic horse outside that you put money in. The horse rocks while music plays, "Row, row, row, your boat, gently down the stream, merrily, merrily, merrily, merrily life is but a dream." Two little boys were rocking on the horse together. The mothers, in their flip-flops, with tattoos all over their arms and backs, one with red hair, sort of 1940s, were talking as mothers do, knowing and nodding. But just the

thought of my father in his navy blue suit with pictures of tigers and skulls running up and down his legs and a carefully placed earring under his fedora—well, I just can't imagine. There's nowhere I'd rather have a baby than Williamsburg. So many bars and parties.

With a baby?

A lot of people are taking babies to bars. There's even a mothers' cocktail hour at Ciao Bella. I met a lot of moms. There were margaritas. I had a Coke, but that's cause I drank too much the night before. Prenatal yoga class is a few blocks away. They have regular mothers' meetings. The place is called Go Yoga. They compare baby carriers. "My baby's bigger than yours. I breast-feed more than you."

July 30, 2003

PARK SLOPE AFTERNOON

LOCATION
Park Slope, Brooklyn

RENT
$975 (rent stabilized)

SQUARE FEET
600 (one-bedroom apartment in four-story prewar building)

OCCUPANTS
Dana Sherwood (art teacher), Karen Mancuso (editor, *HX*; *HX for Her*)

Your cherry-red-and-white table makes me think of June Christy when she sings that song about apple pan dowdy. You say your life is in the kitchen and you love to cook! I bet you both read stories in the food section about the lonely life of a blueberry or the misunderstood spotted mushroom. You have cutout illustrations of food on your kitchen walls from a 1950s home economics class. The Swiss steak is out of focus. On the back of the picture of liver, it reads: "dietary allowances for boy or girl." The percentage for girls is higher. Liver discrimination! So here you are in Park Slope among the literati. You say you found your big, airy, tidy apartment after looking at two others. The realtor was panting and said you had to give him cash immediately. He drove you right to the ATM in his car.

[DANA] We had to take out $1,000 and give it to him. [KAREN] He was a jerk. [DANA] You know how they are.

This was six months ago?
[KAREN] Yes, and a good friend who just moved to Park Slope got a one-bedroom smaller than this and it costs $1,400. Ours is just $975. [DANA] An apartment downstairs the same size is renting for $1,200 now. In a few months, prices have gone up so much. [KAREN] You constantly see young couples, kids, and real-estate brokers walking around Park Slope together.

What a sight!
It's such an amazing community. [DANA] People are so happy to be living here. [KAREN] There are gay couples, tons of interracial families. It's very friendly.

It sounds like a planned liberal community. How did you meet?
[DANA] I went to Clark University in Massachusetts. [KAREN] I was a sophomore. I didn't know Dana. [DANA] You knew Heather. [KAREN] You recognized me. I was in a bar in Manhattan last February. [DANA] I was here on a working trip with a friend. I was living in California. I knew I wanted to move to New York. I saw Karen and I said, "You look familiar." [KAREN] Then when I went to California, because my brother's ex-girlfriend is from Santa Cruz, I called Dana.

You said you go to stoop sales a lot.

[DANA] I get a lot of art supplies. There're these old ladies in Park Slope who'll say, I'll sell you my acrylics for five dollars.

How sad—all these aging women artists who don't paint anymore!
No, it's grandmothers with these paint-by-numbers set kinds of things.

Here's your matchbook collection that Dana got from her cousin in Connecticut. There's one from Lester's Family Shoe Store and another from Frances Brewster, Distinguished Resort Fashions. That's the kind of place where my friend in high school's mother got the strapless floral with the big skirt that she wore one Fourth of July, and after about five gimlets told the guests, "You can't squeeze blood from a turnip." She was talking about her husband. Here's a matchbook that says "Noel." It's so early sixties. The design is so long and low.
[KAREN] I don't notice these things.
[DANA] You're a words woman.

August 4, 1998

GREG MILLER

TURTLE DIARY

LOCATION
Turtle Bay, Manhattan

RENT
$803.30 (rent stabilized)

SQUARE FEET
264 (studio in 1920s walk-up)

OCCUPANT
Thomas Aveni (graphic producer and digital designer)

Dag Hammarskjöld Plaza Park is right near here. He was the second United Nations secretary-general. What a peacekeeper! He died in 1961 when he went to stop the fighting in the Congo and he and fifteen others perished in the night when their plane crashed near the border between Katanga and Northern Rhodesia. I've always been taken with Dag, but I couldn't sit in the park because it was raining. Which then brought me to the Japan House, which is all black with dribbling fountains inside, so I meditated a bit and adjusted the insole in my shoe. You are so lucky to live near the U.N.—the center of international excitement.
I haven't been since I was a kid, on a field trip. I grew up in Smithtown, Long Island.

If I lived here, I'd go all the time. I remember the gift shop from my youth. I got miniature carved wood camels and they were linked to each other with small gold chains. There used to be 60 nations who were members and now it's 190-some. There's no room in the Secretariat—well, it is pretty thin—only seventy-two feet thick—so the Japanese architect Fumihiko Maki is designing a $330 million addition.
Security's pretty intense now. I park my car on Beekman Place. I know all the doormen around here. We save each other parking spots. I moved here in 1995.

The Trump World Tower, all mirrored gold. I wanted to visit the World Bar, but you have to walk up all these stairs. [*I look around.*] You don't have a lot of possessions.
Yeah.

You do live here, don't you?
Sometimes I stay in Florida for a month. My friend Ellen has a place in Hollywood, near Ft. Lauderdale.

You don't have any books.
I love to purge.

You do have these two enlarged magazine covers with women on them.
One was from a party I went to. The other was out in the trash.

Who are your neighbors? A lot of doors have American flags. This building looks like where someone would have a secret hideaway.
I've seen models come in and out, but they're just transient models. The woman before me was here for seventeen years. She's Asian. She

used to work at the Waldorf. Then she moved downstairs because she was tired of walking up the stairs. Here's a list of what I thought would be interesting to you. [*We look at the list.*]

Ginger.
You know, from *Gilligan's Island*. She walks her dog around here.

Is she glamorous?
You can still tell she's a movie star.

Ray Liotta.
He has a light-yellow Rolls convertible that he parks on the street. He's so hysterical. I've seen him in slippers at three in the morning running out to get cigarettes. I always say hello.

Cindy Adams.
She was downstairs in Summit doing a review.

There are so many dark, grown-up, expensive restaurants here. Probably for U.N. officials having affairs, though I'm

sure Dag never did. You listed the Fubar.
It's a hangout on 50th Street. You can go play pool. When Ellen from Florida comes up, we go.

Then there's Katharine Hepburn's apartment. One of those townhouses with hidden gardens on 49th. There's a "for sale" sign in front.
Not too many people I know could come up with three, four million at this point. The double-deckers come by every five minutes. We could throw water balloons at them if we wanted to. Greg Brady's on the list. He's ridiculous. He was at some party. It was actually closer to the theater district. I don't think he qualifies for this neighborhood. I've taken my mom to see Broadway shows. The bus goes west on 49th. Every Sunday, I'm at my mother's on Long Island. I mow the lawn. [*We discuss some more names on the list.*] I go to Spring Street to visit my friend. If the parking situation here is bad, I go down there for an hour.

May 26, 2004

DUMPLING HOUSE

LOCATION
Chinatown, Manhattan
RENT
$1,000 (rent stabilized)
SQUARE FEET
300 (three rooms over restaurant)
OCCUPANTS
Adley Atkin (graphic designer; illustrator), Chris Madak (freelance art and technology consultant)

It's not very big, is it?
[CHRIS] It's like a quarter of an apartment. [ADLEY] It's even smaller than I thought it was going to be. I moved in last month. We know each other from Hampshire College.

So here you are above Joe's Shanghai and thousands of bubbling dumplings.
[CHRIS] One of the most obnoxious things about living here is that the line to get in the restaurant goes halfway up the stairs when it's cold. The restaurant ventilation occasionally shakes the building.

I did hear a noise coming up the narrow, Old World back stairs.
Our teakettle rattles. You have to go on the roof.

I don't want to.
The roof actually smells like dumplings. I'm vegetarian. I was walking up the Bowery one day and I saw a crab escape from one of those tanks in a restaurant. He got out by standing on the back of a lobster.

Isn't that like life?
Is it?

How many of you young non-Chinese are living in this neighborhood—not counting artists who got lofts in the seventies?
I've only seen maybe four non-Chinese people around. [ADLEY] If you go around Canal, I've heard there are more. [CHRIS] I wondered if we were encouraging the gentrification of the neighborhood. The rates of Chinese immigration are still really high. I think we're kind of a drop in the ocean.

My friend A. lives near here over a secret mah-jongg parlor and he hears the tiles clicking all the time and once he found a solid gold bracelet outside the building door and he thought somebody won it in a game and now he wears it all the time. It's a link bracelet and I told him that's what women wear but he doesn't care. It makes him feel rich. Anyway, a local real-estate agent told me that most of the property is owned by members of the Chinese community and that they are loathe to sell, which is great because that means Chinatown will stay Chinatown with its red and gold dragons and durian fruits, but the agent also said that owners are not resistant to developing condos or tripling rent. I love how intensely focused people are down here. They are very much involved in the

bustle of their own world and selling roots and lily bulbs and they could really care less about anything else. Chinatown is a great place to come on a lonely Western holiday because you realize that the world hasn't stopped and the people on the street could care less about, let's say, Valentine's Day.

I love that. On Canal and Mulberry you can get food for a dollar. My girlfriend used to live here. We found it on the Internet. We actually thought it was a joke 'cause we'd never seen a Chinatown listing.

What's that door downstairs?

It's like the herbalists' storage closet. The two businesses above Joe's are a law office and an herb and tea store.

No, not that one—the silver-vaulted door outside of that regular apartment door.

We were conjecturing about the door—that people leave the door open and still get ventilation.

But you don't need a vaulted bar cage to guard an apartment.

It's the only thing that makes sense.

Who lives there?

A hipster kid.

Oh, darn. So there's no mystery. It must have been there when he moved in. Though maybe the hipster kid is a front.

[ADLEY] I've run into him a couple of times. Whatever he does, he comes home with Barneys Co-op bags. His apartment is twice as big. I've heard some phone conversations, Rod Stewart coming out. [CHRIS] It's not what you bargain for when you move to Chinatown.

What was he saying on the phone?

[ADLEY] Oh, I wasn't listening in.

March 23, 2005

TAMARA ROSENBLUM

TEN PIECES OF KIELBASA

LOCATION
Greenpoint, Brooklyn

RENT
$800 (market)

SQUARE FEET
300 (two-room apartment in 1915 house with siding)

OCCUPANT
Suzanne Schulz (associate producer, Hibiscus Films; program director, DocuClub)

Love all that pink pork in the stores on Manhattan Avenue and how everybody on the street is speaking Polish, and saying words like "brushky schusky." Their language always sounds so smoky in the bedroom, like some Polish film director is twirling a cigarette and telling you about the revolution, hours into the night. Though in your neighborhood, I see mostly families and men wearing hats with small brims.

I've only lived in Greenpoint four months. I thought about joining the hundred percent Polish gym, ninety-nine cents a day, but I don't know if I could work out with the giant Polish he-men. Before I moved here, I was in *all* these places—I'm from Long Island—like Park Slope without a lease. Then I had an illegal sublet in a Mitchell-Lama and I had to leave in a day, and then an apartment where I spilled some shampoo that stained the marble floor a little and the housemate kept my whole $600 security deposit. So I wanted to have a place where nothing like that would happen. Though here my bathroom is in the hall, which leads to not wanting to go to the bathroom in the middle of the night.

That print of the *Tambourine Dancer of Sorrento* in the hallway outside your door bears a resemblance to you—well, that is, if you wore white peasant blouses.

The painting is my landlord's. He lives across the hall from me. He's from Poland. He gave me a half-eaten box of clementines for Christmas and filled the other half with cookies. On Valentine's Day, he presented me with a lovely bouquet.

Has love blossomed?

This morning he came over and gave me all these plants. The other day he fixed my doorknob. He's in his seventies. I'm twenty-five. He looks a little bit like a younger version of the pope. He wears very charming outfits, like a tweedy jacket with a tweedy hat. Currently he's been wearing his Florida shirt, a Hawaiian print. He just went down to Florida; there's a whole Greenpoint contingent in Miami. He lives alone. He really seems to enjoy the bachelor life. He's very well respected in the community. He's always showing me copies of the Polish paper when he's in it. He took me to the Polish Slavic Cultural Center for lunch. His daughter and two granddaughters joined us. Then he took

SYLVIA PLACHY

me to this Polish deli because he had ten Polish student musicians staying with him. He bought me ten pieces of kielbasa, but I told him I don't eat meat. He doesn't speak English. We really have trouble understanding each other. A month ago he took me to Lincoln Center to a concert. I was originally supposed to go to a friend's art show in Williamsburg, which was just on one night, but I said, "*No*, I'm going to go out with my *landlord*." We went to Lincoln Center on the subway. He was really impressed I knew how to transfer. The concert was Polish music. In the end, everybody stood up and sang this Polish song and they raffled off a television set. These women from Poland were on the subway on the way back; I could tell they really liked him. For the first couple of months, he gave me juices. He gave the two guys upstairs juices, too. They've gone out with him, but less than I have. My landlord has a garden out back, raspberries and eggplant. He told me he has parties back there. Any time I have a night visitor, I tell them to be quiet and I stuff a pillow in their mouth. I'm afraid my landlord's going to hear them. I don't know why. I'm an adult and all. He goes to bed at ten. After that, I'm pretty safe. His bedroom is on the other side of the house. If he's in his living room, he'll poke his head out and see what's going on. My kitchen wall is the same wall as his bathroom wall. Once he said to me I shouldn't smoke because I have a beautiful face.

March 20, 2001

MR. SOFTEE

LOCATION

Whitestone, Queens

RENT

$0

SQUARE FEET

1,600 (two-story 1950s house)

OCCUPANT

Stuart Cohn (producer, MTV news and specials)

Whew! That number 7 train. I think I was drugged. So was everyone else. We were dozing off like in *Sleeping Beauty.*
They overheat the cars.

Whitestone was like the valley of death last summer, what with the deadly encephalitis mosquito and then all those news photos of fumigators standing over inflatable swimming tanks and blasting out the larvae with pesticide sprinkle. Weren't you scared?
Nah.

Let's not waste any time and go right to the combination dining room and wood-paneled den area with the avocado mod tablecloth, the Chinese-style buffet cabinet, and small porcelain animals. This is your parents' house, but they've been living in Delray Beach, Florida, for three years, so you have the run of the place.
Yeah.

Your stuff is *everywhere*. Your knit hat's on one chair, another's on the living room floor, your socks are on the kitchen counter near your mother's Farberware electric coffeepot. You've been home alone here three years, but you haven't always lived in the house of your parents—former high school teachers—in this mainly Catholic Irish and Italian neighborhood. You left in 1974 to go to SUNY Binghamton and then got an apartment in Carroll Gardens in the pioneer days, 1981.
I lived with someone, but then she went crawling back to the East Village. I had a nice floor-through for $400. The landlord raised it to $440. I thought it was too expensive.

Then the L.A. years, 1990 to '96, commissioning music videos for Hollywood Records, driving on the Disney lot, going past the guard with his thumbs up. You lived in a wooden Craftsman-style bungalow with orange, fig, and lime trees in Atwater Village, the cool side of the city. You said it's like living in Brooklyn, but then after a few years everything was not so cool, because you realized in L.A. you have to be hooked up, in some sort of relationship, otherwise you just sort of drift—that noir dread stuff really exists.
I didn't plan to rob or kill anybody.

So you came back to New York for a visit, got involved with a woman at a party, moved back here, broke up. *Que será, será.* Anyway, it's three years later and now what? Are you going to sit in

that Eames chair forever, near your pile of _Rolling Stone_ magazines, opera CDs, and Mets scorecards from almost every game since 1963, sitting there watching ESPN, day in, day out, or are you going to buy a place, which I know you've been dwelling on, though I can't really see you living in that 1920s co-op apartment you were looking at in Jackson Heights and hanging out in the neighboring tearoom where they like to play the music from _The Wizard of Oz._

Now I'm thinking maybe Brooklyn. I met this woman and she said, Stuart, we've _got_ to get you to DUMBO. But I like having a backyard, a lot of space. I like all the memories of being in this house. It's not like I think consciously about when I broke my front teeth when I was four. But it's more like a kind of secure feeling. But my mom is going to sell this house by spring, so I'll have to find something. Unless she sells it to me. Today I saw this apartment in Astoria for $1,500, but it's like a third-floor walk-up. What's up with that? I'm going through what everyone goes through in New York. Everything costs a lot of money and nothing seems to be worth it. Of course, I don't have as much in common with adults in this neighborhood. People my age here have kids, go to church. I don't live near my friends or anything. My home life is not like a social life. But Mr. Softee does still come around.

Would he come to DUMBO?

I doubt it. Fuck DUMBO.

February 22, 2000

SANDRA-LEE PHIPPS

WHERE THE RICH PEOPLE LIVE

LOCATION
Forest Hills, Queens

RENT
$950 (sublet)

SQUARE FEET
780 (studio apartment in prewar co-op building)

OCCUPANT
Karen Russo (financial coordinator, Levy Group)

I was on Austin Avenue, your main shopping street. Two women in their eighties, wearing dark glasses, were walking near Chez Moi with the rhinestone evening gowns and the one woman said, "Oh, when she sings 'I am what I am—dah dah dah,' it is so sensational." But you know, Forest Hills is so medieval—gables, leaded windows, Pre-Raphaelite sex. Well, it would be if one had sex here and then dressed up as Lady Guinevere or King Arthur, depending. On the other hand, the neighboring Forest Hills Gardens, based on an English garden community of healthy nonindustrial feudal life, is all about feeling held, contained, protected—all warm, brown-red brick walls.

I wanted to live in Forest Hills my whole life! I just moved here last summer. My father grew up in Forest Hills and that was one reason. My grandfather was a jewelry designer. We did holidays with my grandparents. My grandfather used to have a tree he'd hang from the ceiling with little boxes. Inside would be jewelry he made for us. I was born in Ridgewood, Queens. We lived in Jersey as a family from '87 to '91, in a condo in Hillsborough. That was a hick town, kind of a culture shock, frankly. Then my mother—she was a cook for a church—picked up my sister and myself and moved back to Ridgewood. She figured there would be better jobs for her. She wanted to be closer to her family. My mother was Austrian. In Ridgewood it was very European, a lot of Yugoslavians, Romanians. I always called it "Little Bosnia." I went to Manhattan Community College. I was in the television field. I didn't really know what I wanted. After college I was living in the Bronx. The Bronx—oh, it was terrible, East Tremont by the zoo. I moved to be on my own, have a roommate. No, he and I are not still friends. I lost my job, moved back to Ridgewood in October 2001. One day I came home and found my mother on the couch. She'd had a heart attack, passed away, fifty-three. She was beautiful. No one knew she was sick. My father lives in Jersey. He's manager for the Men's Wearhouse, in Totowa.

Men's Wearhouse! With that man in the television commercial with the gravelly voice! George Zimmer! "You're going to like the way you look."

CARY CONOVER

My father resembles George Zimmer. I met George at the Christmas parties. He's for the legalization of pot. The party was at the Marriott Marquis.

Were they all in their suits?
Yes! The greatest employee of the year gets the Aloha Award. He got to go to Hawaii.

Your friend Ana's visiting, eating meatball Parmesan at your dining table with a big Eiffel Tower on it.
Ozzy Osbourne has the same one. It's on his show. Ana and I met working at Old Navy. She lives in Harlem. We just had martinis.

So, more about Forest Hills.
It brings back my childhood. You know how certain smells remind you of certain times. Burning wood brings me back to New Jersey and being a family. I walk around Forest Hills and smell the fireplaces. I think of, like, Holland. No, I've never been to Holland. The smell of celery reminds me of the West Coast. Ana and I were driving down to Tijuana and I kept saying, "Do you smell the celery?" A few weeks ago, I was driving with my dad down Union Turnpike. When I was a kid, I used to imagine the rich people that lived on the right side. The other week, I realized I now live where I thought the rich people live.

You're singing now. You have a great voice.
All my life, I had this dream I was going to become famous. I had this balcony in New Jersey and I used to think my first concert was going to be on that balcony. I'd sing "Somewhere Out There." It's from *An American Tail.* I used to do it on the fire escape in Ridgewood.

March 26, 2003

BURIED TREASURE

LOCATION
Vinegar Hill, Brooklyn

RENT
$850 (market)

SQUARE FEET
1,000 (two-story nineteenth-century back house)

OCCUPANT
Nick Terry (abstract painter; media projects coordinator, American Museum of Natural History)

The most terrible thing happened. I was walking along these quiet, sunny streets thinking how civilized the industrial DUMBO–Vinegar Hill area has become over the years, but then I saw this crowd of people across from the red and yellow Dorje Ling Buddhist Center. A man who works at the furniture factory nearby was there with blood on his forehead, and he said—he speaks Chinese—that a strange man on a bicycle threw him on the ground and attacked him with a knife. Then all these police cars came.
I think I know him. He's such a nice man.

As I walked a few blocks to your street with all the ancient storefronts—one with "Barber Shop" letters smudged out on a window—only a cat was moving on the ripped-up cobblestones. Then I noticed you have a violet glass doorknob and a mysterious garden full of big yellow and red autumn leaves. Inside your house—the brick floors, wood beams, simple table, white bed, bowl of bananas—it all reminds me of a house that belonged to an Iranian artist in another city.
My wife is an Iranian artist.

You have a wife! You didn't tell me. Where is she?
She lives on the Upper West Side. Maryam Amiryani, she's an artist. She has a studio and apartment there. She does come to visit. Actually we go back and forth. Neither of our places is big enough to have a work space for both of us. I paint upstairs here; to paint, you need to be alone. I renovated all this before I met her, but her persona has had an influence. I moved here seven years ago. I'd just come back from a year in Asia. I'd grown up in Westchester, lived in Williamsburg. I ran into a friend who'd seen the place and thought of me. I saw it the next day, fell in love with it. It was great luck. The main thing is you'd never know it's here. It's really tucked away from the street, like something in the south of France. There's a sense of an enclosed, very simple sanctuary. This structure itself is brick, which has a sense of solidity that is becoming more and more rare these days. Vinegar Hill is just a cluster of a few streets east of DUMBO. This was probably a back house where an Irish worker lived when he worked in the Navy Yard. This was a large Irish community. To lure more Irish over, the developer called it "Vinegar Hill" because they thought it would be a strong memory for the Irish. Vinegar Hill was

the name of the place in Ireland where the Irish had their climactic battle during their rebellion against the British.

I read that thousands of Irish died in the 1798 battle. Then I also read that since this Vinegar Hill was a navy village it was bawdy with brothels, and they say gold coins were buried by Captain Kidd underneath the cobblestones. The area declined with the Navy Yard, which was closed as a military shipyard in 1966. We have a neighborhood association. Monique Denoncin, the president, is the grande dame of the neighborhood. I'm sure she'll look into what happened to that man. We don't see each other a lot, but we're tight. We've gotten trees planted, which

is good for the air because of the Con Ed plant nearby. Have you seen Admiral Perry's former house? He was the Navy Yard commandant. It's around the corner.

Let's go! [*We walk there.*] It's so big and white—with a gate like a mansion in a seventies movie mystery—three sports cars inside. I just realized your sanctuary is surrounded by the former house of a North Pole explorer, the 1,390-unit Farragut public housing project, a Con Ed plant, Jehovah's Witnesses buildings, the Navy Yard, fancy DUMBO lofts... The juxtaposition is crazy.

November 27, 2001

BILYANADIMITROVA.COM

MOONY'S ON THE FIRST FLOOR

LOCATION
SoHo, Manhattan

RENT
$320 (rent controlled)

SQUARE FEET
350 (one-bedroom apartment in
tenement building)

OCCUPANT
Joseph Russo (retired box maker)

Here we are in your apartment with the Detecto bathroom scale, the cookie jar in the shape of a priest, the Rincan radio with aqua trim. You've lived here since you came out of the army in 1944.

I know everybody in the neighborhood, and everybody knows me. I belong to the Knights of Columbus. They meet in the church by Canal Street near the tunnel. Ever go through the tunnel? Then, if I don't want to go there, I go to the American Legion Post near where *The Fantasticks* is. We got a big place in the cellar and everything.

You raised your two sons here. Where did they sleep?

In the little bedroom on bunk beds. My wife and I slept in the parlor on the convertible. My sons are married now. My wife died eleven years ago.

How did you find the apartment?

My wife and I grew up near here, around Vandam and MacDougal. It was before they made Sixth Avenue. I was getting out of the army and I called my wife, who was living with her sister in Flatbush. I said, "Try to find some rooms in the neighborhood." When we first came here, there was only hot water, no heat. I was paying $25.

What was it like around here before it was all Deux Gamins, Le Pescadou, and the Cub Room?

It was always a good neighborhood. There were three stores. One, they sold vegetables. When I was in junior high school, my father lost his job. It was 1930. We had to move to the east side. I didn't fit in with the east side boys. Some of them used to pull jobs, you know, but don't print that.

Do you think they're going to come get you now—sixty-seven years later?

You don't know. Anyway, I went to Oregon with the CCC, the Civilian Conservation Corps. My parents moved back to the west side. I came back and met my wife in Washington Square Park, near the statue. Jeez, I forget the name of the statue. It was like a hangout at night for the boys and the girls. I took her for an ice cream soda at the parlor on University Place. My father always said, "Don't go with girls in the neighborhood." He was afraid I'd go with a wiseguy's daughter and if I did anything bad, they'd throw me off the roof.

GREG MILLER

It was stressful living in either neighborhood! Of the twelve apartments in the building, how many are still rent controlled?
There's only four of us left. There's Moony on the first floor, one guy on the top floor, a woman downstairs. She's here the longest. Then there's me.

So, there you sit, all comfy in your recliner with the green and yellow afghan. How do you feel about the younger people taking over the building?
They're all nice. I just feel sorry for them that they have to pay all that rent.

June 17, 1997

OLD SCHOOL

LOCATION
Bensonhurst, Brooklyn

RENT
$800 (market)

SQUARE FEET
500 (one-bedroom apartment
in house)

OCCUPANTS
Danny Pesce (doorman, Park
Laurel), Amy Pesce (nurse, Guild for
Exceptional Children)

How long has it been like this?
[DANNY] It started off small. [AMY] Then it got bigger.

Almost forty saint statues are in front of the sofa.
[DANNY] We sit in the kitchen. [AMY] All the food is in the kitchen. [DANNY] I get them at Universal Mercedes Botanica. A few of these are not made no more. When I'm going to be an old man, they will be almost extinct. It's not something this generation is into. I'm twenty-seven. I keep to the old school. I don't know why. I'm one of the last young guys going to mass every morning—Regina Pacis Church.

When thieves stole gold from the church, you said, the late Carlo Gambino said, "No police." It was back in eight

hours. I went to Tomasso's Restaurant in Bensonhurst once and there was a picture of Paul Castellano in front. There was a lot of chintz, big wine glasses—the owner was very close to his late mother. He sang "God Bless America." His piano player had this long gray hair. What's going on in Bensonhurst now?
Block parties are pure guido. It's the land time forgot. Ten, twenty years, it's all going to come to an end. Houses are selling for half a million. Chinese, Russians are paying in cash.

In bills?
Yes.

In black garbage bags?
[*No comment*] The old Italians, they're moving to Florida or back to Italy. Lot of their kids are moving to Staten Island, the new Little Italy.

You're holding your stomach. Are you going to have the baby now?
[AMY] No, it's OK.

I was walking along 18th Avenue—it was emptier than I thought it would be but there was Kersner Furs—"Remember Her with a Gift of Fur" and some stole in the window with small animal tails on it. And then, Doris, the store full of mannequins leaning to the side, in satin evening gowns. Their arms are reaching out but they have no hands. You've been a doorman five years. Your father was a doorman for thirty. Your two

brothers are doormen—all in the Lincoln Center area! Are lots of Italian doormen from Bensonhurst?

[DANNY] No. They're all Hispanic now, Dominican. Couple of Irish guys left. It's a dying art. You gotta have some etiquette. I just go with the moment—"Hey look, there's Jackie O, ready for the evening." My father, he put me to shame. He was so natural. I look at the building across the street where he worked. [*His father died last year.*] I sing to my tenants. They say, will you sing "Happy Birthday" to me? We're the hottest building on the Upper West Side, very exclusive. If the paparazzi knew.

Don't you want to live in the fancy building?

[AMY] At night, he's dying to come back to Brooklyn. [DANNY] I get here and I feel like a new man.

Do you wear your hat even when you're a doorman?

I got thirty, all old-style—applejack, fedora. I grew up in the eighties. I really believed it was the fifties. This generation cannot capture the class. My dad kept it that way. He'd have guys come over every night. All we'd do is sing doo-wop, play baseball, and hang out at the OTB. That's all I knew. A gangster'd tell me, "Pick a number, kid." I have like a 14,000-song collection. Frankie Lymon, my favorite.

Why do foo-oools fall in love…why do they fall in loh-ove?

My father won the Apollo seven times. Our whole family sings. I was doing doo-wop in a restaurant on Staten Island. This older Italian lady walks in. She said, "Come with me." I thought I was going to get whacked, this lady in this Cadillac, some Bruno waiting for me. Lo and behold, she brought me to this shrine. It's on Victory Boulevard. That's all I'll say. The candles never go out.

February 25, 2004

When things are bad, I will look at a picture, photographs, "Batman" comics with cities made from green and blue ink and then set on orange fire by evil forces. The Forbidden Planet store is a temple. I will get lost in the colors, in the trees, the scientist in the laboratory staring at a beaker, the sobbing spy. The visual image is what holds when all else does not.

Everybody has that place, above and beyond the subway map—the vase, the wine glass, the bagel, the Empire State Building, even Ground Zero, which has become more than a place of worship but almost a rite of passage, a badge of witness, a snapshot of having experienced the sight of hollowed-out developer's ground that has little to do with the people who had to jump.

Because New York City is so difficult to live in, individual callings are memorable to the interviewer. What is the big pull, the invisible hold in the midst of the petty, the loud, the mean?

I looked at the Unisphere the other day from the 1964 World's Fair. Set in the middle of a fountain, a glorious circle of water shoots, the base holds up 700,000 pounds of stainless steel as if it were the most marvelous paperweight. I could see the women in their hats back then, the men in their suits, going to and from the House of Good Taste and the Fiberglass Wall of Light and reading the plaque aloud to each other with that hopeful mid-century nobody-can-stop-us-now: "Dedicated to man's aspirations toward Peace through mutual understanding and symbolizing his achievement in an expanding universe." It was made at a time when the world started to tremble; they must have sensed the coming fragmentation and inability to stay whole.

CALLING

FIVE FLIGHTS UP

LOCATION
Upper East Side, Manhattan

RENT
$990.50 (rent stabilized)

SQUARE FEET
400 (two-bedroom apartment
in tenement building)

OCCUPANTS
Jon-Michael Hernandez
(actor; director; artistic director,
Huckleberry Productions; admissions
counselor, American Academy of
Dramatic Arts), roommate

You have no use of your legs below the knees and you've lived in a fifth-floor walk-up for ten years?

I suppose it is a bit of a walk. When I first moved here, it took me about ten minutes to get upstairs. I hated it. I thought, I'm making such a big mistake. Now I've got it down to three minutes. I have spina bifida, a congenital birth defect where you are born with a hole in your spine. They corrected it when I was two weeks old. I was completely normal until thirteen. Then I started falling down a lot. They put me in the Shriners Hospital for Crippled Children in San Francisco.

Shriners Hospital! That's the one they used to pass around a can for in movie theaters.

You have to be sponsored by a Shriner. They wear a fez, but not during the day. On the first Saturday of the month, all the Shriners bring ice cream to the kids. By the time I was twenty-five, I was walking with forearm crutches. I'm from Hanford, California, 1930s tract home, southwest of Fresno. My father is an auto mechanic.

Couldn't you have rented an apartment on a lower floor? I mean, you not only walk up and down seventy-five apartment steps every day, but then there are sixteen at your day job and the twenty-five when you are rehearsing one of your plays every night at the Metropolitan Playhouse. Plus you have to take two buses to work, two from work, two to the Playhouse on the Lower East Side, and two home. That's eight buses a day!

My roommate and I—he's a dresser on Broadway; we lead totally separate lives—looked at an apartment on the second floor here, but it was so dark. I looked at so many apartments—one great one had a spiral staircase...

Spiral staircase!

It wouldn't have bothered me, but the apartment was out of our price range. Every two bedroom was. There was a great huge one, but it was in a neighborhood where I would have been afraid to come home late at night. I mean, I can't run.

I came to New York in '91 to study at the American Academy of Dramatic Arts. Coming from California, you hear all these horror stories about how dangerous New York is. I lived in a private residence, the Kolping House, 88th near Lexington. But it was like a dorm room. I wanted my own place.

SYLVIA PLACHY

Didn't the broker for this apartment say anything when he saw your crutches? No, he just wanted the money. The New York housing situation is so bad.

Your living room is the size of a closet. The smallness gives me a lot of freedom. I only need one crutch inside. When I dream, I never have crutches, you know. I'm running and jumping.

I would have thought there would be architecturally perfect subsidized housing for people with disabilities, but when I started calling around, Joan Byron, a housing expert at Pratt, said, "Are you crazy? If the given vacancy rate for New York City is one percent, for people with disabilities, you're talking five percent of one percent. Available housing stock just doesn't work for them. Most housing units in the city are relatively old, built prior to accessibility laws." Elevator buildings cost tons of money. You make too much for public housing. The wait list is eight years. It never occurred to me that you can't really live in Brooklyn or Queens. Not all subway stops are accessible to people with disabilities. By the way, why are there all these Breakfast at Tiffany's posters in your room? My favorite film! It was made the year I was born. I actually live very close to where Holly Golightly lived in the movie. Some days I walk by that building. In springtime they put up an awning—it's the same style, white-and-green stripes, as the movie. I've had breakfast at Tiffany's, too. You remember she said, "If I could find a real-life place that made me feel like Tiffany's, then I'd buy some furniture and give the cat a name."

April 17, 2001

CINECITTA

LOCATION
Woodlawn, Bronx

RENT
$250 (negotiated with parents)

SQUARE FEET
352 (basement in parents' house)

OCCUPANT
Jeff Asencio (actor in music videos, indies, and cable soap "Dark Knites"; pizza deliverer, Italian Village Restaurant)

How long have you rented from your parents?
Three years. I grew up in this house. I've been here ten years altogether. I'm twenty-two.

Are your parents strict landlords?
If I can't pay my rent, they're not going to chop my head off.

Your place is really outfitted! You've got a Panasonic KX-FP200 fax, RCA ColorTrax Plus TV, two VCRs, tons of videos. The walls are covered with cutouts of Spider-Man and X-Men. There are big posters of Demi Moore and Bruce Willis.
I like both of them. They're together. They're making movies. They're powerful.

What's this magazine cutout of a woman bound in a silver metal space outfit?
I just liked it 'cause it was a girl.

You call this the "Dark Knites" basement?
Yeah, the Dark Knites is from Batman. It's the name of my cable show. The Dark Knites is all the people I hang out with. Like Michael and me go on auditions together. There's Jorge and Phil. It's like a little clique, the ones that want to do movies with me and stuff. It all happens in the basement. I always leave my door open. Phil comes in the morning. He won't even wake me up. He sits down, turns on the TV. I could be dead asleep.

Phil's here right now. So is Lucky. While they snooze on the bed and your girlfriend Sophia sits next to you on the futon sleeper couch, let's discuss your former cable show. You said you shot it all over but mostly in the basement.
Yeah, like the episode about two Puerto Rican guys trying to get into the two Italian guys' mob. They have to go through these initiations and by the end of the skit, they end up getting in and becoming official animals.

From watching the video, it looks like they are having a pillow fight. You shot a video of your own simulated crucifixion down here in the basement for an art exhibit. The New York Times called it an "erotic video."
I don't know. I didn't have a shirt on. Jesus Christ didn't have a shirt on.

You keep your archives and memorabilia in a pizza delivery box!
Yeah, from work.

GREG MILLER

There are five blond wooden doors down here. Where do they lead to?

A boiler's in one, a boiler's in the other, one's for the fuses, there is the closet, the door to outside.

How long do you think you'll be renting here?

Not long. I'll move when I make enough money. But I ain't moving far. I ain't going to no Brooklyn or Queens. I think I'll stay in the Bronx. That's where I get all my creative ideas.

But won't you be sad to leave this basement? It's got everything!

Nothing lasts forever. You gotta move on. This basement's cool and all. But someday I'll have an apartment. I'll have separate rooms. You know what I'm saying?

November 4, 1997

HIP-HOP FOREVER

LOCATION

Canarsie, Brooklyn

RENT

$950 (market)

SQUARE FEET

800 (three-bedroom apartment in
two-family brick house)

OCCUPANTS

Rack-Lo (hip-hop artist; CEO of
Spit Factory), Shileena Perez
(telephone representative, 1199
Health Care and Hospital
Corporation; hip-hop artist), Doris
Billips (medical assistant), Christian
(kindergartner)

Rack-Lo, you're a member of the Lo-Lifes, the club that you and your friends started in the late eighties. You got famous by stealing and wearing anything Ralph Lauren Polo. Then one day the theft mob became a music group. Is your zest for Ralph Lauren in the home too?
[RACK-LO] I got some sheets.

You were living in East New York for eight years?
Near Linden Boulevard, about four blocks from Spring Creek. The neighborhood was decent, but the violence was there, the urban life, you know. They sold the building, so we had to get out. It was crucial. We walked around East New York and didn't see anything we really liked. Canarsie's, like, residential. We just moved here last week. We looked for two months. We got it through a broker.

You grew up in Brownsville in Brooklyn.
Yeah. At age fourteen, I was homeless. My mom told me I had to go. I couldn't deal with the rules, you know. I lived on the streets for two weeks, slept in the park a few nights. Moving around, it was real awkward, feeling strange, not knowing where I was going to rest my head, get my next meal from. The experience made me stronger and I learned a lot. Then I went to my Aunt Rebecca's in Marcus Garvey Village, the housing project in Brownsville. My grandparents lived there. A lot of wars were going on, urban wars with the housing project across the street. Lot of gunplay, fights. You couldn't trust anybody. I dropped out of junior high. I was trying to get into the GED program, fifteen going on sixteen. I developed a real tight relationship with the director of the program. Then her granddaughter stopped by the program one day. I had no idea it was going to turn out this way. [SHILEENA] My grandmother used to say, "Oh, he's so handsome, so smart." I thought, "Let me go check out this guy." Once we saw each other, it was love at first sight. [RACK-LO] We never parted from there. That was '89. We got married. I'm twenty-seven now. My sister Doris lives with us. [SHILEENA] I grew up in Flatbush.

So this is your hip-hop home.
[RACK-LO] We do hip-hop whatever we do. We live it. When you come up the

stairs here, you see the Lo-Life history: the photographs, the album covers, *Rack Lauren, Thou Shalt Not Steal, Spit in Ya' Face.* In this room is my company, the Spit Factory.

It's got an Early American style chair, a computer, FedEx envelopes.
It's a start.

Your hip-hop living room has lovely beige couches.
[SHILEENA] Here's the hip-hop bathroom, pink tile, the hip-hop kitchen.

Curtains with apples and pears, pink pottery canister set.
This is George's…

Who?
George! [*Whispers*] I'm not going to call him Rack-Lo. His family calls him Junior.

I expected the hip-hop home to be a little rougher. Do you have a song about your new apartment?
[RACK-LO, *singing*] We moved from East New York two weeks ago/We're in a new apartment/We hardly get any rest/If you look at our new apartment/It's the best/

HIROYUKI ITO

A Polo treasure chest/I got one section for music/One section for sleeping/Every time we do this/We come out even/Now I'm breathin'/There's Polo in the kitchen/Polo in the living room/Polo in the bedroom/ Give me some room to breathe.

November 28, 2000

SACRAMENTAL CACTUS

LOCATION
Chinatown, Manhattan

RENT
$500 (rent stabilized)

SQUARE FEET
400 (four rooms in 1880s walk-up)

OCCUPANT
David Nathan Allen (graphic designer, Lord & Taylor; painter)

All the tents hanging over the bed, it's so psychedelic. Of course, I don't mean to imply...
No, it is. I was art director for *High Times* right at the height of the Reagan drug wars.

That! You have a chartreuse refrigerator and a black bathroom. And a black, fluffy toilet cover.
When I first moved into this building in 1984, they still had toilets in the hallway.

You're near a palm reader.
We've got spas, Chinese businesses, the all-night Bengali place for the taxi drivers. When I first moved in, this building was owned by an Italian. I heard there'd been a mob hit in a restaurant downstairs. The landlord was collecting $200 rents. You could see Gotti on a regular basis.

A Chinese man is sitting in the hall on the stairs reading a newspaper—so hot and crumbling.
One apartment has nine guys living in it, cubicles with three tiers of bunk beds. Downstairs, men and women are packed into one apartment. The guy sleeps in his hallway on a platform. In the summer, my hallway starts to smell. I used to work at the *SoHo News* with three other people who lived here. It's pretty much how I got in. I'm from London, north.

I smell incense.
Nag champa. It's one of those smells that's familiar and unfamiliar, and that's what I find intriguing about it. I was just in Glastonbury, a place I liked to go to as a teenager, being with a big bunch of people for weeks. Once these guys dragged carpets into an old medieval tower. We lived there for a while. After *High Times*, I got heavily into painting—Native American, shamanic. I'll show you this book I had as a little kid. [*He leaves the room. I study the strange roots and cacti growing about the place.*] Here.

Indian Crafts and Lore with drawings of buffalo, moccasins.
It sparked my interest in mushrooms and herbs—peyote, for instance. All this pottery I have comes from the Peyote Way Church of God.

Are we going to have some now?
It was founded by this old Apache who believed peyote should be used by everybody. That was an influence on my work. Prior to 9-11, I was planning

to move out to New Mexico, pursue my painting. I was working down at the New York Mercantile Exchange designing a publication. We finished the week before. After 9-11, work was hard to come by. That's what made me give up half the apartment.

You used to have seven rooms.
In the beginning, I was married. There was room for the ex-wife, the ex-girlfriend, roommates. When I first moved in, it was me and a big cokehead. The rent had been $700. It rose to $795. The Italian landlord sold it to a man in a hat in Williamsburg and this man set about knocking this building apart. Most of the tenants fled. He wasn't fixing the violations. I withheld rent. By '92, I got a rollback from $925 to $795. Then I gave up three rooms if he'd lower it to $500. We've had three brothels in this building and I've reported every one. I walked by a door one day and I heard an old man going—*ah, ah, ah, ah, ah.* They turn on the TV really loud. You saw the pimp, a little Chinese guy wearing thick-rimmed glasses. One brothel was run by an old lady. Old men were the customers. I had a burglary. I fought and struggled with the guy in the bathroom. I finally locked him in and he hit his head on the toilet. I have war clubs, tomahawks I've made and strategically placed around the apartment.... Enki, Enki, come on out. [*The cat comes out.*] He's been living here fourteen years. It's amazing how they stay kittens even though they get old. Here's a painting.

A shaman!
Peyote growing up his legs, snakes going on. The only ghost I ever saw was in broad daylight but that was in Chaco Canyon. My sister saw it too.

What does your sister do?
She lives in a cave in Spain.

June 15, 2005

CARY CONOVER

BHAGAVAN DAS'S ROOM

LOCATION

Inwood, Manhattan

PRICE

$225,000 in 1999 ($880 maintenance)

SQUARE FEET

1,700 (two apartments combined in prewar walk-up)

OCCUPANTS

Emily Horowitz (professor of sociology, St. Francis College), Seth Barron (freelance writer), Marina Barron (six, P.S. 314), Juliet Barron (four)

Is this the temple room?

[SETH] This is sort of the outer temple. [EMILY] Here is Bhagavan Das's room. He's on the road eleven months a year. [*To a child*] Don't tip over the massage table. I do yoga here with his ex-wife. She's the top teacher at Jivamukti. She's my best friend. Bhagavan's current girlfriend is my friend too. We do yoga here.

I saw his Web site. He has a long gray beard. He was born in Laguna Beach and found spiritual enlightenment in the sixties and leads Vedic astrology readings and evenings of ecstatic chanting.

You know how like in India, a family adopts a guru for good luck? We kind of did that with Bhagavan Das. Allen Ginsberg wrote a poem about him.

Bhagavan Das is pretty famous.

He had three kids by two different women, and then he had to get a job. I've been a follower of his since I was eighteen. I said, "We have to buy two apartments so we can have a room for Bhagavan Das." We had never even met him. Two years later—this was after buying the apartment—I went to a concert. He came over and said, "Hey, how ya doing?" I said, "If you ever need a place to stay in New York…" He said, "You know what? I need a place to live." I have my own career, but now I'm his manager, booking agent. His real name is Kermit. When I make plane reservations, it's kind of hard.

When you bought this in 1999, you said it was "a real crapshoot."

I was six months pregnant, I had a baby. We were living in a studio on the Upper East Side. I said, "I cannot raise children up here. It's horrible." I saw an ad—"Build your own palace, ten-room apt." My husband said, "You're nuts." I just came up here, totally pregnant. It seemed kind of creepy, the neighborhood. But the apartment was so great. My whole life, I only lived in rental. I really wanted to own. It nearly killed us to buy it at the time. We had to borrow from everybody. I was working all the time. I had no time to research neighborhoods. Now the grocery is making an effort. They're carrying vegan ham and soy milk. I had started a food co-op here, but…

You and your sister lived by yourselves in high school, you said.

My mom died when I was a kid. I took care of my sister. We lived by ourselves, in Summit, New Jersey. My dad was supposed to live with us. He lived with his wife twenty minutes away. He'd come to visit. On vacation, I figured out how to stay with friends. Seth and I met at graduate school, at Yale.

You became Jesse Friedman's good friend after he got out of prison in 2001 after thirteen years.

One of my interests is helping Jesse. I knew Jesse before the film [*Capturing the Friedmans*, about Jesse's father and Jesse, nineteen, pleading guilty to sexually abusing young boys who'd gone to the Friedmans' Great Neck house for computer classes]. I do work on wrongful convictions. After prison, he couldn't even go to the grocery. We have him over for Thanksgiving, holidays. He loves Bhagavan Das. [SETH] We got Jesse a job. A friend's training him to be an electrician. [EMILY] And an apartment. He got thrown out of his building when they found out what he was in jail for. My neighbor across the hall happens to be Ron Kuby's assistant. We asked her if Ron would represent Jesse. Jesse's filed an appeal to vacate his conviction. When my friend moved out across the street from us, I told Debbie Nathan, who's written a lot about the case. She bought that apartment. Jesse has two-hundred-plus counts of child abuse on his record. He is *totally* innocent.

February 2, 2005

THE SCIENTOLOGISTS

LOCATION
Greenpoint, Brooklyn

RENT
$1,100 (market)

SQUARE FEET
450 (top floor of house)

OCCUPANTS
Camille Acey (booking agent/
promoter), Benjamin Ickies Jr.
(accordionist/composer; director,
the Ambitious Orchestra; library
clerk, 92nd Street Y)

Just after I had a jelly donut at Peter Pan on Manhattan Avenue with the rabbits, I passed the We the People Document Service Center—"Bankruptcy $199, Divorce $199, Living Trusts $399." You live across from a gas station and next to a tire store…and you have heavy purple drapes. Camille, do you work at home staring out at the cars?

[CAMILLE] I used to. I started a temp job at a swimsuit company. It's funny—there are all these old women there who are overweight. I feel like our community here is seventy-five percent senior citizens. Our friend who helped us move did numerology for us.

She concluded?

Organization was going to be an issue. Benjamin and I met living at Flux Factory in Queens.

Is that a live-work building?

They live it up. That's why I quit my job. They sit and read the newspapers for three hours. [BENJAMIN] Half is a performance space, half, these fifteen dormlike rooms. You pay the rent to the Flux Factory. There are two bathrooms for the whole house. [CAMILLE] No, three. [BENJAMIN] That was the executive bathroom. [CAMILLE] It just had a sink, a toilet, and a cat litter box. They had this installation at the Queens Museum. They rebuilt it in the executive bathroom. [BENJAMIN] You could watch surveillance tapes while you were on the toilet. I moved in 2003. It was so cold that winter. Half the house hooked up with the other half. Brian started going out with Liz. Then Dan and Alice Mary. [CAMILLE] They met before that. [BENJAMIN] The point is— I'm giving you gold. These were the circumstances in which Camille and I became involved. [CAMILLE] Nonsense. On Thursday, they have performance monologues. I got up and said, "I've never had a boyfriend." So we went on a Valentine's date, a place called Jekyll and Hyde. I said, "Where did you go to college?" He said, "I didn't. I went to L.A. and studied Scientology." I flipped out. I just can't be a member of a cult. I screamed at him. We got in a huge fight. We ended up making out—no, I said, making up. My mother's from Ghana. I went on vacation. I got malaria. I took this medication. It made me psychotic. [BENJAMIN] She was nuts. [CAMILLE] I thought he could hear my thoughts. He tried to make me think of nine things.

STACI SCHWARTZ

Nine things?

Benign things. He started showing me Scientology things you can do to be organized. More and more, bringing those pamphlets. Now I identify as a Scientologist. Actually I'm glad about it.

Does Scientology have an approach to the home? No? Well, I heard communication is a big thing.

[BENJAMIN] Communication is so big. Before Scientology, I was a mess, spinning around, trying to start a band. After Scientology, I was able to get these tasks completed. Things aren't a mess now in the apartment.

You were raised Orthodox Jewish, Camille said.

Conservative. I swore off Judaism after my bar mitzvah. I was reading from the Torah and some old lady I'd never met before started talking about me, saying, "He's very

talented." Who is this lady and why is she talking about me on a very personal level? I knew Judaism was not for me. Then my mom got into Scientology and she said, "It's important I share this with you."

Is there a Scientology church?

[CAMILLE] You take services there. I have a study packet. It's in Times Square. [BENJAMIN] In Judaism, you have the Bible, the Torah. In Scientology, there are maybe fifty books, a lot of application of the texts...

I have to go now. [*I put on my wrap.*]

[CAMILLE] Oh, we didn't tell you about the backyard.

What about it?

[BENJAMIN] We have one.

April 20, 2005

GOD'S PLAN

LOCATION
Corona, Queens

RENT
$700 (monthly church donation)

SQUARE FEET
1,400 (five-room apartment over Baptist Church)

OCCUPANTS
Recardo Fonseca (sales, Humanscale Ergonomics; deacon, Sunday school teacher, and drummer at Baptist church), Jeidar Fonseca (full-time mother; clerical assistant, event planning), Joileen (eleven), Zuri (seven), Markie (three), Caleb (eighteen months)

What are the mysterious messages written on your living-room ceiling— "QUEENS IS A REAL KING'S EMPIRE" and "TRY AND TOUCH THE LIGHT"?
[JEIDAR] The person who lived here before wrote all over the ceiling and the walls. It's like he was a rap artist. He thought he was Michelangelo.

Your apartment is over a church that has velvet benches, lace on the altar. Recardo, all you have to do is walk out your front door and go across the hall to teach Sunday school. Your daughter Joileen's room has a pink flowered quilt. Radio Disney is playing. What a station!
They play songs from *The Little Mermaid.*

You can hear Ariel in her high voice sing, "Wanting to be a part of your world." How long have you lived here?
We moved here in July. [RECARDO] Before that we were a few blocks away in Elmhurst. That area is to die for. The end of the block is shaped like a horseshoe, Overlook Park. You can see the LaGuardia tower. This whole area is great for kids to go to school. A lot of money goes to East Elmhurst, Corona, in terms of education.

Corona is where Louis Armstrong lived. Corona-Elmhurst is supposed to be one of the most ethnically diverse areas in the world, immigrants from over a hundred countries. Northern Boulevard is hopping—stores, restaurants. And there are so many churches.
[JEIDAR] Almost twenty within nine square blocks. [RECARDO] Some Pentecostal, one Haitian, two or three Spanish. I think there's an increased need for answers, for spiritual food. People want to feel safe.

Recardo, you used to live in Jamaica, where your father was an accountant at a sugar factory. You came to New York when you were twelve, in 1977, and lived in Yorkville Towers. Your mother was a diplomat. Jeidar, you moved from the Dominican Republic at eleven to Brooklyn—Cypress Hills, which was an Italian neighborhood. You left your mother at fifteen because of continuing physical fights and you lived in three foster homes, the worst was...
[JEIDAR] Covenant—imagine being with a major amount of women who were

SANDRA-LEE PHIPPS

streetwise. They only had six little rooms, so the rest of us had to sleep together in the TV lounge with our belongings next to us. It was like jail. The best was Heart's Ease, 70th and Second. That place was gorgeous, brass staircases, an elevator. But they told me I couldn't read the *Village Voice* because there was a photo of a giant…

Sexual organ! Anyway, you said a great force drew you to live here over the church. It started long before, with that first Elmhurst apartment.
[RECARDO] Before we found the Elmhurst apartment, we had seen this other apartment off 108th. We wanted it. I had my money in hand. But we could not get in touch with the landlord, could not reach him. So the next day we saw an ad for the Elmhurst apartment in the paper. We called and clicked like this with the woman on the phone. [JEIDAR] I told her, I'm still nursing, and do you mind having three children in a two-bedroom apartment? She said, I don't mind if you don't. [RECARDO] We went over. She opened the door, she was on the phone. She just let us in without looking. This is a person who lives by faith. Later, she said, "I knew you before I even met you." Something just pulled us in there. It turns out that's where I would meet the pastor of the church we live above now. She was the pastor's wife. They owned the house. And that's how I got my calling. The pastor would set me on the road to become a deacon. We've been blessed tremendously ever since. I was between jobs, too. The job came, everything came. The pastor had always said, "You should hear me preach." Once I came in here, it was home! When God has a plan for you, he has a plan. There's nothing you can do.

October 12, 1999

What, no miniature lamb chops? I slammed the menu shut. I had been hoping. I sipped my vodka and tonic though I had thought about ordering a gin-gin mule. It is so hot tonight. Here I am at Bemelmans Bar at the Carlyle, which has been the *ne plus ultra* since it opened in 1930. Its first resident was Richard Rogers, the composer. "When you walk through a storm, hold your head up high."

I nibbled on a wasabi pea. Then my mind wandered as I looked around at the pale ochre murals with the green scribble trees, white snow dots, and ice skaters. I remembered that the artist, Ludwig Bemelmans—he made the *Madeline* books—came to New York from Austria in 1914 so he wouldn't have to go to reform school. He made a deal that he could live at the hotel for free while he painted the murals. Look, there's a little man with a fur collar. He's getting robbed. Rabbits are under an umbrella. Bemelmans wrote a book about interior decorator Elsie de Wolfe called *To the One I Love the Best* because when he saw her little dog cemetery, more than one plaque read, "To the one I love the best."

It is so hot tonight. Northrop Frye wrote that summer is romance, fall is tragedy, winter is irony, and spring comedy. I was just at the New York Film Festival party at Tavern on the Green. P and I were discussing Žižek near the topiary gorilla. Of course the next day I saw *Regular Lovers*, the new movie from Paris. Everybody in the movie has black hair. Their shirts are white. A man in a turtleneck inhales from a pipe and says, "I never want to be anyone famous or important. I want to be anonymous."

Then someone else says later, "I left the Molotov cocktail in a gutter."

"Are you the one burning cars?"

"Oui."

"How can we make the revolution for the working class despite the working class?"

"Do you want a puff of the bamboo?"

"Morning is Italian. Night is German."

His girlfriend goes to New York and writes a letter. "Here you don't feel too much, just like a lonely animal in the jungle."

I had another wasabi pea. The man at the piano played, "I know you miss the love you lost long ago.... And when nobody is nigh you cry."

SOPHISTICATES

PORN STAR

LOCATION
Catskill, Greene County

PRICE
$22,000 in 2000

SQUARE FEET
240 in 2000, now 800 (three-room
shack with loft office area)

OCCUPANT
Tom Judson aka Gus Mattox
(porn star/actor/writer/composer)

What do I call you, Tom or Gus?
Either.

I began my journey early this Sunday morning, sliding away from the barbarous city in a train along the river, all bandbox blue with a gold light, expectant as if something's going to happen, though the train moves on before it does. There was a swan moving its way north. Frankly, I was so tired....
How do you make a living in porn?
You don't. Except for the producers. I have a pied-à-terre in the city, in my friend's two-bedroom apartment. I pay $200. I share a room with her office. I met her when I was in *42nd Street*. I got this shack after my *Cabaret* national tour. I bought it from a lawyer. She bought it from the guy who built it. I think, in the seventies. She said he moved to a kibbutz. I grew up an hour south of here, regular old 1950s house, in Washingtonville.

What did you do?
I played the French horn.

How did your mother feel when she heard that you didn't get the award for Best Threesome? Was she sad?
We didn't discuss it.

Where did you live before here?
New York. In twenty-five years, I only had two apartments, first at 45th and Ninth, then Third between Second and Bowery.

Did you move here because you yearned to live in sweet and simple harmony with the craggy mountains?
Like a Brueghel painting? No. [*He points to a photograph.*] That was my husband, who died of AIDS in '96. We met in '90. A friend of Bruce's had this house by the Rip Van Winkle Bridge. Bruce was a video editor. He worked for *Entertainment Tonight*. We met at the Russian Tea Room. We would come to that house near the bridge every weekend. Then Bruce died. We had such wonderful times together at the other home. We'd cook, play Scrabble.

I see.
This shack was just this tiny, tiny room when I bought it. I lived in it for about a year. I made the deck. I made the rooms with six-by-six wooden posts sunk into the ground. The walls sit on the edge of the floor.

How do the walls stand erect?
At first it's shaky. As you go along, it gets sturdier and sturdier, and everything supports each other. Cutting through the

wall to make a door was exciting. The floor is one of my great inspirations. When I did the rooms, I knew I could afford either a hardwood floor or knotty pine paneling. What you see is subflooring. I thought, I'm going to stain it and polyurethane it and call it a day.

I think it's the little, pale brown piano that gets me. Then, of course, the sylvan-glade green towels.
The look I was going for was a TV writer from the fifties who has a little getaway.

He would write for *The Alcoa Hour* or...
The Philco Playhouse.

All your shoes are lined with sheepskin.
I just happen to have three pairs of slippers.

How often are you alone?
It can be a week or ten days. With my Web site, I have constant conversations with people from all over the world. I go to the gym in Cairo, I see the same three guys there every day. I'm going to San Francisco tomorrow. I have lead roles in two movies. I actually have scripts to study. [*He serves a lunch of poached salmon and a marinade of cucumbers and sweet onions.*]

What is your motivation?
In one, I play a sheriff who's found some boys stealing. We work something out so I don't have to arrest them. In the other, I work at the leather store in San Francisco. I am sort of the connect character. I've only been a porn star for a year.

I'm so energized by the salmon. I feel I could do a film. In the leather one, is there a revelation in the plot?
The what?

January 26, 2005

ESKIMO HORROR

LOCATION
Upper West Side, Manhattan

PRICE
$162,000 in 1987 plus $148,000 in 2000 ($1,500 maintenance)

SQUARE FEET
1,080 (one bedroom and studio combined in prewar co-op)

OCCUPANTS
Cornelia Ravenal and Mikael Södersten (writers/filmmakers)

This room with the eighteenth-century statue of Vishnu...

[CORNELIA] This room doesn't represent both of us. Some of the kitchen represents both of us. I always thought that New York kitchens should be dark and sophisticated—I am from Washington, D.C. Then when Mikael moved in, he was used to blond, Swedish wood, light and airy. Now this room is the nighttime room. We're also in here in the morning writing together. We rarely come in the middle of the day because we're both in our separate offices. My office is in the Swedish room. [MIKAEL] When we did the bathroom, we were keen on keeping it northern style and that to me meant white and black and we have the harbor... [CORNELIA] To me, the bathroom is Zen and rustic. I wanted a bathroom that brought the outside in. It has almost the same materials

as the roof across the way. [MIKAEL] We have different entrances into the problem but with harmonious results. That integration... [CORNELIA] It's such a little room but we spent so much time thinking about it. [MIKAEL] We began to think of it as the masculine bathroom because we have two. [CORNELIA] But you can't see it.

I won't look. You met at Harvard.

In 1982. We reconnected online in 2001. I wrote him: So are you married, happy, with children? [MIKAEL] I didn't want to send her a reply in which I didn't appear successful, particularly to an American, for whom success is so important. But I had to be honest. My reply: No.

Didn't you live with the Inuit?

During my time in Sweden, one film project took me to the north point of Greenland, where the people believe they live in the navel of the earth. [*We discuss.*] [CORNELIA] When we first got together, we went to the Museum of Natural History. I wanted to show him the people from South Asia, where I have traveled. He wanted to show me the Eskimos. [MIKAEL] I had a grim story to reveal that Cornelia did not know about.

And?

Robert Peary, in order to finance his trip, brought back and sold six Eskimos to the museum. No, not dead Eskimos. But they died by themselves rather quickly from pneumonia, because there's so much bacteria. [CORNELIA] The story gets worse. [MIKAEL] One survives and he sees his father being buried. After that, he was raised by a museum employee. At seventeen, he discovers that his father has not been buried properly but his bones are...

In an exhibit!

[CORNELIA] Yes! [MIKAEL] No. It said that in the newspaper but that may have been rumor. The bones were used for scientific purposes and his brain was put in formaldehyde to be used as a research object. It was a scandal at the time. [CORNELIA] We'd had one date before, when I was living with my first husband who was—Egyptian, six-four. [MIKAEL] He was a tall guy. [CORNELIA] With a very deep voice.

Then you bought another studio, broke down a wall...

I wanted a home office where I could hold meetings, writers' groups. I had also been interested in esoteric design philosophies like feng shui. You have to clear the bad out to let the good energy in. Then Mikael came and that became the Swedish room. [MIKAEL] You have embraced the Swedish style and I am very happy with that. [CORNELIA] The other fusion element—the Swedish-looking candleholder that I found. I wanted to get forty made for our wedding. I sent out an Internet request to a consortium of Indian manufacturers: "Can anybody make these?" A man with a factory outside Delhi emailed: "I can do it!" [MIKAEL] We use candles a lot in northern countries. [CORNELIA] We'll be lighting them soon tonight. [MIKAEL] We're a pale people.

April 27, 2005

BRIAN KENNEDY

GAULOISES

LOCATION
TriBeCa, Manhattan

PRICE
$200,000 in 1996 ($1,200
maintenance)

SQUARE FEET
1,500 (two-story loft co-op in
nineteenth-century former dry
goods warehouse)

OCCUPANTS
Uscha Pohl (gallery owner; fashion
designer, Up & Co.; publisher, *VERY*
magazine), Ellis Kreuger (roommate
and design partner)

**If Marshall McLuhan could see this
loft, it would bring tears to his eyes.
There's a catwalk eight feet in the air for
fluorescent underwear fashion shows,
a gallery space with installations, an
office for magazine publishing, a kitchen
counter that doubles as a sales desk for
gallery purchases, a forthcoming video
projection wall. Then, of course, two
bedrooms, two baths. How is it sleeping
here? Just one gallery opening means a
hundred people smoking Gauloises near
your bath towels.**
[USCHA] I have no home life.

**But it's so glamorous! Plus, your
childhood was in Düsseldorf. And you
worked for Vivienne Westwood in
London, and lived in Paris and Brazil!
Anyway, you moved to New York in**

**1994. In the first month, you came here,
to one of TriBeCa's many five-story dry
goods wholesale buildings that went
up during the mid-nineteenth-century
building boom—as everyone knows, the
nation's biggest port was bustling with
commercial prosperity and everybody
was shopping. You came to visit friends
of friends from Europe who had a loft.
Something terrifying happened...**
I'd never been south of Canal. It was so
confusing. I didn't know anyone. I was shy.
This strange man came up to me and said,
"Can I help you?" I said, "No." My knees
were really shaking. I finally found my
friends' building. I went inside. I started to
go up the stairs. This old man came toward
me like Frankenstein with a walking stick.
He said, "Where are you going?" I said,
"I don't know." Then I came to the door
of this apartment. I thought my friends
lived here. I looked in. It was all dark,
sinister, and brown, like a forties movie or
a sixties boardroom. In the back was a fat,
naked old man playing cards with himself.
I mumbled, "So sorry." I went upstairs. I
found my friends' loft.

**You heard the card player's loft was for
sale. You wanted it even though it made
you feel like Little Red Riding Hood.**
It looked so fascinating. But it took forever.
I got it after an endless court case. There
are four lofts in the building. The ground
floor used to be a diner, but they left last
week. The building was co-oped in the
1970s. I got the apartment from the owner,
the man with the cane. He wanted to sell
so he could settle his debts. The court put
the apartment up for auction. I won. I put

GREG MILLER

the money down. Then the court wouldn't release the apartment. I was calling every day for months. Finally I got it.

I was literally dead by the end. Then we found out there was the hugest rat problem. That got solved, but then there was a flood at three in the morning. It was like the Amazon pouring down the staircase. I said, "Oh no." My neighbors and I were up for hours trying to stop leaks. I went to sleep at five. I heard boots stomping. I woke up with seven firemen around me. I said, "Oh no, oh no." The diner had called the firemen. Their ceiling had come down. Two days later, my phone wires were mysteriously cut.

You fixed the wires.

Yes, but now that the diner has left, the cockroaches are coming out.

January 6, 1998

SALT FURNITURE

LOCATION
Upper West Side, Manhattan

RENT
$2,000 (market)

SQUARE FEET
500 with 1,200-square-foot terrace
(penthouse of prewar former hotel)

OCCUPANTS
Evan Bennett and Silvia Fuster
(architects)

This building is not as luxurious as I thought it would be. The vent in the elevator is coughing. No one is at the desk.
[SILVIA] When we moved in, it looked like a frat house, broken tiles. [EVAN] Asphalt roof. Our first question was, "How strange is this?" [SILVIA] The owner lives in Israel. [EVAN] He comes once a month.

At first I thought you lived in the Milburn Hotel nearby.
[SILVIA] There's a nudist colony on top.

Are they all always nude?
[EVAN] They're regularly partially nude. [SILVIA] Maybe we just notice them when they're nude. Except for the guy writing in a white T-shirt and glasses. He might be nude from the waist down. [EVAN] We get watched just like they do. [SILVIA] We

spent a lot more time out here last year, before the wedding thing.

Weren't you just married in a castle in Spain?
Yes, in my mother's village.

I heard there's a salt mine.
It's been mined since Roman times.

You mentioned that you're going to be designing furniture out of salt?
[EVAN] We're researching the material.

People will want to lick the chairs.
Well, who knows.

Where are you from, Silvia?
[SILVIA] I was educated here. Summers and Christmas, we went to Spain. I grew up on East 75th. I was born in Minnesota. My father's a heart specialist at the Mayo Clinic. We spoke Catalan at home. It's very international in Minnesota. [EVAN] I'm from Aurora, New York. Wells College is there. [SILVIA] We met our junior years abroad. Columbia architecture school has a New York–Paris program. [EVAN] We lived with a group of friends on a houseboat. [SILVIA] It wasn't like a yacht. [EVAN] It was like a big thumb. [SILVIA] With Astroturf. Mr. Fioleau, the landlord, came and took us for a ride. [EVAN] He took our apartment underneath the Boulevard Richard Lenoir.

What is that container?
[SILVIA] An ashtray made of Bazooka gum wrappers in Hebrew. It's full of olive

pits...[*We discuss the dog.*] We moved into this apartment before we had the dog. [EVAN] Our friend Rufus found him wandering around the streets of New Jersey. He gained forty pounds since we got him. [SILVIA] People were feeding him through cracks in car windows like they were on safari.

His head is so big.

He's not supersmart. If he were that big and smart, it would be a problem. His butt is couch height. My parents' building...[EVAN] Has a twenty-five-pound limit.

When he opens his mouth, there's a whole world in there. He's so wanting. There's something restful about him.

[SILVIA] It's very relaxing. You can learn from dumbness. I think mostly he's dumb but not self-conscious. [EVAN] He's dumb but secure. [SILVIA] We're all dumb in certain ways. I'm sure he's talented in many ways.

Now your wedding...

It lasted four days. [EVAN] I got food poisoning on the plane on the way back. [SILVIA] He spent the whole time in the bathroom. [EVAN] I threw up on the snack table. When we came back to the apartment, all the trees had died, all the books had fallen.

You're holding up a jagged fragment of wood.

It's a piece of the coffee table. Basically there were four shelves, forty feet, of architecture books that fell on the floor. The inside wall was destroyed. [SILVIA] The plants outside were all destroyed. It was so hot while we were gone. Climatically it was a hundred degrees. There was so much heat on this box. [EVAN] We thought the walls got so hot and holes expanded and I think the plastic anchors got soft. [SILVIA] We're at the point where the terrace looks better at night.

September 27, 2005

BRIAN KENNEDY

TIGER LILY

LOCATION
Upper West Side, Manhattan

RENT
Under $2,000 (rent controlled)

SQUARE FEET
800 (five-bedroom penthouse with
wraparound terrace)

OCCUPANT
Sondra Lee (director/actress/dancer;
faculty member, NYU Drama
School, Stella Adler, Actor's Studio;
private acting coach)

I'm disappointed. I'd hoped you'd say "Ugga wugga wigwam" when you opened the door, the way you did when you were Tiger Lily in Peter Pan.
Jerome Robbins's *Peter Pan* was a long time ago. I've done a lot of things since 1950-something.

Aside from having Marlon Brando as your first lover and your many performances, including the La Dolce Vita orgy scene where a balloon swung from your ponytail, you got this apartment from your second ex-husband. Good work!
I've lived here about twenty years. I think he married me because he wanted my furniture. He was the nameless producer. We called him Mr. Wonderful.

It's hard to focus because the apartment is so dense with objects. The blue room
is exploding with photos. Plus you have crystal bottles, silver teapots, pieces of alabaster, and so many birds' nests.
Birds' nests are very delicate. Each species makes a different kind of nest.

Lots of the lampshades are covered with silk and lace scarves.
It's very European. It softens the light. The violet cut-velvet scarf over the hall lampshade is from *Places in the Heart*. I went to the set person and said could I have it at the end of the shoot? She said no. Then she gave it to me.

What are your favorite things to watch from the terrace?
I love the little boats that go by. And the sun in the summer. It's like Japan. You see this red circle dropping quickly, into New Jersey, I guess.

The kitchen is full of hundreds of teapots, Moroccan baskets, and pig figures.
When I moved in, the kitchen was cockroach heaven. Then it was followed by mice you wouldn't believe. We couldn't even have people over for dinner. I'd put the food out and it would be crawling with animals. I had to rebuild the cabinets.

You're so full of get-up-and-go. So many people can't even pull themselves together to get in a cab to go to Bed Bath & Beyond to buy a soap dish.
You have to do things for yourself. Even before the building management changed the windows, I changed mine. When it was cold, there would be ice inside. This

building is in total disrepair. I wish they'd let us just paint the hallways ourselves. Rent control is kind of a joke. You may start out low but you pay for every improvement in the building.

You've created a perfect place.
There have been bad robberies. I was away doing a movie in 1982. I was told to come home immediately and bring a friend, a doctor, and a detective. It was a bombshell. My paintings were destroyed. These guys took bottles of wine, broke them. It took about a year to get it back in shape.

Even Neverland had its pirates.

April 1, 1997

GREG MILLER

THE PLANNERS

LOCATION

Fort Greene, Brooklyn

RENT

$1,700 (market)

SQUARE FEET

750 (second floor of nineteenth-century brownstone)

OCCUPANTS

Georgeen Theodore and Tobias Armborst (architects/urban designers)

A red glow comes from the brownstones at this time of night. Your stone steps are pink. Yes, I'd love to sit on the terrace. These drinking glasses, so wide and low!
[GEORGEEN] They're from Barcelona. [TOBIAS] We took about half a year to find just the right apartment. [GEORGEEN] When we were in Cambridge and knew we wanted to live in New York, Tobias said, "The only thing I want is a terrace." Of course Tobias grew up…

Where the Rhine and the river Düssel conjoin, in Düsseldorf, with his sculptor parents in an art nouveau house…
[TOBIAS] It was more *Gründerzeit*, late 1800s, a very rich period when all cities grew. [GEORGEEN] No, It was kind of art nouveau, a new period of flourishing. Here, on the terrace, we have a view of the Masonic Temple. It has this faded glory. We see the little red blinking antenna on top of Brooklyn Tech, feel the waves coming out. The G train sort of rumbles underneath. There are all these different systems pressing up against one space, the urban intensity of things. [TOBIAS] We have a beautiful caterpillar. It's in that box. [GEORGEEN] It's turning into a butterfly right now. [TOBIAS] It was in our dill plant.

Tobias, you just helped your firm design four ferry landings on the East River. Georgeen is working on a master plan for a Rutgers neighborhood study, doing some work in Savannah. It seems everyone is an urban planner today!
[GEORGEEN] We are urban designers, not planners. [TOBIAS] In the United States, clearly, planning is thinking about dividing land to sell it. In Europe, it's different because the land was initially owned by kings and churches. [GEORGEEN] That's a little unfair description of what planning is in the U.S. A main tool of planning is zoning—how much you set on one block, what you set back. It is about separating incompatible uses. Years ago, skinning cows would be put separately because of the filthy conditions that compromise quality of life. [TOBIAS] The modernist idea of urban planning was to separate the functions. Cities crowded people, so, go to the country. [GEORGEEN] The first thing you see in one of Corbusier's houses is a washbasin—to cleanse yourself of the city. [TOBIAS] Now people are going in the opposite direction.

BRIAN KENNEDY

Your design company, Interboro [with Dan D'Oca and Christine Williams], was a winner of the L.A. Forum's Dead Malls competition. You proposed a future for a 1970s mall in Fishkill. Dan said you are all more interested in how city life emerges without big plans, endogenous development, recognizing that things form, build off of each other, out of mess is where the good things emerge. He said Jane Jacobs believed in the importance of mess. You know, Rem Koolhaas wrote about this steaming garbage dump in Lagos, Nigeria—the dump being "the lowest form of spatial organization"—and "on its surface lived a community.... This was the dump as housing."

[GEORGEEN] Koolhaas was a writer before he was an architect. I think we're not as much into mess as Dan, but what we're excited about are the little things

that have their own logic, building on that. In the Dead Malls project, we saw flea market vendors using their trucks to create roofs. There's a certain logic to that, a beauty in the myriad ways people make do. [TOBIAS] There was a Chinese laundry, the only one of the stores left over in the mall and, outside, a bus stop for people going to Atlantic City. [GEORGEEN] Both functions coalesced. [TOBIAS] This laundry guy could sell the bus tickets just because he was the only guy on the site. [GEORGEEN] But then there were all these empty parking spots because the mall was dead—a symbiotic relationship. So many who do urban design try to create new worlds. [TOBIAS] Like the New Urbanists...

Dan said they don't see what's exciting about the suburbs and they're "no fun."

September 3, 2003

BOUGAINVILLEA

LOCATION

Upper West Side, Manhattan

RENT

$1,800 (market)

SQUARE FEET

525 (one-bedroom apartment in walk-up)

OCCUPANTS

Sharon Simpson (writer/producer), Hugh Raffles (anthropologist, UC Santa Cruz)

Tell how you bought a California beach house and had nervous breakdowns.

[HUGH] We were living on Ludlow and Canal. [SHARON] This great 1,000-square-foot loft. Everybody said, "It's just like a movie set." [HUGH] I was a graduate student and we had just been in the loft six months when I got this really good academic job in Santa Cruz. What can you do? [SHARON] I said, "There are only two places I'd be willing to live—New York or the Bay Area." [HUGH] Now, don't be mean about Santa Cruz. [SHARON] We're there for about two weeks. [HUGH] Paradise. [SHARON] Sea lions. [HUGH] Pelicans. [SHARON] People lovely all the time. [HUGH] Genuinely lovely, though Sharon hasn't been there for a while. [SHARON] I've only lived in cities, as has Hugh. [HUGH] Sharon grew up in the middle of Belfast. I grew up in London. [SHARON] We met when we were twenty—twenty-five years ago, University of Warwick in England.

[HUGH] We were earning way more money than ever before. [SHARON] Way more. [HUGH] The rental market is really expensive. Santa Cruz prices are comparable to New York's. [SHARON] That was '99. We did what everybody does—try to make sure you're OK when you're old. [HUGH] People said the only security you could get was to buy somewhere. The university gave really good mortgages. [SHARON] We're horrible brats because we had all these advantages there. The whole looking for a house! First of all, we're not even American. We had no idea of what middle-class Americans live in. We'd always lived in New York, ten years.

[HUGH] Our realtor [*He makes quotation marks in the air.*]—that's a real California thing—Bernice. [SHARON] Poor Bernice. [HUGH] She'd pick us up in her Mercedes. [SHARON] We'd walk in these houses—huge rooms, high ceilings. We're used to tiny apartments. [HUGH] We got agoraphobic. Bernice said, "You like it?" [SHARON] I said, "Are you serious? We're not going to live in this!" [HUGH] Eventually we found a house. It was going to be $300,000. The idea of owing somebody this much money...[SHARON] We're not credit-card-debt people. [HUGH] We had to put down $10,000. [SHARON] Fifteen thousand. [HUGH] Because Steve lent us...[SHARON]...our best friend...[HUGH] It was like emptying our shoe boxes to get this. I just cannot understand how with $15,000 you can buy a house for $300,000. This is supposed to be a good thing. There's something really fucked up about that. Everyone says it's all about the tax break. [SHARON] We're puritans about that. If you earn a lot, you should pay a lot of tax, subsidize people who don't earn a lot. [HUGH] If you can afford to buy a house, why should you pay a lot less tax than people who can't? Where is the logic in that?

We find the house. [SHARON] And we love it. [HUGH] It looked like an apartment. [SHARON] New Yorkers would say it's just perfect. [HUGH] Bougainvillea. [SHARON] Roses. [HUGH] Five blocks from the Pacific. [SHARON] Hummingbirds. [HUGH] Snails. [SHARON] Hugh used to rescue them in the morning in a bucket and set them free in the ocean. [HUGH] There are a lot of murders there. People smash snails against the walls. [SHARON] We're vegetarians. [HUGH] The day we moved in, our realtor came over with the keys. Bernice said, "You have such a beautiful garden." [SHARON] I thought she meant in the back. On the corner, we had the whole of the street, with these little dwarf maples. [HUGH] Two magnolias. [SHARON] Bernice said, "That's going to be a lot of work." I said, "Hang on a minute. We didn't buy the street in front of the house." [HUGH] What about the city? Doesn't the city do this? [SHARON] The moral is never leave Manhattan. Our friend Greg said, "You need a weed wacker." [HUGH] The fights. [SHARON] Our fights were so public. We'd throw the weed wacker at each other. *You* take the *fucking* weed wacker. Every Sunday morning, we'd be so resentful. We just wanted to read

a book. [HUGH] Sharon left. We discovered why nobody else was fighting about cutting the grass. They'd hire workers. [SHARON] We just couldn't do that. [HUGH] It would take us half a day. These guys could cut it in thirty minutes. [SHARON] In the end, we did that. [HUGH] I'd hide. I was so humiliated. [SHARON] We felt so guilty, we also gave them the same amount of money we were paying their boss. [HUGH] When you own a house, you make all these compromises. People would walk past. Their dog would pee. [*Hugh wags his finger.*] You turn into one of those suburban Republicans—complaining about property taxes, checking real-estate prices. You become invested in this whole system that you really just hate. [SHARON] I'd tell you not to look at the prices. [HUGH] My fear was we wouldn't be able to sell. We'd be trapped there forever.

Sharon left. It was that or our relationship. [SHARON] We came to New York for a vacation—May 2001. My friend Ellen was subletting her apartment. I said, "Would you consider subletting to me?" I hadn't even talked to Hugh. [HUGH] We'd been living together twenty-two years. [SHARON] You were great. It took you an hour. We put the house on the market. I moved back to New York, September 9, 2001.

[HUGH] We had to sell the house. I would have died living there by myself. The drama—way more than buying. You audition realtors. It's like the primaries—they tell you what they're going to do for you. They just appeal to your greed. [SHARON] Remember the Palo Alto couple? So much plastic surgery. [HUGH] And Justin Thyme from Thunderbird Realty.

We know what song they play when he comes in a room.

It's like this whole show. You feel bad but then they make $20,000 at a time. They come in, give you a really high price, justify it to make you feel good. [SHARON] They say, "Oh, we looked at comparison prices, factored this in." You fall for the whole thing. [HUGH] Two weeks later, they come back all very serious. Like they're in *The War Room*. [SHARON] It was happy, happy Judy [their realtor] in the beginning. But then it was, "We have to talk to you guys." [HUGH] They say, "What you've done is, you've gone in too high. We've tested the market and the market clearly, well, the market knows that we're doing something wrong because no one has been to see the house." [SHARON] The market knows.

Judy's doing this open house. [HUGH] There's a big ink stain in the middle of our couch. She said, "Oh, my pen leaked." We'd never spent real money for furniture before. She said, "You can just wash it out." [SHARON] There's still a big bleached spot. [HUGH] You sign this paper agreeing they're your realtor. You have to. We were really, really desperate. [SHARON] We had to pay Steve back. [HUGH] Judy starts slashing the price. Sharon's gone by this point. Judy and I can't stand each other. Then Judy says, "I think this is what to do." I said, "Judy, this is my money, not your money." [SHARON] It's so out of character. He never says things like this to people.

[HUGH] Every time people came around, I was just like a performing monkey. Forget about integrity. You buy a house—it feels like the end. Yes, we sold it. Actually I sold it. Judy made loads of money. Yes, we made money on it. I almost think we'd feel better if we lost money. [SHARON] We did well and we hated that.

[HUGH] Now we have an apartment in Santa Cruz. I'm so happy. I also have an apartment in New Haven because I have a fellowship at Yale. [SHARON] Now we have three apartments. This year's the anomaly. Now New Haven is...[HUGH] I completely disagree. New Haven is *totally* fine.

February 11 and 18, 2004

BRIAN KENNEDY

All the men are made of alabaster. They are praying and have no heads. It is the Altar Predella and Socle, Spain, 1456–58 by Francí Gomar.

I was up at the Cloisters near Washington Heights. The Cloisters are not really medieval, though the art and monuments are. They were built in the 1930s when women wore little velvet caps with a feather and lived in half-timbered houses in Riverdale. John D. Rockefeller Jr. wanted a proper setting for the collection he bought from a sculptor who had gathered up all this medieval art that had been abandoned during the French Revolution.

I went to the gift shop and fingered the unicorn neckties. What man would want to wear one?

I had to sit down in the Cuxa Cloister and think about this. In the warm sun, I leaned my head against a pink marble column. A monk ran by. He was looking for the cruet, the ewer, and the cross. He had given his attention to the espaliered pear tree.

I was embroidering a piece of wool with silk and gold thread. I had just finished a pansy, a pomegranate, and a columbine. Father Francis was in the garden. He was planting herbs, Our Lady's Bedstraw and Scotch broom, feverfew. That's in case somebody had a fever.

I copied a manuscript and read Jeanne d'Evreux's tiny prayer book.

Then I rubbed two kindling sticks together, added some paper and gold. There was a bit of fire. I picked up the broken parts of the world.

FANTASTIC

FOREIGN LEGIONNAIRES FOR DINNER

LOCATION
Boerum Hill, Brooklyn

RENT
$1,600 (market)

SQUARE FEET
2,400 (loft with 600-square-foot roof garden)

OCCUPANTS
Leslie Thornton (filmmaker; senior lecturer, Department of Modern Culture and Media, Brown University), Thomas Zummer (creative director, Sunshine Digital; writer/illustrator/cartoonist; developer of Internet conspiracy-theory games)

How long have you had the top of an Algerian tent tied to a sprinkler pipe in the middle of your loft?

[LESLIE] Five years. It's a set piece for a film I'm working on, about a turn-of-the-century woman explorer who dressed as a man and converted to Islam in Algeria. She was the lover of many powerful sheikhs and died at twenty-seven in a flash flood. I work on a film in a very impromptu way. It's best to already have the set. If the actors are around, I start filming. When I made *Peggy and Fred in Hell*, I turned my apartment into Hell. But it was disturbing

to come home. There were piles of old machine parts and fifty loaves of Wonder bread and eggs.

Why is the tent made of purple silk?

It is based on the same tent given to the Colonel, a key character in my film, played by Ron Vawter from the Wooster Group. It was Ron's last role. I filmed him having Foreign Legionnaires over to dinner. That's when the tent was bigger, four-hundred square feet. There were a couple of opera singers and belly dancers in there. We had sex scenes. I also use the tent as a guest room. There are candles, oil lamps, brass coffee urns. The rugs are from Morocco and Algeria.

Wouldn't you rather just live in the tent?

Yes. I'd have a TV and VCR in there. I live like that in Providence when I teach during the week. Simply. The rest of the loft is so complicated. The complications partly come from Tom and the tons of library that come with him—about eight thousand books. He's still unpacking five years after we moved. And then I have closets full of costumes. The furniture and things on the walls are set pieces. Then there are the plants, a hobby of Tom's. Most are from seeds Tom picked up when we were traveling. He has seeds from Brazil and the Bronx. He likes the seed and then when it becomes a plant, he's perfectly content to let it die. I say he tests plants to destruction. He says it makes them stronger.

What's this ladder with the Christmas lights?

It's the cats' ladder with all their toys on it.

GREG MILLER

Do you like the neighborhood?

I don't go out much. People come over. All my friends have keys. But I do like it here—we're on the edge of Brooklyn's Arabic shopping area, Atlantic Avenue. Tom is well known and beloved on Atlantic.

Where did you live before?

An apartment in Fort Greene that was formerly a hair salon/bordello with a tacky Greek motif. One whole wall was floor-to-ceiling mirrors with marble arches. There were gigantic godlike figures in the nude.

And what was that film called?

Oh, that wasn't a set. Just a weird home.

May 6, 1997

DANCING SHOES AT HOME

LOCATION

Washington Heights, Manhattan

PRICE

$265,000 in 1998
($930 maintenance)

SQUARE FEET

2,050 (three-bedroom apartment
in 1911 co-op)

OCCUPANT

Michael Burke (lighting person
for film/television)

Here we are at the Grinnell—so triangular and that twenty-foot archway, the empty courtyard. I read that the site was part of George Bird Grinnell's estate. He was "the father of American conservation" and the Grinnell Glacier is named after him. Schwartz & Gross were the architects, popular among the affluent and creating buildings for the rising middle class.
The toilets are made by Grinnell. This was the dining room. Now there's a stuffed emu. Here's a sugar sculpture.

Let's go on a tour in the early-morning light—ah, peacock chenille bedspreads, broken-glass angels, Judith Scott's yarn sculptures, baby shoes made out of Camel cigarette wrappers by prison artists, a "Cooky Jar" folded from magazines and legal paper by the *Golden Venture* Chinese immigrants who were interned in Pennsylvania, and a book on Ghana coffins because you are ordering one in the shape of a Converse sneaker. Tell how you found the apartment.
We were filming *Gloria* in the building, the original Cassavetes, in 1980.

She's always drunk in the living room.
No, that's *Under the Influence. Gloria* is Gena Rowlands being chased by the mob because she takes this little boy who witnessed a hit. I thought it was just a really cool building. I had wanted to buy the place across the street. I went to the police department. They were not very enthused about the neighborhood then. At the time, I was living with two girls. I just filed this building in the back of my head. I moved to 104th and Central Park West and lived there for eighteen years. At this point, 1998, real estate was going crazy again, so I said, "I'm going to put my apartment on the market, I'm not going to be flexible," and seven months later, two bids came in an hour. I got even more than the asking price. Everybody said, "Michael, you're crazy, you'll never find a nicer place." I had to go to New Orleans for Jazz Fest. Every year I go. I said, "I'll look for an apartment when I come back." I drove up to the Grinnell, left a note with the doorman—"If anyone is interested in selling, please give them my number." This really became a long story but three months later, I ended up buying this. The money I sold my co-op for on

Central Park West, I got this and a house in Louisiana. I flipped the one place and then I got two.

You sound like the guy in *The Usual Suspects*. "He'll flip you."

Yeah. All my family lives in Jersey. I was born in Hoboken. My father's a gaffer, my sister, my brother-in-law. A gaffer is the head lighting person. There're all these cliques of gaffers—Italian, Jewish, Irish. They call my father Red. There's Rusty, Kelly, Kenny. When I first came in, they called me Dancing Shoes.

Your girlfriend lives in Houston.

We met in New Orleans. She has a jewelry store in Houston. She just bought a house. Last week I was in Texas painting her bedroom. I'm all over the ice when I'm not working. My wallet lives in New York—I do the lighting on *Law & Order: Criminal Intent*. My soul is in New Orleans. I went there in '89 to work on *Miller's Crossing*, fell in love—the music, architecture. At some point I knew in another life I was there. I was then involved in a relationship with someone down there. I worked on *JFK*, *Pelican Brief*. The prices of homes were so incredibly inexpensive in the early nineties. I bought this one in the Lower Garden District, funky neighborhood. I started fixing it up and renting it out. My next-door neighbor was selling his. So I bought that, sister houses. They're my retirement fund. My girlfriend and I have a house we rent in New Orleans 'cause we can't afford the rent I charge. We live with this little air conditioner in the window.

September 17, 2003

THE MODELS SAY

LOCATION
Ridgewood, Queens

RENT
$700 (market)

SQUARE FEET
1,000 (floor of 1920s
two-family house)

OCCUPANT
Gary Speziale (artist; circulation
assistant, Bobst Library; master's
candidate in religious aesthetics,
Gallatin School, NYU)

Mommy!

It's the Mommy Room—the kitchen. The
Madonnas are in this room. There are a lot
more madonnas but they're not up now.
[*He holds up a small Madonna statue.*] This I
found so cheap, I cannot tell you.

You have all these drawings of nude men.

I've had a lot of models come here to
pose. Some are not sure how to react to
the religious imagery all over. They're
comfortable with their nudity and sensuality.
You could put them in the sexiest pose ever
but they're uncomfortable posing as Jesus.
I'll look at them and say, "Oh, you know
who you should be."

**What a charming Italian Polish
neighborhood this is—a hobby shop
and little blond brick buildings, but
you have to take the M train to Fresh
Pond Road.**

The models say, "Oh God, I never took
that train before." They like it when they're
here. They're used to posing in dirty, cold,
nasty studios. I'll go to the European Coffee
Bar here and sketch. I'm like the mascot of
the coffee shop. No, I don't ask the local
people to model. I really like working with
local people but I just don't want to go up
to them. I wanted to put an ad in the local
paper but the paper wouldn't take the ad. I
said, "I have a long track record with you.
When I lived in Ridgewood from '89 to
'94—I have receipts for the ads." I showed
them my receipts.

Tell about the exploding radiators.

In '97, my friend and I moved into an
apartment in Ridgewood before I got this
one. We weren't even unpacked and all
the radiators exploded when they turned
on the heat for the first time. We were out
until two in the morning but everything
was destroyed. The room was full of
steam. The only solace was that a lot of
my work was in a show at the time. When
I moved here, this entire apartment was
the color of Gulden's mustard, high gloss
tempered by a lot of cigarette smoke. A
prison guard lived here. My friend and I
first moved in together. I love her dearly,
but two designers—it didn't work. We'd
have knockdown, drag-out fights over paint
colors. She moved.

Where are you from?

Edison, New Jersey. First I did the living room in really dark olive. I went from there to the clean studio, all painted in blue grays. I was going for the Medici Chapel. The dropped ceiling has inscriptions all around it—"To be with art is all we ask." That's from Gilbert and George, the photographers. The bedroom has, "Don't ever forget—not never—that Jesus Christ is your savior." My friend's grandmother told her that when my friend was going off to law school. The "not never" is very Sicilian.

The kitchen is gray green. You want the Martha Stewart paint names—Georgia Mist, Quaking Aspen, Porch Ceiling Blue. I really prefer her paint. I could be the salesman for her. It's cheap. It's exactly the color they say it's going to be. Even when the little kid at Kmart is mixing the paint, it comes out on the money. The hall is Apple Butter, Driftwood, Mercury Glass on the ceiling. That's the best color because you can put any other color near it and it's completely changeable. The bathroom will either be Egyptian bulrushes or something neoclassical. But I can't do the bathroom until I graduate. Here are my file folders—green for the bills. Yellow—clippings. Red—the house. Orange—the art. My friends will say, "Can you help me with my apartment?" They're doing it beige. I say, "*Drama*, not Dramamine."

January 28, 2004

LA BELLE ÉPOQUE

LOCATION

Greenwich Village, Manhattan

PRICE

$79,000 in 1995 ($530.19
maintenance)

SQUARE FEET

500 (studio in 1930s co-op building)

OCCUPANT

Charles Busch (actor; playwright;
novelist; journalist)

**You say your colorful apartment is
very *Umbrellas of Cherbourg*. It is so red
in here.**

I call it "Gigi red." When I moved in two
and a half years ago, I had to make a rash
decision with the painter. I said, "Just off-
white and we'll call it a day." But I'm not
an off-white person. So a friend said, "Let's
do color!" Well, we spackled, ragged,
varnished, and glazed. Now we're not
speaking. I was getting very Barbra
Streisand while my friends were doing all
the work. Anyway, we made it red. But it's
a very sunny room. I knew that red would
look good at night, but it might have
looked like an East Village club in the day.
You have to be careful. After I saw *The
Birdcage*, I was telling a friend, "God, that
film was so clichéd—as if every female
impersonator lives in an overdecorated
apartment." Then I caught myself.

The alcove is purple.

I thought if I made the alcove an entirely
different color it would convince me it's
not really a studio. Of course, the hall
wallpaper is a trip down the Yangtze in a
sanpan at dusk.

**You are an Orientalist—so many pillows
on the bed!**

An astrologer who was doing charts of
famous drag queens—I can't imagine
how many that would be—thought I was
into the occult. He pointed out my crystal
balls, the Haitian pyramid, the Indonesian
masks for warding off evil spirits. There's
a store on Bleecker that sells the masks. I
said, "I'll take that, that, and that." The
owner said, "Let me tell you about the
tikafucatikakooka." I said, "It's okay, I just
like the look."

**You see everything in the neighborhood
from your three windows.**

It looks like Paris, especially the little park. I
used to watch the construction crews—the
blond dyke and the muscle man with the
cherry picker. The last night, when they
were laying down the asphalt, I went
outside. I wanted to stand next to them. I'd
watched them so much, they were stars to
me, but I didn't know what to say. Something
like, "Oh, it's an exciting night, isn't it?"

Where did you live before?

On 12th Street, for fifteen years, in a
horrible tenement building. It was my first
New York apartment. I ended up paying
$1,000 a month. There was hardly ever
heat or hot water. I love this neighborhood

GREG MILLER

so much, I had to live in a two-block radius. It was galling to find out the difference between a studio and a one-bedroom in this building is $100,000. I could only afford a studio. The price was so low I was afraid it was going to be a *Rosemary's Baby* situation. The building went up in 1936. I heard Lauren Bacall lived here once.

Patrick Dennis's real-life Auntie Mame lived across the street.

I'm just trying to keep up with tradition, babe.

April 22, 1997

JAN FINDS THE TABOO

LOCATION
Greenpoint, Brooklyn
RENT
$1,800 (commercial)
SQUARE FEET
1,400 (raw loft in factory building)
OCCUPANTS
Amy (freelance producer; artist's assistant), Andy (musician), Andrew (Web designer), Brian (record company employee)

We can't say what your last names are, because you are living in a commercial space that is not for residential use and you are not supposed to sleep here, though you can be here twenty-four hours a day working on your Web sites and such and "taking naps," like hundreds are doing all over Greenpoint and Williamsburg these days.
[BRIAN] That's correct. [AMY] If you drive around the neighborhood, every other building is full of artists living in commercial spaces, factory buildings. When Brian's mother came to visit from New Jersey, she said the hall to the loft looks like a prison.

It's long and skinny, five feet wide with a metal floor, and there are all the doors
to the other cells—I mean lofts. Cell Block D.

But the most important thing going on here is the indoor Polynesian village that you are building. When it's completed, each one of you will be living in your own Polynesian-inspired, bamboo-covered hut that will have two windows and its own door. Two of you will be living in second-story huts.
[BRIAN] *And* we're going to have ten-foot palm trees, a bamboo-bridge walkway, and a Hawaiian wet bar below.

For the luaus.
Then, as you come in, there's going to be a common living room, a workshop-garage area for our bikes and tools, a linen closet…

Are you re-creating the suburbs?
Actually, I framed houses for two summers in New Jersey.

What is your budget?
All said and done, $5,500. It's divided between three of us. The fourth person, Andy, is just renting from us for $800. That means three of us are only paying only $333 each.

How did you arrive at the indoor-village concept? Most loft livers just make rooms. You're not architects from Rotterdam or something?
[ANDREW] No, we were trying to find an easy way to divide the space. We were going by Home Depot and we saw

these sheds. They're only five hundred bucks. Brian and I got to talking and the idea evolved into more than just sheds. It should be a structured village where everyone's home would look like a house, the computer area could look like a school, a library building—Main Street, USA! But then we ended up deciding on a Polynesian tiki theme. I guess Brian and I watched the Hawaiian episodes of *The Brady Bunch* too many times. They go to Hawaii. Mr. Hanelei traps them in a cave. The whole thing starts because Jan finds the taboo, this eight-inch-tall wooden tiki man, that brings bad luck. When Peter Brady hears this, he says, "Bad luck, come and get me." Then this heavy wall decoration almost falls on Peter. Jan finds a spider in her beach bag. Every time they have these accidents, Hawaiian music in the background goes toodle loodle loo. You never saw that episode? It's a three-parter.

There's a lot of construction going on here.

One of us lives on an air mattress. I live on a bed that was donated by one of the Polish construction workers who was here before us. It's a *Battlestar Galactica* mattress with little spaceships.

How fun.

Not if you had to sleep on it. We're living in filth and we wake up with paint chips on our faces. I don't know how many mosquito bites I have. We leave the windows open and there're no screens. We've got factory windows.

When's the bamboo coming?

The bamboo is coming much later. You can get it if you go to bamboopoles.com or something. I ordered a Hawaiian-lady lamp on eBay. But the dude never sent it.

September 12, 2000

THE SWEET LIFE

LOCATION
Harlem, Manhattan

PRICE
$38,000 in early 1980s

SQUARE FEET
4,000 (1886 Queen Anne–style brick house)

OCCUPANTS
Michael A. Cummings (quilt artist; program analyst, NYSCA), boarder Kevin Powell (writer for *Vibe*, MTV, HBO)

Your house makes me think whispering willows are outside the window instead of the B subway stop. What a parlor! And so dense with such beautiful claret brocade draperies, pink damask wing chairs, Ashanti funeral urns, rubber frogs, and a crystal chandelier with a red jewel. Then there are all the mahogany doorways, brass doorknobs, and...
[MICHAEL] The house itself was built more for the working class. I consider this plain Jane. Would you like some peppermint tea?

I believe I would. [Doorbell rings.] Oh, it's our mutual friend, the architect John Reddick, whom you met...

[JOHN] At a Frida Kahlo exhibit in the seventies, long before Madonna knew about her.

This house is technically in Sugar Hill, which sounds like you live inside a china bowl full of sparkling sugar.
After World War I, well-to-do blacks moved in. The topography gave them this panoramic view of the city. For people living here, life seemed sweet.

Michael, you lived in West Village apartments for ten years. Why move?
[MICHAEL] I needed more space to develop my art. I started going to brownstone-revival seminars. I read a book on how to buy a house with no money down. It was written by two women who had met at a brownstone-revival party.

Are the parties wild?
I've never been. I looked all over Harlem, which I thought I could afford. I felt like the gal in *Follies*. [*Michael and John sing, "I'm just a Broadway baby..."*] I'm walking up and down Broadway, St. Nicholas. I'd look at houses before work, four times a day on weekends. I'd go down to City Hall. They've got books listing hundreds of houses with addresses and owners. I'd write to the people but I couldn't find a house. After a year, I almost gave up. This was the early eighties. Mortgage rates were sixteen to eighteen percent. Prices were going up. Finally I located this one. Rain was coming through a hole in the roof. With my trusty how-to-buy-a-house book, I bargained with the owner. My mother

GREG MILLER

whisked here from L.A. to see the house. She said, "Michael, what have you done?"

How much did renovation cost?
A lot. The house is now valued at $180,000. If I could only move it below 96th Street, it would be worth $600,000 to $800,000.

You have three floors of rooms and so many places to sit.
I have all these chairs but I really don't have people over because I'm so busy working on my quilts. So I have all these empty chairs.

Looking at your storytelling quilts with the figures of jazz players, fireflies, and
wild cats, Rousseau comes to mind. He had a sort of quiet mystery the way he created, the hundreds of greens, the lushness of the composition well layered with images.
You know, I approached my house like a collage. I told myself for years, "I'm going to be working on the house and I won't be able to do my art. So I'll treat the house like a shadow box." And I did. I brought it to life.

December 30, 1997

PURPLE PETUNIAS

LOCATION

Chelsea, Manhattan

PRICE

$110,000 in 1997
($852 maintenance)

SQUARE FEET

800 (duplex co-op apartment
in tenement building)

OCCUPANTS

Richard Watts (money trader,
Norddeutsche Landesbank),
houseguest Marika Maiorova
(recent film school graduate)

So, every day at three o'clock you walk out of the bank where you sit in a big glass trading room with forty phone lines talking to twenty-five brokers at a time about interest rates and you come downtown to your tenement building and walk up five flights of carpeted stairs—the building was renovated in the eighties—and you walk into your apartment with the hoopskirt hanging from the skylight, and the bowls of 1950s Christmas ornaments in shiny emerald green, pink, and midnight blue and you slip on your Dolce & Gabbana beach clogs and there, waiting for you on your second floor deck which looks so California with the wood planks and purple petunias, is Peewee, your Chihuahua.

[RICHARD] He's such a gentleman.

You lived in a $1,500 one bedroom on 37th and Fifth for eight years. You bought this two and a half years ago. It took a while to buy. You were picky.
I only wanted to be within such and such blocks, facing a certain direction. I had my dream apartment. I looked every Saturday for two years. One day I said to my broker, "You better find me an apartment today or I'm going to spend all my cash." He took me here. It's across from the projects. I said, "My mother is going to kill me." Then I went in and saw the fireplace, the skylight. When I saw the deck, that was it. Coming from Mississippi, I needed some outdoor space. I'm a little farm boy.

The critic Dave Hickey was giving a lecture at the Columbia School of Architecture on Las Vegas, sex, and Flaubert, and he said the spaces people and architects like most are the ones that first made them happy. For him, it's a low, darkened bungalow. For others it could be a white modernist house with walls of glass and clear blue rectangular pools and all built-in furniture and a heliport with a pink helicopter and a room full of Superman and Batman comic books and a closet with a hundred Comme des Garçons skirts—white—and a visual imaging room with the latest up-to-date projection devices and also a room full of gold coins for rolling around in.
I grew up in a ranch house with two grandmothers who sewed quilts all the time. I've always loved velvets and fabrics.

You were in the navy for four years, in Sardinia, in the resort town that you said was built by the Saudi billionaire who was involved with Imelda Marcos. You came to New York in 1987. Marika's been your houseguest since December. [MARIKA] I'm from Georgia, which was a part of the Soviet Union. I lived in a big apartment. No, we didn't have samovars. Georgian culture is more Asian. More of a backgammon culture. My happiest space is that old apartment. Big rooms, lots of big lamps. Lot of grandparents and parents. The door was never closed. [RICHARD] My house was like that, kids were over all the time. This is an open house, too. People are always here. More often than not my friends meet here rather than go to clubs. There's Alan, an aspiring Romanian model. Alisa, she was a model in Russia. [MARIKA] She's just beautiful. [RICHARD] We have Ivan, who's an aspiring Dominican actor. He wants to play the guy who dated Zsa Zsa Gabor and married Barbara Hutton. That's the core group. Sometimes there are three, four downstairs, others upstairs. We take a lot of pictures. Then everyone looks at the pictures the next time. [*He shows photos from leopard-covered albums.*] Here's a party. There's Marika. She made her silver dress in fifteen minutes. We served sugarcane and bananas. That's Anita, the one in leather pants, holding a cigarette, another dear friend. Here are three stylists. On New Year's Eve we had a party in an hour's notice. The only thing we served were carrots. [MARIKA] My mother called from Georgia. She said, "You have to dress in white and have carrots because it's the year of the rabbit."

June 15, 1999

SANDRA-LEE PHIPPS

ONE THOUSAND RHINESTONES

LOCATION
Flatiron District, Manhattan

RENT
$1,455 (rent stabilized)

SQUARE FEET
3,000 (loft)

OCCUPANT
Marvin Schwam (founder and president, Gay Entertainment Television; executive producer, Party Talk; co-owner, American Christmas Decorations)

How come your loft has more riches than all the temples of Asia? You Marco Polo, you!

I used to manufacture Christmas decorations in China. My trips to the Far East were extensive. Right behind you is a globe with dots on the 120 cities I've been to—well, the major cities. I didn't put dots on places like Poughkeepsie.

What would we call this area with the jeweled seating platform, the flying Burmese dragons, the crystal ball, the chubby burgundy velvet couches, the Coramandel screen, and the New Orleans street lamp?

I don't know.

The bathroom looks like a golden shrine.

I put a Thai door frame on the outside. I'm building a dome for the top.

You have a seven-foot columnar aquarium.

Don't you love it?

And you have a golden ox!

I know. Whenever I am traveling, I have a motto: If you like it, buy it. I never think about anything too much. Everything is by instinct.

Your doorways have canopies and trim.

Well, when a maharajah passes through a doorway, it has to be adorned. See this elephant? I made it myself. I'm rather proud. I took a cement garden sculpture and made it into an Asian relic. One thousand rhinestones I glued on it. I'm thinking of the jewelling of garden ornaments as a whole new business.

This big black bell?

Actually I bought that in Seattle. This pottery I made. I took a course.

You can do so many things!

It's all visual. That mirror on the wall is made of 690 pieces of glass. I took a course in how to cut glass. This table underneath the glass top is a wooden door from Africa. One of my sons just started a business putting imported African arts into contemporary furniture. My other son runs my display business. We're a bunch of entrepreneurs. Here's my office, with my elephant chairs.

Your bedroom is most splendorous of all! Silken burgundy tassels on the door knobs, burgundy carpeting on the walls and floors, giant blinking balls hanging from the ceiling, and Chinese lions flanking the platform bed, which I just tripped on because the carpeting's so thick. Was the loft always this way?
Oh god, it was rubble, a warehouse. By the way, I spray-painted the lions with car paint. Anyway, I got the loft in 1978 when I started my acrylic-painting business. That was after the display business. I got orders for thirty paintings for a hotel in the Catskills, I needed a place to make them. The painting business was an offshoot of my side business painting stripes on walls in Long Island kitchens...and now, over here....Where are you going? We just missed my moose horns that I got in Alaska.

I have to sit down. I feel faint from all the globetrotting.
Would you like anything to drink?

Just a strawberry Twizzler will be fine. You have jars of them all over.
I have them at my business, too. Clients like them.

September 16, 1997

GREG MILLER

SHIBORI

LOCATION
Chelsea, Manhattan

PRICE
$375,000 in 2000 and 2001
($900 maintenance)

SQUARE FEET
850 (two connected studio
condominium apartments
in high rise)

OCCUPANT
Eve Kosofsky Sedgwick (author,
*Epistemology of the Closet, Between
Men*; professor of English, CUNY
Graduate Center)

**Your essay "Is the Rectum Straight?"—a
favorite! You are one of the founders of
queer theory. Where are all the books?**
I gave away hundreds to students. I was
teaching at Duke, living in a big ranch
house. In '98, I was moving to New York
and I knew something had to give. I have
potlatch fantasies. Potlatch is—Indians in
the Northwest have parties where they give
away everything. A family might do it every
five years. There's a lot of real wealth in
terms of their art and weaving. It's not just
"This is extra; take it."

**You were living then with a male friend.
But you have a husband who you haven't
lived with since 1972. Though you see
each other on weekends.**
Hal Sedgwick is a professor of visual
perception at the SUNY College of

Optometry. We got married in '69. We
were living in a commune. In '71, I started
graduate school at Yale and we started
having a commuting relationship. He had
a studio in the Village, where he still lives.
The house in Durham was big, sixties,
full of walls of windows, and it made me
very happy to have the permeability of my
spousal relations and my friendly relations
and my relations with my students. It was
just kind of utopian and very gratifying.
The whole idea of one family, one
mortgage, one social unit just gives me
the creeps.

**Yet you always had the oneness of the
one husband you see on weekends.**
There's an image in Winnicott, the
psychologist, of a child being so confident,
being held by its mother, it doesn't have to
think about primary relationships all
the time.

**I was telling a friend that living with
someone gives a sense of a proscenium,
a constant threshold. She yelled,
"No, it's not like having a piece of
real estate. It's having another will in
the same room with you, that doesn't
always do what you want it to."
Anyway, I believe that true home is in
the mind.**
I've lived in so many places. When I
finished graduate school in '75, I bounced
around for quite a long time, so I didn't
have any external sense of a home and it
became very existential or Zen. I'm still like
that. The first night in a strange place, I'll
have trouble sleeping. The second night, it
will feel like where I belong.

JAY MUHLIN

I've stripped down my apartment: a bed, a laptop, an alarm clock. It's as if I'm traveling at home.
One of the places I lived was outside Utica. I had taken ten days of vacation. I got back, started looking for a cookbook. I couldn't find it. It was perfectly easy for me to believe I didn't have cookbooks. I had no object permanence. It's a term from Piaget, the developmental psychologist.

Your family home: Dayton then Bethesda. It's all in your book *A Dialogue on Love*, which I almost stayed home and kept reading instead of coming here. What's on the walls?
Shibori's a two-dimensional surface, fabric or paper. You build it up in a three-dimensional way, then just float ink on water and let it do what it wants to do.

Now the breast cancer discussion.

In '91 I was treated for breast cancer but it was still localized. In '96, it metastasized to my spine and other places. It was clear that it was incurable. Since then, it has been pretty stable. Cancer adapts to whatever environment it's in. The point is to keep it confused.

Not give it a home. The big round African baskets?
These have deconstructed kimonos. I've never paid attention to the nonverbal before. Because of the cancer treatment, it became harder for me to write and articulate. It's called chemo brain. I've discovered the physical world. Texture really has a kind of ontological primacy to it. I feel alive if I'm feeling something with my finger.

July 30, 2002

FAMOUS CHAIRS

LOCATION
Chelsea, Manhattan

PRICE
$325,000 in 1995 ($398.88
maintenance)

SQUARE FEET
1,100 (loft in former theatrical
storage building)

OCCUPANT
Kar-Hwa Ho (architect and designer,
Kohn Pedersen Fox Associates)

My god, you have a red foam chair like the ones in the space terminal scene in *2001* **where the woman scientist says she's been calibrating the new antennas at Chulinka and Dr. Haywood Floyd says he's just on his way up to Clavius though he's not at liberty to discuss why one of the rocket buses was denied admission.**
I know. Here's the ribbon chair that was in *Diamonds Are Forever.*

That's the one in the scene where Bond meets Bambi and Thumper, the female assassins. Bambi says, "I'm Bambi." Thumper says, "I'm Thumper." Then they fight Bond and throw him in the swimming pool. Was this loft always one continuous white space with a perfect ten-foot-high white ceiling with thirty-six recessed pinpoints of halogen?

Oh, it was awful, dark, dingy, cut up into tiny spaces, pipes with cobwebs—not something I jumped at. Three years ago I'd looked at thirty-five, forty lofts. I'd been a student in a small apartment on 14th Street. I knew I had to buy, nothing would be the perfect space. So I did a whole gut job.

Your sheets have a French poem on them.
It rhymes. Now, the original bathroom was very long and narrow. I changed the tiles to limestone. I used frosted glass panels to divide up the space. When I light the glass from behind, the wall becomes transparent. From the front, it becomes opaque. In this bathroom, I can collect my thoughts. I like to hang out in the tub.

You're a modernist! And you have Issey Miyake exfoliating gel. It's mysterious how light it is in here. Yet all your windows face only a light shaft.
Instead of setting the shades within each window, I hung the shades a foot back so they are perceived as one light wall, to diffuse the light equally. Even the closet has a translucent glass wall. So it's not like walking into a dark closet.

Where a monster could be waiting. I hate that. Claustrophobia is such a big problem in New York. I read in the *Fresno Bee* that claustrophobes should sniff green apples because the smell makes rooms seem bigger. I just realized all your chairs and tables are famous—Jacobsen, Noguchi, Gehry. Even your appliances, well, except for

that refrigerator with the simulated wood handle.

I ran out of money. I get a lot of furniture at flea markets. In Singapore, where I grew up, I'd always been exposed to design. My dad and grandfather are architects. Five uncles and an aunt are architects. Somebody's a town planner.

Do you all get going on one big Lego set?

It's hard for us to get together at the same time. I do have a lot of sixties and seventies furniture. I guess it's because I grew up with all this American pop culture, watching *The Brady Bunch* and *The Mary Tyler Moore Show.* I just found out my swivel chair was in Ted Baxter's bachelor pad.

I bet it's the episode where he has a crush on Chuckles the Clown's daughter!

Relax.

February 10, 1998

GREG MILLER

BABY TEETH

LOCATION
Park Slope, Brooklyn

PRICE
$115,000 in 1986 ($500 maintenance)

SQUARE FEET
700 (one-bedroom co-op apartment
in prewar building)

OCCUPANT
Jim Gelfand (artist; creator of
Where I Live, a limited-edition book of
photos and poems)

Your apartment is full of small objects all over the floors, the chairs, the plumbing. There's even a baby in the kitchen sink.
Yes, I've been working on my project for ten years, since I bought the co-op. See these tarot cards on the living room floor? They are traveling toward the wall. The railroad logos are traveling to the mah-jongg set. As you walk along, there are a few hot spots. Be careful not to step on…

Oops, I think I just stepped on…
the Persian camel that is lying on its side on the living room rug. I tried to warn you. Of course, hovering can be obnoxious.

Yes, of course. Now the radiator…
This was the radiator. Now it's an altar to American Indian stuff. I had to have it turned off. A sacrifice, but…

Don't you get cold?
The building is full of old people so it's overheated.

I'd like to sit on this chair, but it has a pope doll on it. Are all the chairs occupied?
Most.

The view outside of the turn-of-the-century house and flowers is blocked by a huge totem pole.
A tough choice but I decided it was okay to sacrifice the view.

Can you open the window with the row of crack vials on the ledge?
No. They would fall off and so would the Clarabell puppet riding a bicycle on the fish wire. The closed window was another considered choice.

It is a little warm in here. There's a Basquiat T-shirt stretched over a Scrabble board that's placed in front of the music speaker, blocking the sound.
It just takes away a little of the sound. Things get more interesting in the hallway. My baby teeth are on a barrel.

You had a lot.
About thirty.

Can you sit at the kitchen table?
No. Another sacrifice. The kitchen chair has a T-shirt pinned to it.

What's with the stove?
The gas was turned off years ago. There's a

watch on the burner, a T-shirt over the oven.

You said you use the bathroom sink even though there are jawbones around it.
I don't use the shower. There's a telephone dial on the nozzle. The tub is an ode to an unsuccessful Upper East Side suicide. See the handbag and the high-heeled shoe? I shower at my health club. Here's a photo of a lizard coming out of a person's ass. There's some raw stuff here in the bathroom. A bathroom's meant for that. Yes, I use the toilet.

What is on the dresser in your bedroom?
My old retainer for my teeth, photos of myself. There's a baby doll in the train in the center of my carpet. . . . Well, by the time you get to my bedroom, you realize I have no children. This is the desk I never use because I write in bed when I'm half dreaming.

I think I need to sit down.
Go sit on the couch. But sit in the middle. I hate it when people don't sit in the middle. They need to see the room properly.

Do you have a working telephone?
In the bedroom.

Can I sit on the end of the bed while I make the call?
You could, but I would really prefer that you stand.

September 23, 1997

watch on the burner, a T-shirt over the oven.

GREG MILLER

Today a washcloth and undershorts are hanging in the airshaft—all the laundry of strangers, and the laundry that used to hang from the strangers who died. The airshaft is so gray with the crumbling buildings. The rooms face each other's backs, what is past, not forward.

The city is dusty with layers of the lives before—a stationery salesman drinking whiskey in the afternoon, an actor who didn't make it, a husband who grew cold. People live in buildings where the original function is gone—the whirr of knitting machines, sail makers, and sex.

"Haunted" comes from "hanter," which is distantly related to the word "home."

What was the memory cloth they talked about in *Batman*? I don't remember.

The city is haunted by Dutch people. They started the whole thing in the 1600s. There were the Van der Voort sisters who couldn't stop ice-skating until they died in 1880. Figure eights all day long. People still see them on the pond in Central Park in their velvet skating outfits. Way up, near the George Washington Bridge, is a narrow path with stones and scratchy trees. No one is on it, mostly. And who was David McKean? He died of yellow fever "in the midst of his usefulness" on August 7, 1795. His gravestone is in St. Paul's Churchyard.

It is not only the city that haunts. People carry memories of other places. Walking about, they think of, in a flash, the colonial house in Michigan, the mango someone peeled, a day in the South, a root beer drive-in, all the memories of rooms.

The past looks over, protects. The dancer doesn't know that he is being watched by General Sherman as he runs for Lincoln Center.

HAUNTED

IN THE DARK

LOCATION
Stapleton, Staten Island

PRICE
$100,000 in 1998

SQUARE FEET
3,300 (fifteen-room 1835 landmark mansion)

OCCUPANT
Peter McNally (senior computer analyst, HIP), his sister, April Entrieri (real-estate manager), her children, Anthony, Frank, Tara, and Kelsey

You mentioned an occurrence...
[PETER] I was sitting in the den and I looked over and saw a body sitting behind my sister. We saw him about five times—a short kid, with a little derby on his head.

I'm not a professional parapsychologist— haven't published any monographs on cold spots or anything—but let me ask, does whatever walks here, walk alone?
I don't know, but on my very first night four years ago, I heard a moan that made my hair stand up on my head. I went to the hall and said, "Whoever is here, you can *no longer* stay here. You *have* to go into the light." It was such a sad and sorrowful sound. Just so you know I'm not nuts, a woman came to deliver a pizza one night.

She used to live here. She said, "Do any strange things happen here?" But she wouldn't tell me what.

This is a tough case—the kid, the moan. Maybe the moan was Susannah Tompkins on her wedding night. She lived here in 1835. Or it could have been her father, the former governor, who, by the way, pushed for the abolition of slavery. Maybe he was visiting and moaning about some political problem.
I don't know, but the land belonged to Cornelius Vanderbilt. This was a wealthy seafaring area, prominent shipping tycoons.

You said your plumbers wouldn't go in the basement unless you went with them.
That was because of the rats. When I got the place, it was an active, falling-down crack house—garbage up to the waist, old cars in back, ten-foot-tall weeds. Somebody'd planted bamboo. I could have killed them. I got on my knees, pulled every frigging tree out.

You mentioned you dabble in spells.
Oh, nothing much, just a little candle magic. I'm a computer analyst. I'm going to have some mediums come to the house this spring.

I didn't think Staten Island was going to be so spine tingling when I went up that 1950s mint green escalator in the Manhattan terminal, got on the ferry, watched people eat peanuts, and listened to a woman with a guitar sing, "Hello, it's been a while," then saw

some pizza places upon disembarking. So, you grew up in the Stapleton Projects here in the late sixties.

It was great: 150 kids outside every day playing ring-o-lario. Later I lived in twenty-five places—Williamsburg, Hell's Kitchen—every neighborhood before it was hot.

Now you have a landmark house! The New York Landmarks Commission wrote about it in 1973: "Tetrastyle portico with Corinthian columns rising two stories to an entablature below an overhanging spring save." How much to renovate?

When it got over $100,000, I stopped counting. I'm still not done. I invited my sister and kids to live here, gave them the big part of the house. I took the servants' quarters. Just got digital cable. Now I can watch *Queer as Folk.* I light the fire, listen to some Barry White. I've got a seven-month-old kitten who goes into heat every two days.

Are there a lot of gay bars in Staten Island?

A few. My Crisco Disco club days are over. The whole North Shore here—St. George, Tompkinsville, Stapleton Heights—today is a mishmash of people: Rastafarians, Ukrainians, Turkish, Arab, gay, straight. Foreign restaurants are opening. Everybody's working together to make a community. As soon as I finish work on my house, I plan to become very involved in community action here. My neighbor just contacted Starbucks to open a place. We need somewhere to go at night.

So does the little kid in the derby.

February 20, 2001

SYLVIA PLACHY

GIMME ANOTHER

LOCATION
Long Island City, Queens

RENT
$900 (market)

SQUARE FEET
1,300 (former corner bar)

OCCUPANTS
Richard Howard (musician;
marketing associate, United Way of
Tri-State), Mary Potts (copywriter)

**So, this place used to be a bar starting
back in the fifties. I thought it would be
like, "Hey Lou, gimme another, schlurp,
schlurp." Then Belle walks in after the
guys knock off from the factory. "Hiya,
Belle, you're looking swell." "What's it
to you, Buster?" Then she says to
someone else, "Let me tell you a thing
or two, Mr. Smarty. I'm goin' over by
Carl. Carl wants to dance, don't you,
Carl?" People are bouncing up and down
on the dance floor. On the other hand,
my friend who lives nearby said, "It's
so Kierkegaard in there, staring at the
tile floor and thinking about despair
and *Either/Or*." So I thought it would be
like that but it's so…eighties, almost a
little tiki.**
[MARY] The red devil lights. [RICHARD]
The same woman had it for years. She let
the lease expire in '89. When it closed, it
was called "Just a Pub." There's an old guy

in the neighborhood. He said he used to
mop the floors for cash.

**They'd say, "Hey kid, over here." Oh,
never mind.**
The neighbors said a lot of mafia types
were hanging out here.

**Mafia types are so boring, with their
predictable, dopey crimes. I was
thinking more of people committing
adultery that leads to doom and ruin.**
[MARY] Adultery's cool.

You have so many bar chairs.
[RICHARD] I got eight stools from Gothic
Cabinet Craft.

**My friend said you keep the cat box
behind the bar. He knows because he
came to your Wednesday night jazz
sessions. He said the jazz was of a
really high caliber, not self-indulgent
nonsense. Then he said that when Mary
came home, you were thrilled over her
purchase of extension cords. There's
something so verboten about living in
a place that was meant for commercial
public life. You get to stay up all night in
it. No bartender making the rules.**
I've lived here long enough [since February
2001] that I don't have that feeling of living
in a place that's not a living place. Mary
moved in in early 2003.

**I just noticed the string of lights around
the bottom of the bar.**
[MARY] We got this idea from Casimir in
the East Village. We don't go to bars a lot.

Richard said you both don't drink very much.

That's why we met on match.com.

Isn't it redundant to go to a bar?

There's almost a weird, sick pleasure in watching people throw money around in a bar, all crowded and noisy. We have our own private bar. We watch *NOVA* on PBS. People give us a lot of bar-themed gifts. I thought about doing some Bavarian elfy stuff. [RICHARD] We have a three-compartment sink, a giant exhaust. [MARY] When I first met Richard, I thought, "Oh, he must be another one of those ladies'-man jerks." [RICHARD] She didn't even see this place until our third date. [MARY] He had this comforter on the bed, Tarzan leopard skin. [RICHARD] My boss gave it to me. [MARY] Yet he's the nicest, sweetest guy. [RICHARD] We met at Barnes & Noble in Union Square. [MARY] I didn't expect him to be so handsome and I ran up the escalator. On our second date, I was all

pretending it wasn't Valentine's Day. "Let's go to the Native American museum," I said. Later, he ran in this bodega and got me some tulips. But then later I thought, "Oh, those are sympathy tulips. He knows I'm a woman and I'm alone." I was living in Jersey City, flowerless. The third time…[RICHARD] We saw *Black Hawk Down* in the neighborhood.

I've never understood why they wore all that noticeable equipment to carry out the mission.

[MARY] His friends were over, drinking beer. I'm thinking, "I wish they'd leave."

But then…

[*The pages flip by on the calendar.*] He got me a KitchenAid mixer for Christmas.

Oh.

[RICHARD] Mary loves to bake.

November 10, 2004

249

MADONNA COMING OUT OF THE BATHROOM

LOCATION
Upper West Side, Manhattan

RENT
$857.17 (rent stabilized)

SQUARE FEET
288 (studio apartment in tenement building)

OCCUPANT
Brian Selznick (writer and illustrator, children's books)

I know you used to live in the same apartment as Madonna, but before we get into that, let's talk about where you live now. At this moment, one of your two windows is wide open. There are bright green plants on the fire escape. The afternoon sun is twinkling. 1560 WQEW is on. A man is singing "You do that voo-do that you do so well...." You have a six-inch pink plastic house on your desk. Is this place rent stabilized?
The dollhouse?

No, your apartment.
Yes.

Why do you have these houses and dolls' heads around?

So I can draw them for my books. Wait, I have to get something out of the oven. I'm baking a heart-shaped lock for the front of the house. Seven years ago I was working at a children's bookstore around the corner. A friend of mine found this apartment but the appointment to see it was too early for her. I got it instead.

Do you like living on the Upper West Side?
I like the park and the museum. I live on the Zabar's block, so the food is good. But I mostly eat dumplings and egg drop soup from Ollie's—to go. I used to live in one of the four bedrooms of a giant apartment on Riverside Drive. I was always told my room had belonged to Madonna.

So you and Madonna weren't there together?
No, but I know someone who was. I had always heard all these stories—the landlord said there was a photo taken of Madonna coming out of the bathroom, though I never saw it. I heard there had been a mural in my room that Madonna's friend painted. It was like George Washington slept here. I did the drawings for my first book in Madonna's room! I've been telling the story for years. Everyone laughed at me. Then I went with my boyfriend to a party. I was talking to this woman, Roby Newman, about past apartments, as people do at New York parties.

The same Roby Newman who is a producer on WNET-TV's multipart CD-ROM on the history of the Jews from biblical times to the present?

GREG MILLER

That's right. I mentioned to Roby that I used to live on Riverside Drive. She said she once lived in that exact same apartment too, and her roommate was Madonna! I couldn't believe it because I had lived in that same apartment!

We have to call Roby immediately. I'll do the talking. [To Roby on the phone] Roby, you've got to tell us how it was being Madonna's roommate in 1980. Don't hold back!

[ROBY] This was before she was famous. I moved out four months after she moved in. Not because of her. In fact, she was very untroublesome as a roommate. She was very neat in the kitchen, which was a good thing because there were cockroaches. [*A five-minute conversation follows.*]

So Brian, Roby said Madonna mostly wore a ripped T-shirt and black baggy shorts, she didn't listen to music that much, and she talked on the phone all the time. You're still excited about all this?

Of course!

October 28, 1997

SPRINGTIME IN THE ROCKIES

LOCATION
West Harlem, Manhattan

RENT
$227.46 (rent controlled)

SQUARE FEET
700 (four-room apartment in tenement building)

OCCUPANT
Eleanor Murray (retired lingerie buyer, Bloomingdale's; office worker, CCNY)

All these buildings named Loraine, Regina, Corinne. Ionic columns, too.
I got a spur in my heel. I don't live on Tylenol all day. I'm not a pill popper.

Right now we're outside sitting on the steps of the building next door.
I sit here every night. My landlord put in the gate and took away our corner three years ago, before John died. All our life we sat there. John was a supervisor on Macy's platform, watching over the trucks. I was born here in this building on West 135th, September 27, 1922. I met my husband right on this street. We were fifteen years of age. We belonged to the same crowd. Everybody on the block had crowds. We used to go around together. We liked each other until the day he died. He lived up the

hill in a corner building, 1512 Amsterdam. The neighborhood in my day, from my birth until 1950, was eighty percent Irish, the other was Greek, Italian, German, Jewish—all very nice. [*To a kid*] Hiya, Kenny. Do I know everyone on the block! I know a lot but I don't speak Spanish. The block is now eighty percent Hispanic, nineteen percent black, one percent white.

You know demographics like the planning department.
I had six children. I lost my seventh. I had a miscarriage. Eleanor came, 1950. Daniel came January 20, 1953.

The one who raised the pigeons on the roof across the street.
The bird man.

How many birds?
Ha! Five hundred. Since he was ten. Then my beautiful daughter Jean. Her husband died six months after mine. Then came Neil, then Barney. My last child passed December 24, 1990, Timothy. He was twenty-eight. He worked for a modeling agency. Nice boy, they all are nice. When I graduated high school, I became assistant buyer of lingerie at Bloomingdale's. I stayed home nineteen years with the children. My mother was super of this building for fifty years. She died at ninety-nine.

Did she have to keep the building clean?
Ha! She was in the days of coal and ashes. She had to make fires in the big boiler. She had to take out the garbage. She had to mop the building every day, roof to stoop. She cleaned the sidewalks. My father, he

never did things in the building. He was a foreman in a warehouse, 27th and the Hudson, the Terminal Warehouse, forty-two years. He was never absent one day. I was born in the basement. When I graduated high school, my mother took the apartment upstairs. Me and my older sister didn't want to live in the basement. We were overcrowded, all of us in three bedrooms, living room, and kitchen.

People complain today about being crowded.

I had to let it do. I always felt bad that I couldn't give my children more comfort, eating and sleeping. We had one bath, four sons in one room. My one daughter stayed with my mother in the basement. I'm also a singer. I sang in the Horn & Hardart Children's Hour. I was eleven. I sang "When It's Springtime in the Rockies."

Let's hear...

[*Sings*] "When fish gotta swim and birds gotta fly, I'm going to love one man till I die..." I was madly in love with my husband. He was intelligent, handsome, friendly, kind. Did you see our high rise up the block? A beautiful building. [*We go upstairs to the apartment.*] I was baptized at the Annunciation Church. I made my Communion there, married my husband. Orlando Gonzalez was our best man. My mother was Hungarian. My dad was from Croatia. They met in 1907 when they got off the boat.

Here's a photo of you in a smart suit.

Yeah, I dressed bea-uuutifully. I had mink, furs, everything. At Bloomingdale's, you had to dress nice. That painting is called *The Lacemaker*, by Vermeer. This is the seat I sit in every night and watch television.

September 7, 2005

CARY CONOVER

MATT'S GRANDMOTHER

LOCATION
Williamsburg, Brooklyn

RENT
$1,800 (commercial)

SQUARE FEET
5,000 (industrial loft in former sweatshop)

OCCUPANTS
Jude Tallichet (professor, Tyler School of Art, Philadelphia; visual artist; drummer, Ultra Vulva), Matt Freedman (sculptor; cartoonist; writer)

How long have you been here?
[MATT] Five and a half years. We just signed another five-year lease.

How is the space divided?
Two thousand square feet is our work space. Eight hundred is for living. We sublet the rest to two other artists.

I noticed you have a minyan of rabbis on your shelf.
[JUDE] Matt made them, and thousands of other characters: woodchucks, baseball players, violinists, et cetera, out of cast bronze, clay, and other materials. The rabbis are plaster.

What's your favorite thing about living here?

We're not sure—maybe that it's big enough for indoor barbecues.

What do you hate?
Aside from the landlord? The lack of amenities. There's no heat or light—those are the worst things.

No light?
We have light bulbs. We just don't have natural light. There are only two windows in the living space; they're heavily covered with plastic because of the cold.

You must have *some* heat.
We installed gas blowers—they're so loud. It's hard to hear Leonard Lopate over the blowers. All artists listen to Leonard Lopate on the radio—you can go from one studio to the next without missing the program.

What else is upsetting?
Constant leaking…but that's also the good side. Because it's constant, you don't worry about it. If you were in a nice place and something broke, you'd be worrying all the time.

How many times have your cars been attacked?
Two cars have been broken into seven times and stolen twice. They stole them even with the Club. Now we're down to one car.

Who else lives in this neighborhood?
This isn't cool like 11th Street—that's all artists. Here there are mostly industrial spaces.

GREG MILLER

Do families live around here, too?

[MATT] Some, mainly Dominican and Puerto Rican. The Hasidic neighborhood is to the south. This neighborhood used to be Jewish. When my mother sent me my grandmother's table, I had the spookiest feeling that maybe my grandmother worked in a sweatshop in this same building a long time ago.

What did she do?

Bessie Freedman made belts, and they make belts downstairs now. You know, she worked her damnedest to get down to sunny Florida. Now her grandson is living where she started.

There is a gray mist in the kitchen in the shape of a woman holding a piece of poppy-seed cake!

That is definitely her.

February 18, 1997

WHEN JOHNNY COMES MARCHING HOME

LOCATION

Greenpoint, Brooklyn

RENT

$1,300 (market)

SQUARE FEET

760 (top floor of Civil War–era brick house)

OCCUPANTS

Kirsten Swenson (art critic; PhD candidate and teacher, SUNY Stony Brook), Stephen Shapinsky (teacher, P.S. 31, Greenpoint; musician, The Line and Sinker Trust)

This desk—leather panels, pressed gold borders.

[KIRSTEN] My friend's father's girlfriend was very close friends with this Russian-literature professor at Hunter. The professor passed away and left everything to my friend's father's girlfriend. And my friend invited me to come to the Park Avenue penthouse and just take whatever we wanted. I got the desk, the Chinese rug. She lived in one of those gorgeous brick buildings, small windows, prewar. Similar to ones in movies from the forties, Hitchcock

films—not as spacious and extravagant as one would think, very small kitchen, finely detailed. No, I don't know if she lived with anyone.

Did you find any love letters?

No, just this letter exchange with the Soviet government.

Didn't she have anyone to leave her things to?

She was quite old. Nobody survived her, I guess.

This table is lit with blue and amber panels.

Stephen made it. [STEPHEN] With very little know-how, you can design pieces of furniture. Kirsten liked a friend's George Nelson knockoff. [KIRSTEN] It was a reissue. [STEPHEN] We thought it wouldn't be that hard to knock it off ourselves—some plywood from the neighborhood, the foam store on East Houston. Kirsten did the cushions and there you go. [KIRSTEN] Fake Nelson hairpin legs from eBay. [*Stephen measures the apartment.*]

A metal tape measure being pulled out. It sounds like something is happening, something is going to be built. I wanted to talk about the Byzantine Catholic church near here, where I first talked to you outside on a brilliantly sunny Sunday and you were talking about getting married, though not there. Then I started reading about Byzantine Catholicism but I realized that I only cared about the way the light was on that day, far from Manhattan. You are

BRIAN KENNEDY

so near the water. Stephen, you look so conflicted.

[STEPHEN] Everybody has this ambivalence and frustration about the waterfront because it's so close but so underused. [KIRSTEN] It's just an industrial wasteland. [STEPHEN] If they ever develop it, it will price everybody out. [KIRSTEN] Some of Stephen's students live across the courtyard. Sometimes we're spied on. We hear them call, "Mr. Shapinsky." [STEPHEN] It sounds more like Mr. Shapeeeeensky." [KIRSTEN] After a class on sentence construction, you could hear them yell, "Mr. Shapinsky, what are three kinds of sentences?"

We got this apartment because the realtor confused our application with that of a much higher-income couple with no cat. It is quite a bit nicer than most dumpy places we saw. Then we met the landlords and we got along so well. Our landlady likes that every unit has a teacher. [STEPHEN] They don't like the terms "landlady" or "landlord." [KIRSTEN] We try to say "landpeople." My old landlady, she sort of kicked me out. I started dating Stephen and

he made more commotion. So I was asked to leave. I was paying almost nothing. Then, when we got this place she and her sister were sort of miffed that we had gotten an apartment on the most prestigious block in Greenpoint, part of the historic district.

People get so excited when their house has a past. I was really depressed once in New Jersey and one of those home shows was on, *Secret Walls* or something. People were popping up with newspapers they'd found in their house—1856! 1929!

Here, we're just passing through. We sometimes think how people lived in this building during the Civil War. One time Stephen imagined a wounded Civil War soldier coming home to this apartment.

In his dusty blue uniform. I once lived in a former Civil War hospital in another city but only for a week because I could just hear the amputations.

The whiskey amputations.

November 19, 2003

MOAN

LOCATION

Garment District, Manhattan

RENT

$900 (market)

SQUARE FEET

1,100 (loft in a four-story
commercial building)

OCCUPANT

John Nova (photographer)

You said your loft used to be a brothel. You know, everyone tells me their apartment used to be a brothel.

It was. My neighbors found flyers stuck in the floors. See, here's a flyer with the address. It was called "Heaven on Earth."

Oh, the flyer has a photograph of a woman with a large chest who isn't wearing any clothes.

It was a Korean brothel, I think, though some of the writing is Chinese. The city shut it down in '94 or before. I moved here in 1995. The building was all boarded up. The landlord was eager to get people in because he was losing money. I had to go to the city and prove I wasn't going to open a brothel. The city was difficult to meet with. They stood me up three times. Finally, I said, "Look, I don't need this apartment." The head superintendent came running out and apologized.

So did he ask you, "Are you going to open a brothel?"

He did say just that. Though I'm not the stereotypical brothel-looking guy.

Well, you grew up on a farm in Pennsylvania. Anyway, you got the apartment.

Yes. Here are photos of how it was when I moved in. You could see where the small massage rooms were from the studs for the walls. I figured the bigger room that faced the street was the madam's room—all light and airy and secure. There was a double open shower area for the johns. There was this disgusting red carpet. All the windows were blacked out with contact paper. It was a mess to remove. There was a makeshift pipe and crack vials under the sub floor. There were used condoms, vomit in the corners. The conditions were deplorable. There were locks to keep people in as well as out. The city required that I remove them. If there was ever a storybook reason to abolish prostitution, this was it.

Was this all part of a big cleanup campaign?

I don't know. They recently closed another place. It was called "The Big Banana." The weird thing was, after they closed the top three floors, The Big Banana reopened as a video store on the ground floor. Anyway, I got my landlord to give me a five-year lease. I knew I'd have to put a lot of money into it. It needed a lot of work. I spent $3,000. I figured I wasn't going to commit to just one year. Since then, I've demolished the massage rooms, removed the carpet, painted the floors five times, added a kitchen, got rid of one of the showers.

GREG MILLER

It's really beautiful. Do you still feel the aura of the former occupants?
A friend came to stay and was convinced a succubus lives here. That's a sexual spirit, or something.

It sounds like your friend reads Milton. So is the spirit so pervasive that everybody in the building—the video makers, the tailor—do they have sex all the time?
No. Just the opposite.

May 27, 1997

BACK FROM THE DEAD

LOCATION
Crown Heights, Brooklyn

RENT
$2,000 (commercial lease)

SQUARE FEET
2,700 (former machine shop)

OCCUPANT
K. C. (artist; film editor; bartender)

Be careful with that knife.
I found it buried behind the wall. I was thinking it was a murder weapon or something. I found all kinds of stuff—trinkets, rosaries. Lot of Hasidic clothing was in the space. I discovered the history of the building through different clues in the walls. I moved in over a year ago. I had to put down $4,000, plus a hefty broker's fee—$3,700. I got the place with a roommate—and his credit rating—but he's gone now. But I'll be getting more roommates. I can't tell you my real name since this is a commercial space and technically I shouldn't be living here. My plan was, I wanted to get a space big enough to fix up an old sailboat to travel around the world. I wanted to document the experience on film to send to classrooms throughout America. I haven't gotten the boat yet. Or the camera. The first year here I had no heat, no running water, no locks. I had to open the front door with a crowbar. I've been on rent strike close to a year. It was so cold, I'd make coffee and within minutes it would be slush, ice. I've woken up in my sleeping bag with snowdrifts up against me. Snow comes in through holes in the walls; the wind makes the drifts. Now I have heat. But I had to do most of the plumbing myself, bring all my appliances in. My neighbor came to me one day and said, "Listen, man, feed yourself first and then spend money on materials." I earn $250 one week and I think, "Oh, great, I'll buy some drywall."

You have multiples of everything! Three couches, six radios.
Most of these things don't work, actually. The junkyard guys bring them to me. They're always excited when they get me stuff. This is an isolated little industrial area. People living around here are Dominican, Haitian, Pakistani, Muslim. Some homeless people too. There are a lot of empty lots around.

You have a pirate's chest.
I got it in Albany. My friend got arrested and went to jail. He wasn't paying child support. All his friends swarmed in and got his stuff. I went to SUNY. I'm working on a film now about some of the more memorable times of my life. There are a couple of things. I've died twice.

Here?
In L.A. My mother has a propensity for finding haunted houses. We've always had the presence of a ghost in our home. This one place was particularly disturbing. It was on Martel Avenue. My brother and I were

always playing Atari back then. Anyway, so there were these ghosts in the house. One day I came home from school, the ghosts threw me down the stairs and I died and...

Do you smell gas?
Probably. I have to fix my oven. Let me turn off the main valve.

What about the second time you died?
I was three. I basically overdosed on Robitussin.

When did you move from L.A.?
When I was in sixth grade, in '90, my father was closing his gallery in L.A. and opening one in New York. Though my parents had gotten divorced when I was a year old, they were still friends. My father got a house on Long Island for everyone to live in—he thought it would be better for everyone

to be closer together—my mother, my stepfather, my older and younger brothers, my father's grandparents, and my father and his lover. I didn't move right away. I had very close relationships with my friends in school. So while everyone was getting settled, I stayed in L.A. with an ordained Buddhist monk. When I came to live on Long Island six months later, things in the house were already falling apart.

You're living underneath a five-ton crane. If that big iron hook fell down, it could...
I haven't had time to fiddle with it yet. I have a lot to do here. I have floods fairly often. Water runs like a stream through the living room area. One night, there was a book, a bag, and clothing just floating away.

March 13, 2001

MICHAEL KAMBER

Where is everybody? Even the hot sun is gone, just some cool clouds. It is a Saturday in late summer. Everyone has gone to his country house. I have the Seagram Building practically all to myself. It is like a sleek black suit—tall, dark, and elongated. I sit down on a green marble slab. A man walks by in a purple T-shirt drinking a can of Diet Coke. There goes another man in a purple shirt. Now comes one in a navy blue stripe. There are about seven people on one side of the street. That's so little for New York. The chubby couple, with tattoos and cigarettes, have their arms around each other.

"Dramatic Twist in Aruba Mystery" reads the headline on the *Post* in a box.

Who knew that there were so many green glass buildings on Park Avenue? There is a roaring, moaning, from a motorcycle, but it's not as bad as on a regular day. With everyone gone, all the better to see the flowers in the median. Sartre wrote that Park Avenue is "sad"; maybe he meant further north.

There goes a long white limousine. A woman toddles by in pink iridescent high heels, barely a strap across her foot.

Two men are mopping the Seagram steps, one in yellow rubber boots. He's using a machine that has "Sun Glo" on it. It's on wheels, making a noise.

What's in the Stefano Ricci window? Long, black, men's crocodile shoes and a matching crocodile briefcase. All the blue ties. Walter Steiger shoes are alone in their window, gold tapestry and big bows. The doorman at 475 Park Avenue in his dark green hat with the gold trim is just kind of standing there.

Something is always missing in New York. With so much going on, not everything could last. Not everyone could stay. Julius Gumpertz left Mrs. Gumpertz one morning in 1874. He went to his heel-cutting job at Levy's workshop and never came back.

Then people die. The Ridiculous Theatre, Charles Ludlam as Camille, "Oh Nanine, where are the days when we laughed."

MISSING

THE MURDERS

LOCATION
Long Island City, Queens

RENT
$550 (rent stabilized)

SQUARE FEET
400 (studio in red brick prewar
building with forty apartments)

OCCUPANT
Savvas Kaminarides (national sales
manager, Bottega Veneta)

First, we have to understand how you came from Arkansas to New York by way of Cyprus.
My father taught economics at Arkansas State University. My parents, who are from Cyprus, didn't want me to acclimate to Arkansas. Then, after college, I wanted to move to a city where I didn't have to have a car. So here I am.

Why don't you live in Manhattan?
When I moved to New York eight years ago, I had no job and wanted cheap rent. I also thought I'd connect with the Greek community in Queens, which is very large, but I never did. My friends mostly live in the city. Though I've met some neighbors, it's always been in a time of crisis, so to speak. Because I'm on the ground floor, people think the super lives here. My bell is always ringing. Once a man was stabbed and Rose came to my door for help. Now Rose and I say hello to each other.

You mentioned that someone jumped off the six-story roof.
That's how I got to know Lucy and Sal. Their kitchen overlooks the air shaft where the body was. I think they discovered it and called the police. It wasn't a resident. Then there was a neighbor who was murdered. That's how I got to know Belle, his wife. But then she moved away.

Hmmm, I always thought the people in these little houses with the rosebushes lived such happy lives! You know, you are just a few blocks from the Kaufmann-Astoria Studios and the Museum of the Moving Image, which has on exhibit Bette Davis's wig block, Ben Hur's chariot, and sandals from *Quo Vadis*.
I go more often to the Noguchi Museum. I also like the Socrates Sculpture Park. There are never any people there. At least no one from Manhattan ever comes. School kids climb the sculptures. There are high school lovers making out. But now they're building a discount store next door.

Do you eat in the neighborhood restaurants?
I like the pizza parlor. It's run by an old-line Italian family from Queens. They never leave their twenty-block radius. And I like the Cuban place underneath the train. There used to be more Latin and Brazilian restaurants, but now there's been an influx of Pakistani and Bengali restaurants. We have a mosque around the corner.

Do you plan to stay around here?
I'd like a one-bedroom in the building.

I hear plastic wheels outside, children on skates and bikes.

I hear mostly dogs. The building is full of them. One woman has five pit bulls. The woman who owns the botanica with the religious objects has a white dog she walks every day exactly at nine. I always know what time it is. Right now there's a scandal. Dog pee was found in the vestibule.

Notes were left. A dog named Sammy was accused.

Do you think something will happen to Sammy?

I don't know. Maybe I'll meet a new neighbor.

April 15, 1997

GREG MILLER

THE MAN WHO WASN'T THERE

LOCATION
Fort Greene, Brooklyn

RENT
$1,159.84 (rent stabilized)

SQUARE FEET
624 (duplex apartment in
turn-of-century building)

OCCUPANT
Gabriel A. Tolliver (writer; producer;
founder of GFR Media)

Your neighbor was CIA?!
That's what Steve said.

Who's Steve?
My super, who lives next door.

What was the neighbor like?
He got in around '96. I moved here in '94.
He kept really odd hours. I'm very attuned
to sounds. The shades were always down, no
lights. I'd ask my super, Steve, "What's with
the guy across the hall?" Steve said, "He
works for the CIA."

How did Steve know?
Steve has the scoop on everybody. It was
weird, in the summer before 9-11, the guy
just up and moved. He'd cleared out the
apartment, but he hadn't turned in the keys.
Steve couldn't get in for a month. When he

did, the place was just torn up, full of trash,
bank statements.

If you're a spy, you cover your tracks.
It was almost as if the guy really didn't live
there. He just came and went.

**Do you think he was using it as a
lookout? His windows face the subway
entrance.**
Who knows what was going on in the area?

Maybe it was a front?
And he was checking out organizations.

What did he look like?
Portly black guy, very unassuming. You
wouldn't look twice at him on the street.
He didn't give off an air of tough guy. He
very much kept to himself. So being CIA
kind of made some sense. Once I even
slipped a note under his door. At one point
in time, I was thinking of a career in the
multimedia aspect of the CIA. This was
after NYU. I was very into that electronic
warfare, hacking and stuff. Though I'm not
a hacker. I slipped a note under his door:
"I understand that you work for the Central
Intelligence Agency and I was interested in
hearing about your experiences." His being
African American and all.

What happened?
Nothing.

Did you tell Steve what you did?
No.

Maybe we'd better talk to Steve.
He's on patrol.

JAY MUHLIN

Patrol?

Doing work on the various buildings.
[*He calls Steve: "Steve, hi, someone's here talking about that neighbor I had—well, this is just a little information reporter thing," and hands over the phone.*]

Steve, how did you know the guy was CIA?

[STEVE, *on phone*] The building office told me.

Of course! They want to know who your employer is! Did you see him much?

Any packages that came for him, I'd take them. No, I don't know where they came from, all different places. [*We hang up.*]

Did he ever have any visitors?

[GABRIEL] He was by himself all along.

Four years! Wasn't he lonely?

I don't know. He had very wary eyes, always taking in a lot. Once I saw him coming from the pizza place with a slice in a bag.

Did you ever hear anything through the walls?

I heard the TV. It seemed like it was movies. I did hear him once like crying out loud, sobbing, like he was having a very private moment.

Even spies have emotions.

[*The doorbell rings. A very large deliveryman is outside the door.*]

Oh, God.

It's just a package for a neighbor.

April 2, 2003

MARGO'S COUCH

LOCATION

Chinatown, Manhattan

RENT

$2,400 (market)

SQUARE FEET

1,080 (early 1900s walk-up)

OCCUPANTS

Andrea Lindstrom (coordinator, harm-reduction needle exchange), Chris Jordan (media artist), Jamie Favaro (assistant director, George Washington Bridge Outreach Program, Urban Pathways)

I just found this crumpled-up mystery paper on the crooked stairway.

[CHRIS] This is the first time I've ever seen graffiti in the halls. [ANDREA] It said, "Lil' Wang."

Such a lovely breeze is coming through the window. Chris and Andrea, your room looks out at Wei Wei Fashion and Chinatown Lumber.

I do all my shopping on East Broadway.

I concluded this morning that East Broadway is my favorite street in New York, well, maybe in the world. First, the old _Forward_ building, all sandy-colored with the Doric columns. A DOB work permit said it's being converted to "class A apartments."

[CHRIS] On both sides is a place for chickens and it smells awful.

The thought of living in the old _Forward_ building is so exciting—Isaac Bashevis Singer coming through the brass doors with his manuscripts. "The Bintel Brief"—"Dear Bintel Brief: My husband is so terrible. Do you think it's fair?" Seward Park is equally wonderful. I was thinking that when my friends are at their summer houses, I could come to the park. Then I'd go to the tidy East Side Café for a snack.

[ANDREA] We've been in the neighborhood six years, first at Orchard and Canal. We moved from Minneapolis. It is so different from Minneapolis.

Yes, it is. Shall I tell you about my journey here? OK. Usually I get so disturbed by the empty fabric stores with the words "cotton and wool" rubbed out where the clerks would flop down long, dusty bolts of jersey on the cutting tables and then I'd think about the man who probably owned it and then the son who worked there but never cared as much as the father and now everybody's in Florida or something, but because of this beautiful day, it didn't make me as sad as it might have. The garlic on the vegetable stand was brighter; the rhinestone turtle pillbox in the souvenir store was sparkling madly. The pirate ship made of beaded pearls looked proud. There was a big pineapple made out of gold coins. I don't know if it was real money—if so, an expensive pineapple.

Your semicircular white couch looks like half of Saturn's ring.
[CHRIS] It's Margo's couch. We read a stoop sale ad—"Everything must go in TriBeCa." We went to this woman's house. [ANDREA] A beautiful studio. [CHRIS] She was sitting there kind of sad and her friends were there. She said she had just gotten a divorce and couldn't stand to look at anything from the marriage. We said, "How much for the couch?" She said she had it custom made—$300. I said, "OK, pinch me." Her friends were saying, "You can't sell it for $300."

You can't go back on what you say.
She did. [ANDREA] We got it for $400. Her ex was a lawyer. She was selling his books.

Anyway I hope Margo's laughing it up on a new couch now. Where did Jamie come from?
[JAMIE] I was at Columbia. I got a master's in social work in May and I found this on the Internet and I hit it off with Chris right away on email.

Did you have other roommates before?
[CHRIS] Andy and I moved in with a good friend, a first-year law school student. [ANDREA] It was way too stressful. But we love her. [CHRIS] We had three other roommates, six to eight months each. [ANDREA] There was Julie, then Donna, Caroline… [JAMIE] I've been here since May. [CHRIS] A year! We'll have to celebrate.

Do you all eat together?
[ANDREA] Rarely. Chris and I make our own food and Jamie has hers. [JAMIE] Chris makes awesome breakfasts.

Jamie's room is so beautiful—that rose coverlet, the pink roses, the sun coming in.
[CHRIS] I love that room. It's quiet. You get the southern light. It's the warmest room in the house.

May 4, 2005

CARY CONOVER

269

LOST PLACENTA

LOCATION
Williamsburg, Brooklyn

RENT
$2,100 (market)

SQUARE FEET
750 (railroad apartment in four-story building with siding)

OCCUPANTS
Miles Thompson (computer programmer), Louise Newdack (paper conservator), Baxter Gray (fourteen months old)

Your placenta…

[LOUISE] I had Baxter at home. We lived on the Upper East Side then. I think home birth is a lot more common in New Zealand. We're both from there. It was a long labor but it was good, forty-five, fifty hours. No, no pain medication. You've just got to get through it. [MILES] The apartment was at 77th and York. We got it because, oh, we knew some South Africans who were moving out. Not that they were South African had anything to do with it. So, Baxter was born there. The placenta was also there. We put it in the freezer. You don't want to just chuck it out in the rubbish. We thought we might find a garden somewhere to plant it. We moved out on the 26th of December. It was very cold. We were very disorganized, we were going to New Zealand for a month the next day. The upshot of it all is we

locked the apartment, put the key under the door. We realized we left the placenta and the gin in the freezer. I didn't know whether to call the landlord and say we left some haggis. [LOUISE] The placenta was in a Whole Foods bag. I was kind of sad we left it. But that was also a little sign because that's where he was born and that's where the placenta stayed. [MILES] It's a New York thing, the freezer. [LOUISE] If we were in New Zealand we would have planted it in the garden. That's what people do. It's easier in New Zealand because you often have a garden. [MILES]. I always imagine Baxter coming back to the place he was born in.

The placenta is everyone's first home. You heard about this neighborhood six months ago from a woman you met in prenatal yoga. Your whole family has different last names!

[LOUISE] Actually we'll all be one name soon—Gray. We chose Gray for Baxter because we couldn't decide whose last name to go with. At the time, we thought maybe we should just have a new one. The midwife was very confused when we had to write out his birth certificate. We kind of want to get back to New Zealand by the time Baxter needs to go to school. We've been here just over two years. We came over for a change. Basically Miles worked for a company that was expanding all over the place.

You said you miss New Zealand, how it's so fresh.

Clean air, green hills.

JAY MUHLIN

Here you are in the neighborhood with more environmental problems.

[MILES] Toxic chemicals. I saw a sign: "This neighborhood will explode."
[LOUISE] It's very industrial here. That's what gets me down, very ugly.

It's funny how it's perceived as the coolest neighborhood, well, mainly by people under thirty, and yet visually it's so homey—siding, awnings, housedresses. That garden next to you with all the plastic butterfly pinwheels whirring madly. On the way, I stopped at JS Pastry Polska Cukiernia on Bedford for a sugar roll—plastic doilies, little aluminum napkin holders, a mural of water rapids, and the orange-and-black sign "Yes, We're Open." The only sound is the hum from the soft drink cooler. I prefer it to Verb, which was really hopping—a man selling *Tales of a Punk Rock Nothing*, girls in lingerie packed next to each other on the wooden benches. Verb is so seventies—potbelly stove, wood floors, strummy guitar music. Then, down the street, a man on a lawn chair was opening a government check envelope with a knife.

[MILES] There's a gap between the young hipsters and the older Polish. There's more happening for babies around here. There's going to be a new little play area called "Play Williamsburg." [LOUISE] Then you get all the Tibetan nannies.

June 18, 2003

LONG GONE

LOCATION
Upper West Side, Manhattan

RENT
$1,120.67 (rent controlled)

SQUARE FEET
1,550 (eight room apartment in
prewar elevator building)

OCCUPANT
Linus Coraggio (artist)

How much steel is in here?
Less than a ton.

How long have you lived here?
Since 1969. I've been on the block since
1967. My parents lived here. They got
divorced. My mother stayed. She moved out
in '87.

Where is your father?
In Santa Barbara. He's 92. He's Henry Brant,
the composer. He won a Pulitzer in 2002.

**Inspiration for us all! You said there are
only five rent-controlled apartments left
of the more than thirty units.**
The building's being sold this month to
make condos. People are being given buyout
offers—$20,000 plus the opportunity to
move into a smaller apartment downstairs
and two years' free rent. A neighbor said,
"Why would I want to move to a smaller
apartment?" They told her, "You get a new
kitchen."

**You might as well go right to a nursing
home.**
This is sort of the main gallery room. I
made these chairs. I don't pay for metal. I
find it, refashion it. This is my gentrification
piece from 1984, *East Village in Decline*.

**Blinking red lights inside falling-down
black steel tenements.**
It's meant to be read from left to right—
near decay to absolute decay.

**Downtown New York's getting to be
just about consumers, not creators—
people who ingest all day long. Your
piece captures the nesty darkness of
the Village of long ago.**
The way the garbage would pile up in front
of the buildings.

**Sigh. If your father's name is Brant, why
is yours Coraggio?**
I told you on the phone. You want me to
explain that again?

It works better for the column.
It's my middle name. It means *courage*. My
father thought I'd need that. I used to have
a studio at Gas Station, from '86 to '95, at
Avenue B and Second.

With the Plymouth Valiant on top.
We had a forge there. I taught welding.

**Was welding all the rage? It's important
in making medieval weapons.**
There are two kinds of people—those who
weld and those who don't. The rent at Gas
Station went from $600 to $5,000.

It was an art gallery by day and, by night, God knows.

It was also a pot drop for AIDS patients. Now it's a condo building.

Where do you weld now?

Outside a tire store in Bushwick.

Aren't you cold?

The welding keeps you warm mentally. I can start fires if I need to.

Do you see yourself moving to Bushwick?

I had this offer to buy a lot for 28,000 bucks. I thought of putting a trailer there.

Wouldn't it be lonely in the trailer?

Well, I live alone.

Always?

Yes, in this apartment. Bushwick is still the Wild West. I saw a middle-aged woman fire a revolver in the air.

Did the sheriff come? Let's look at your scrapbooks, titled *Life of Linus*.

I have different categories. Here's my first sculpture, ten bicycles welded together.

All these shots of you holding hoses.

That's an art welder. Here's another gentrification piece, *Landlord Crucified on His Own Tenement*.

So much art and writing is about gentrification. The moment of change— a dramatic subject for narrative. Who are all these people lying on the ground?

This was a performance piece at Pizza-A-Go-Go. Each model represented a different country that had a nuclear bomb. At the end there was an explosion. Here's an article from the *East Village Eye* . . .

The *East Village Eye*.

Long gone.

March 9, 2005

BRIAN KENNEDY

PEARL STREET MYSTERY

LOCATION

Financial District, Manhattan

RENT

$3,200 (market)

SQUARE FEET

1,600 (loft on top floor of 1840s former sail-maker shop)

OCCUPANT

Patrick O'Rourke (owner, Big Apple Lights)

They've been missing since November 1997. What happened?

No one knows.

Michael J. Sullivan—fifty-four, dancer, part-time museum clerk. Camden Sylvia—thirty-six, painter, real-estate agent. Together six years. They used to live here. Then, on or after Friday, November 7, they vanished. How do you fit in?

In '92, I stayed here for a couple of months to take care of Michael's cat. I believe at the point he had joined the circus. I'd been contacted by a friend of Michael's. I became a sideline character. Police said it's very unusual for two people to disappear at the same time.

I always wondered if they'd run away. Though when police came in, they found Michael's wallet, passport, videos rented that day, including Addicted to Love, and a receipt from J&R. The focus of police scrutiny was the landlord. Remember that news photo of him in his lock shop downstairs, the endless wall of keys?

No.

Camden and Michael reportedly gave the landlord a letter that Friday, also signed by other tenants, threatening to withhold rent unless he turned up the heat, a constant problem.

Yes.

Landlord Robert Rodriguez, fifty-six, repeatedly denied involvement in their disappearance. Then he vanished for two weeks. He lived with his family on seven acres in Wawayanda, New Jersey. He was a Cuban émigré, rumored to have had some kind of CIA involvement in the sixties and to be an expert safecracker. Police never found a clue linking him.

I've never been interviewed by the police. According to a neighbor, they brought corpse-sniffing dogs in here, found nothing.

There was a good reason for the landlord's disappearance—the indictment a year later: twenty-nine counts, for laundering more than a million dollars through his security and alarm installation business. He pleaded guilty on federal and state charges of tax evasion, credit card fraud. He

was paroled last August after four years. He never broke while he was in the slammer. Not about that or the unsolved '91 disappearance of a former employee in his security business. Maybe these disappearances were just coincidences. The assistant D.A. won't talk. He just said a criminal investigation is going on. Did you ever meet Camden and Michael?

When I moved to New York in '77, I worked at Dance Theater Workshop. I may have met Michael there but I don't recall seeing him until the day in '92 he came back from the circus. I was here vacuuming. He climbed in through the front window. I was a little surprised. We chatted a bit. He thought he was going to go away again the following summer. Two weeks before—I'd already given up where I was living—he said he wasn't leaving. He had fallen in love. That was '93, the last interaction until I read that they were missing.

That front-page photo of them in the Hamptons, all in white, smiling—she's about to eat an hors d'oeuvre. They were probably at someone's party. What did you think?

I met Rodriguez, the landlord, once in the hallway and he seemed very pleasant. I never ever thought I'd be back here. At that point, I had a loft in Brooklyn, which I did not like. In '98, Michael's friend, who had power of attorney, called and offered me a sublet here.

The rent's no longer $304. A new landlord, the father-in-law of the lawyer who shares an office with Rodriguez's

lawyer, paid $250,000 in '99, according to public records. Rodriguez had bought it in '93 for $205,000. Wait, remember the sneaker floating in the cove?

No.

In 1998, a Fila, Camden's size, with a white gym sock and a foot inside was found in the Battery Park Marina. She and Michael were runners. But then the foot didn't match her DNA. I heard a psychic who looked like the one in *Poltergeist* came here. She went into a trance and said, "They're waiting to cross over after retribution." What does that mean?

Justice.

How was the loft when you moved here in '98?

Everything had been gone through with a fine-tooth comb. Boards pried up. Camden's mother had taken a lot of her stuff.

Camden was from Cape Cod, studied art at Hunter.

Michael came from Chicago. He had a sister there, I think. At the point I was given the lease, I turned over Michael's effects to his power of attorney. I paid his back rent, certain legal fees.

Michael was poor, people said. When there was no water in the building, he washed in the fire hydrant. He moved to Pearl Street in the late seventies. There's a Thomas Struth photograph of the street from then—desolate.

It was very different years ago. The streets were very dark.

Michael was such an artist of that time, financially able to hang on. He ran off one year, joined a circus. Camden's day job was selling property to the affluent, who were ultimately pushing out people like Camden and Michael.

When they vanished, they were paying $304 a month, one-tenth of the market worth. This was governed then under the city Loft Board rules—slightly different from rent stabilization.

This street was called Pearl because it was paved with oyster shells. Early on, it marked the water's edge. Captain Kidd lived nearby in 1696.

He did?

In a mansion with Turkish carpets and chairs from the East Indies. Clipper ships came and went with silk and gold.

This was a sail-manufacturing building. Sails were pulled up through the floors to be inspected for safety.

Thus the giant wheel near your kitchen. I was thinking about Rodriguez, the focus of scrutiny, though police never found a clue. It is so incomprehensible that on a bustling Friday afternoon one person could either shoot two strong people in a ground-floor store or kidnap them. It just never made sense. Let's say a person's in a rage because tenants are complaining about heat. The tenants threaten to go to the law about his business problems—maybe Michael's come across incriminating mail that's been accidentally put in his box. And let's say the person snaps and screams,

"I've heard enough about the friggin' heat," and pulls out a pistol. There would be blood everywhere. How could one person dispose of two bodies? Of course, if someone had a hold over undocumented workers who could help...I don't know. Also, the tenant to silence would be Chuck Delaney, who's the Loft Board representative. But the whole tenant-landlord struggle, New York's most tired joke, was overplayed in the media. This crumbling building was freezing long before Rodriguez owned it and nobody disappeared then. [We reflect.] Things seem pretty calm around here now except for some unexplained spots in the photos you took, the lights that go off without explanation, the bottom of a glass that fell out when a dinner guest wouldn't stop talking about the case, and the— wait. What's that sound?

The air conditioner.

And how about the fire?

The Thursday before last Halloween, the building next door was gutted. It took four and a half hours to put out. It was an electrical fire, according to the Red Cross. They thought this building would go. They woke us at two and we had to evacuate.

I'm still perplexed. People just don't disappear in bourgeois bohemia. Though there's a Chicago story: a well-liked forty-year-old filmmaker fell in love out of the blue with a woman no one knew. To his friends' surprise, he moved west with her in 1993. Two years later, he vanished. It took five years

but they found him. His remains were
in the crawl space of a basement in
Cheyenne, Wyoming. He'd been shot to
death. Police believed the woman was
the murderer. It turned out she was in a
cult. You never know.

July 6 and 13, 2005

RESERVATION FOR SEPTEMBER 12

LOCATION
Upper West Side, Manhattan

RENT
$350 (informal sublet)

SQUARE FEET
189 (room in 1920s single-room-occupancy hotel)

OCCUPANT
Adam James (singer/songwriter; performer, *Our Sinatra*)

This hotel is like where they might do illegal organ removals—chipped green doors, bathroom down the hall, old beige linoleum, signs about terrorism in the elevator, and no food delivery persons allowed. The woman at the desk sounded so tough. Though the lobby does have a coffered ceiling and marble walls, however cracked.

They also post INS notices whenever there's a change in rules. There are a bunch of immigrants here—East Europeans, Brazilians. I don't know why so many Brazilians. I think one got a room here once. When new Brazilians come, they get a room. There are rooms that are half t his size.

Maurice, the manager, on the phone, said rooms cost $50–$75 a day, $475 a

week. You're sort of house-sitting for a friend who's on tour, you said, though you've been here off and on since 2001.
I moved here the week before September 11. I was in this room when it happened. It had been my dream to come to New York for years. I got this grant. Then Broadway was shut down. I was auditioning, looking for apartments.

I can see you coming through the chipped green door—another day, another dollar—singing a song about your woes.
My shoes were wearing out. Then I met Norah Jones. This was before her album was released. She was giving me advice on neighborhoods. I've become a professional house-sitter. New York turned me into one. I take care of a friend's cats when he's away. He's a cabaret singer. Another singer, when she and her husband go to their house in the south of France, I stay at their apartment—85th and Fifth. It's got a grand piano. I was just at 51st and Seventh. That friend is on tour with *42nd Street*. This is how I survive. It's only me, not like I have a family to cart around. The charm of house-sitting is you become other people. When you're living in other people's spaces with all their stuff, you try to tactfully...just seeing the stuff they own—that's interesting.

I don't know. I once sublet someone's apartment for a month and it was in this scary 1930s building and she had all this stuff—appliances and water filters and the closets were bursting with thick sweaters and it was hard to breathe. There isn't room for two

CARY CONOVER

people in one person. Who can absorb a stranger's life? It's too much! Then I would listen to this Julie London album over and over—"You'd be so nice to come home to..." But I was alone all the time except for her neighbor, who would invite me over for cocktails. That's all he did all day, have cocktails. He had a liquor cabinet. It was a horrible experience. Where are you from? Canada. I grew up in the suburbs of Toronto. My dad's a folksinger, high school teacher. [*I stand up.*] Do you want to sit in the chair for a while and I'll sit on the bed?

No, this is fine. I just needed to stretch. I have to tell you about a Nexis search that revealed a news article about this hotel. There was this man, a Cuban immigrant who had left just before Castro. He was married to a mayor of a nearby town in New York and he worked at a bank on Wall Street and disappeared after September 11, though his office was eight blocks from the Trade Center. But once a month, he had stayed at this hotel—your hotel—which the paper referred to as a "shabby genteel tourist hotel." He usually stayed on Wednesdays. He came late, left early, and paid $60 for the night. He was always alone. He had a reservation for September 12. When they asked Maurice, the manager, what the man did there, Maurice said, "We don't ask those questions."

January 21, 2004

279

LET ME TELL YOU ABOUT ROBERT DE NIRO

LOCATION
TriBeCa, Manhattan

PRICE
$40,000 in 1994
($2,000 maintenance)

SQUARE FEET
about 2,000
(loft in former warehouse)

OCCUPANT
Reno (comedian)

The first time I saw you was Tuesday, the morning of the horror. You'd left your home, eight blocks north of the World Trade Center. You were sitting on the stoop of your good friend Pat's house on Sixth Avenue waiting to meet up with more friends, surrounded by giant water bottles and a confused crowd who'd heard there was a bomb scare near the apartment building that has Souen, the macrobiotic restaurant, downstairs. It's the next day, Wednesday, and we're talking again. You've made your way north to the Village apartment of your friend, photographer Lisa Silvestri. Describe your journey from TriBeCa to the Village.

I'm in bed, me and my dog Lucy, and I heard a noise and I said to Lucy, Oh, it's just a suicide bomber, a little joke. Two minutes later I heard my answering machine—I *never* get up until noon—the Trade Center blew up. Everybody ran outside; we knew we had to get money and water. Well, the Korean deli near me—we boycotted it last spring because they exploited their workers. And what I hated about them, after Kennedy Jr.'s death, the deli owner was bringing in trucks of flowers and selling them right off the trucks. Anyway, so we have this fucking, fucking emergency, and me and my neighbors have to get big things of water, get them to people, get to Saint Vincent's to help. And I have to go to *him* to buy saltines.

So the incomprehensibly giant nightmare tragedy didn't soften your feelings, like a friend of mine who is no longer mad at her mother?

Hah! Let me tell you about Robert De Niro and the newsstand on Hudson where we gathered after the first plane hit—the *only* personal store left in the neighborhood, run by Mary and Fred, two old Commies. De Niro's bought a bunch of spaces around here, like that fuckin' TriBeCa Grill. For weeks we've been huddled in a ball because we hear De Niro wants the newsstand out by September 20, and we've been fighting it, writing letters, and it's our only place left in a neighborhood marched over by millionaires. So after the first plane crash yesterday, where are we? We're all gathered at the newsstand—our last moments of neighborly love.

Then, you get north to Lisa's apartment in the Village, all your friends come over to Lisa's to eat and sleep.
[LISA] It was like Noah's Ark, dogs and cats and animals. [RENO] Our friend, Lisa P., she was so freaked out, she's our big-deal tough defense attorney. [LISA] But cooking was her way of dealing with things. [RENO] She made us this genius meal.

Later, like Odysseus, you're going to try to make your way back, though you said you aren't sure what you want to go back to.
I don't know what to go back to. It's just a damn apartment. [LISA] We're not throwing our arms around our buildings. [RENO] Our friends—we're trying to decide whether to get together and leave town, but I don't feel I can leave my home.

This whole thing brought up the question of what is the sense of home. Is it being inside one's actual apartment? With every bomb scare, every new development, it removes a sense of a center, causes a panic about where to go. My TV friend lives in Astoria, and he said, "I don't know anyone in my neighborhood. I went to be with my friends in Manhattan." I went to stay with a friend, though we fought over the one telephone, over the email, whether to stay inside and be claustrophobic and informed or go out and be part of life. I talked to a man from Australia who has a fancy loft facing the Trade Center and who saw, from his window, the hundreds of bodies jumping and falling. I asked him, "Will you be able to feel that this is still your home with the memories of what you saw from it?" He said, "No, that's not the issue so much. My wife is in California right now. She's an actress. We just want to be together, there or here. That's our sense of home."

September 25, 2001

WARTIME

LOCATION
Park Slope, Brooklyn

RENT
$0 (temporary)

SQUARE FEET
600 (one-bedroom apartment in nineteenth-century brownstone)

OCCUPANTS
Barbara Zinn (executive search consultant; aspiring education policy analyst), Jenna Zinn (first grader, Corlears)

Park Slope has never looked more nineteenth century and civil with its gaslights, finials, and turrets than it does right now. And so far away from that smoky hell where you came from, with broken windows and your home covered in ash. You just arrived tonight in a stranger's brownstone, having had to flee Battery Park's Gateway Plaza— right across from Ground Zero—where you lived for eighteen years. I have to summarize the following because there's so much in your story—everyone's story. If they were all told in a documentary film, five minutes per New Yorker, it would be an interminable horror movie. Anyway, you were not in your apartment when it happened. You were beneath the World Trade Center, trapped on subway stairs with a hysterical, stampeding crowd. You eventually got out, fled north

to get to your daughter's school in Chelsea, crying off and on. Once there, total strangers and friends, exhibiting the purest display of unflickering humanity, were coming over, telling you you could stay with them. I was thinking about how emergencies are a test of character. You realize who the generous ones are.

One of the friends called Citi Habitats. This woman called in minutes. I was sure she was in social services, but she was in PR. Two hours later—she apologized for the delay—she found me this beautiful apartment, offered to us by people who had never met us. We can have it a month, maybe two, for free. I have lost everything. My entire client base was in my computer. The jury's still out on whether the data can be retrieved. Yet it's impossible to feel hopeless. Total strangers handed me shopping bags full of clothes, fifteen at least. I had to tell them, *stop*.

As of this writing, no one can live in Gateway.
I've gotten in three times already. There was an army sergeant barking orders at us. He said, "Do you *hear* me?" I said, "*Yessssssssir*."

It is wartime. But maybe he was upset because he wasn't ordering soldiers around, just a bunch of apartment dwellers with rolling suitcases that everybody used to take in car services to and from airplanes. You, yourself, in your banking days, went to South America at least once a month. Now,

MICHAEL KAMBER

for thousands of Battery Park evacuees, it's a humbling, bumpy roll from subway to home.

We had to climb the stairs—it's a thirty-five-story building. They told us we had to clean out the refrigerator—I didn't—close windows, and get back down with stuff, in fifteen minutes. I stayed forty; what are they going to do, arrest me?

Then you had to scrape the ash off the Barbie dolls, which in another country might have been a potato. This was in many ways a middle- and upper-middle-class evacuation—an experience that took away the fat. The future?

I could never bring my daughter back there. My lease expires this month anyway. The apartment looks like it's been raped. That ash could be asbestos, human ash. I just remembered I had a ton of clothes in the former dry cleaner. I have a Fendi mink in storage. The odor down there is really bad, something I can't explain. I'm just going to leave the beds there, everything. But I won't move out of the city. I will not abandon my daughter's school. I'm from Bethpage, Long Island. When I first moved to Battery Park in '83, I was the third person on my floor. There was no working elevator call button. When you wanted to go down, you stood at the shaft and yelled, "twenty-three down." Gateway was the first building down there. It was beautiful, peaceful. I remember I'd sit on the esplanade reading the Sunday *Times* and be the only person out there. Over the years, it became people of all ages. There were summer programs, African drumming for families, everything. I feel like I've seen Battery Park through its inception to its decline. To see the decline, on top of everything else that's happened, it's heartbreaking.

October 9, 2001

RECURRING DREAM

LOCATION
Gowanus, Brooklyn

RENT
$675 (market)

SQUARE FEET
400 (two-room apartment in 1880s house)

OCCUPANT
Ed Woodham (producer; teaching artist; cocreator of *The It Factor* on Bravo)

We're having a second interview on the telephone. During the first interview, two weeks ago, I was more preoccupied with whether you had ever seen the Loch Ness monster in the Gowanus Canal, since you live a block away. But that was before planes crashed into buildings, made the city crumble the way it does in little boys' comic books, and left the rest of the world—as of this conversation—in a state of terror that won't go away. How are you feeling now?
I feel numb, like I'm waking from a sleep. I guess when you bring up the Gowanus Canal again and the monster, it reminds me of the recurring dream I've had since I was a child, about running into a department store and grabbing a bike in order to get away from the explosions. I grew up in Atlanta with the Cuban missile crisis and my head between my legs in a hallway to do duck-and-cover from the atom bomb. That never left me.

When we talked a few weeks ago, it was a warm afternoon. We sat in your kitchen with the ceiling fan turning, Cuban music playing. I was in a cool, green Eames chair; you were in a yellow one. The apartment was so tidy and calm. Does it feel the same way to sit in your house?
It does not. The sound of the second plane was right outside the window, something I'll never forget. I was watching it on TV and I was hearing it outside.

Were you at home a lot during that first horrible week?
Yes. It's my sanctuary. You saw my house. The items are few and functional. It offers me solace, the space does. Of course you question that, too, knowing it's so precarious—any structure. I didn't go into Manhattan. I spent little time in the street, really. I occasionally turned on the TV, watched the updates, until I was full.

Have you seen your wonderful landlords, who gave you a box of candy and a card when you moved in four years ago and only raised your rent twenty-five dollars in all that time?
No, they live in Staten Island. But I'm sure they're all right.

We also talked about the little brown heater in your kitchen, standing proudly on its four legs.
I haven't thought about my little brown heater lately.

I *have*, a *lot*. You called it a "grandma heater," and said your grandparents had one. They lived in a weathered wood home with a tin roof in the depths of Texasville, Alabama, no central heating. Uncle Elmer lived there, too. He was a bachelor. You had wonderful memories of sitting on your grandmother's porch and eating big Sunday dinners. You'd have fried chicken and hush puppies and corn bread and lima beans and iced tea, and just pass out afterward. Don't you want to go back to that? Right now, for the first time in my life, my head is twisted around on my neck longing for what was safe and warm, though maybe it's just a temporary feeling. The emotional climate, depending on the news, seems to shift every five minutes lately.

No, I don't want to go back. It's like a dream to return to yet another dream. It's time to face the reality of the world that we live in.

I hope that reality includes reading that newsletter you showed me when I visited. You had found it during an Internet search for a play you're working on. The newsletter is called the *Grey Play Round Table* for concerned human owners of African Grey parrots. They think their parrots look like "knights in shining armor"; they have a chat group on the Web. We looked at the article on "Wing Clipping: When Is It Too Short?" Then we stared at the photos of these people sitting around a patio table in south Jersey and another group in Salinas, California, with their parrots perched on their forefingers. I just hope those people will be sitting around the table with their parrots for a long time.

October 2, 2001

JAY MUHLIN

I'LL NEVER FORGET

LOCATION
Bronx Zoo, The Bronx

RENT
$0 (complimentary housing)

SQUARE FEET
1,750 (pen with quiet area)

OCCUPANTS
Dasher, Dancer, Prancer, Vixen,
Comet, Cupid, Donner, Blitzen
(reindeer)

I have to whisper.
[CUPID] Come closer.

**Some animal people would be so mad
if they knew I was interviewing you. I
waited until Jim Breheny, the special
animal exhibits director, left to give
a talk on the changing role of the
modern zoo. I told him, "I'm not some
anthropomorphist." But Jim said, "We
all are." I hear you arrived December 2;
you stay until January. So it's like you're
on a Columbia fellowship or something,
though you're not at Columbia, you're at
the zoo. This is a spacious corral.**
Our quiet area is in the back with the hay.
That's where we reflect.

What's Lapland like?
We're from Milltown, Wisconsin.

Wisconsin?!
We like it. We live on a nice reindeer farm.
We're a subspecies of caribou.

You're very polite.
All of us reindeer are.

You're so short!
Three feet. But our antlers are tall.

**You have the most of any reindeer here.
It's like a tree growing out of your head.**
[*He clears his throat.*] It's quite a rack. I'm
the only male here. We usually have more
elaborate antlers than the females. Only the
reindeer with the best antlers are picked
to come here. If you break your antlers,
forget it. Though if we break our antlers
once we're at the zoo, they don't send us
back. They're not that ruthless. See, the
antlers itch a lot once they finish growing;
outer skin dries up, blood supply stops. I'm
not a doctor or anything—I learned all this
from Jim. We rub our itchy antlers against
branches for relief.

**You're doing that right now—banging
your head like crazy. You don't want to
end up like my friend's grandmother's
husband, who itched so much he
jumped off a building. He owned a tie
factory in the Bronx. Jim said you look
like cows without your antlers. What's
it like to fly? You're so earthbound with
your hooves.**
We do *not* look like cows. Anyway, flying's
only one night a year. Rudolph's in just for
that. Boy, what an experience flying is. One
time, I saw the Little Prince. I've seen the
Man in the Moon.

JAY MUHLIN

Do you ever see any airplanes?

Please, I'll never forget that morning. Santa was making us new harnesses. He was watching CNN in the other room. He came in and told us what happened—we have lateral vision, so it's hard for us to watch TV. I thought Dasher was going to have a breakdown. And poor Prancer. Never in my years as a reindeer...Well, I don't want to get emotional in public. But let's face it, things will never be the same.

This is the most beautiful zoo. Have you seen that Congo exhibit with the bird soundtrack and the gorilla that sucks her thumb?

Are you *kidding*?! We're working until nine at night. I've been wanting to get over to the gift shop. I'd like to get a leopard-print scarf for my aunt. We have to stay here and listen to the children sing "Rudolph the Red-Nosed Reindeer"—*over and over*. They sing in those high, screaming little voices. They've had no life experience. They have no idea what they're singing about. I don't know if you should print that. Oh, go ahead, what's free expression if not this?

I like how you just stand there and breathe heavily. How old are you?

Old enough.

So, is New York different for you this visit?

No, actually, it's got the same magical twinkle. They can't take that away.

December 25, 2001

CROUGH PATRICK

LOCATION
Lower East Side, Manhattan

RENT
$906.59 (rent stabilized)

SQUARE FEET
300 (two-room apartment in tenement building)

OCCUPANT
Sue Weston (social worker)

Spitzer's Dress Store is down the block, as is "Esther Apt 1930," carved in stone above the door. Esther must have been the builder's wife—or girlfriend. Your stairs do not match. A sign on the wall reads: "On July 20th, power will be turned off....Sorry for All Incontinences."

There's so much about this building. There's spit on the stairs or chicken wings or cigarette butts.

Are the red streaks blood?

They paint something, wipe their hands on the walls. We send our rent checks to a P.O. box in a very wealthy town in New Jersey.

Who's your landlord?

Landlady. We were on good terms. There have been a couple of brief episodes. I used to have a refrigerator that wasn't self-defrosting. So I happened to wedge some frozen food in, pierced something so Freon

was pouring out. I said, "I need a new one." So she wheels in this refrigerator, she and her two lackeys. By the way, she took a valve off this radiator and never came back for two or three years. I'm sorry I'm talking so fast. I open the refrigerator and a hundred cockroaches come pouring out. She said, "Listen, I buy you a bug bomb."

How would you describe her?

She's tiny. She always wears nice makeup. She often wears a cap, like when people go on a boat, like on *Gilligan's Island*. She's from Taiwan. There was a day when we were still on friendly terms. We had to get a key. We're walking down the street, she's holding my hand. We used to have a door in front of the building that flapped in the wind. Last year, there was an attempted burglary—my apartment and the people's next door. I came home, the door was jammed. I called, thinking she's going to hightail it over. She said, "You have to get a locksmith." I said, "Who?" She said, "Get someone from the phone book." These people damaged the door so badly, it took the locksmith two hours. I decided to deduct $400 from my rent. I wrote her a letter. She went ballistic. I said, "Take me to court." I had so much proof against this woman.

Our relationship went poof. Then she calls with this story that I've been late with my rent. I said, "Where's the proof?" She wants to charge me $25 each time. I said, "End of discussion." She brought me over to her office, closed the door. It was a little intimidating, let me tell you.

The Hispanic family upstairs used to have live chickens. At night, I'd hear this constant pounding. A lot of the people here, for extra money, will cut chickens into pieces. Now, upwardly mobile Caucasians are moving in. Nine years ago, eight guys were across the hall in this same-size apartment.

What's clinging to the stair window gates, like droppings?

It's disgusting. I get mysterious piles of sand behind the radiator. I recently had an infestation of mice. I went on the Tenement Museum tour. Those apartments look exactly like my place. I can't believe I've lived in these conditions.

You're leaving.

I'm moving to Ireland. I'm getting married, a man I met in passing. I have cousins there. Last year, when I was in Dunmore, a town in Galway, I wanted to climb Crough Patrick, a mountain people climb in penance. It's where Saint Patrick spent like forty days thinking about the Irish people. It's a tricky, kind of scary mountain. As I was chatting about doing this hike, PJ came into my cousin's house. He said, "I'll take you up Crough Patrick." So we got to the top and had a bottle of wine. The priests would probably look down upon that. PJ said the mountain spoke to him. He's building a house in Connemara, all stone faced. It's property he'd bought eight years ago, after he worked on the tunnel from England to France.

He was under the ocean?

Welding. He's also a sculptor. He came back and bought this property. The house has four bedrooms and a view of the ocean. I'm walking out of here on September 11.

August 31, 2005

Hooves on the road, clip clop—there goes a white horse. From the carriage, surveying it all, a man in a short-sleeved shirt, a woman in a blue dress. He holds her hand. The horse's head is bobbing up and down—another day, another dollar.

There are hundreds of shades of green in Central Park: pine, apple, olive. The Angel of the Waters fountain water is green. The bronze of the four cherubs is green. Sneakers are padding along, bicycles, cars, taxis, people running, waddling, limping. Everyone is here: Alice in Wonderland, Hans Christian Andersen, Balto with his tongue hanging out—he was on the dog team that ran seven hundred miles to bring the serum to stop the diphtheria epidemic in Alaska. The roots of the tree go far and wide.

Central Park was the first in the country to make a large huge open space, 843 acres, for everybody to come to and be together in a perfect organic world—hello Mrs. Cloggle. Hello, Mr. Reneul. All the rich, all the poor—and then they would be enlivened by growth and grass.

New York City, in the midst of the hardships of life and housing over the decades, was full of such visions. People were always trying to make life better. There was the busy building of cooperatives in the early part of the twentieth century—speculators, prophets, architects seeking garden cities, and labor unions making affordable housing for their members. The city has other group living situations. Some are not sought after, some rehabilitative, and some the result of the progressive housing movement of the 1960s. Many are newly formed with the zest of youth and art, bohemia's eternal recurrence.

What's the big mysterious dark green truck moving fast with the peeling side, no lettering? The back looks like it could unload troops. Leaves are blowing in the wind, a cool night in summer. On the ground are small plaques—The Tree Trust: Gertrude Heimer, Pin Oak Tree 2001; Phyllis Kamner, Saucer Magnolia 2000; Ralph Lauren, Black Cherry 1993.

I had to sit down on a bench. I just happened to have a copy of *Lost Horizon*. I read about the Valley of the Blue Moon: "Never had Shangri-La offered more concentrated loveliness to his eyes; the valley lay imaged over the edge of the cliff, and the image was of a deep unrippled pool that matched the peace of his own thoughts."

I look for the carousel that goes round and round. I see a brick building. Where are the flying horses? Where is the organ playing the Wurlitzer music rolls? A man is setting up a telescope to look at the constellations: "Of *course*, the carousel is closed at night," he says. "It's for *children*."

UTOPIA

DIAMONDS ON THE WALLS

LOCATION

Long Island City, Queens

RENT

$451 (rent stabilized)

SQUARE FEET

900 (five-room railroad apartment in 1915 building)

OCCUPANT

Debbie Van Cura (human resources consultant; president, Greater Astoria Historical Society)

Nice spoon collection! You have three wall displays in the dining room alone! These yellow brick Mathews row homes, like the one you live in, are so funny looking—twenty-five on each side of the block and they're all identical. They look like a photo of an accordion orchestra where a hundred people are holding the same accordion. Anyway, in 1904, German immigrant Gustav X. Mathews had a dream—healthy, affordable housing for Everyman! With determination on his brow, he filled Queens with blocks of three-story six-family homes—some 2,500. He was shooting for more but then there was the Depression.

My grandparents bought this building in 1924 for $19,000. They brought their things over from Manhattan on horses. I grew up in the apartment downstairs. The one I'm in now was my grandmother's. When she passed away in 1983, I moved back. I've always lived in this building, except for five years.

Five years? You must have been beside yourself not living in a Mathews home.
I was in college. I moved into an apartment with a girlfriend. We said, "Oh, let's try something new." We wanted to live near Astoria Park. It was a basement apartment and it was damp. When it rained it would flood. Mathews homes don't flood.

Of course! Mathews homes have a window in every room, a backyard for every building. Mr. Perfect apartment builder! You told me you heard Mathews was so committed to housing for the working class that it's rumored he turned down MetLife's offer to build middle-class Stuyvesant Town. And his love for quality housing was so strong, he reportedly couldn't go through with attempts to build tract housing. Ah, you have Czechoslovakian piano rolls— Muziky Muziky!
My family is Czechoslovakian on both sides. There are a lot of Czechoslovakians around 19th Street by Ditmars. This block of Mathews homes is very ethnically mixed today—old Irish families, Germans, Italians, some Chinese, now Mexicans, Guyanese, young kids from Manhattan.

There was a man sitting on the stoop in his shorts singing. I think he was Italian. You said rents are up to $800. Oh, your friend Bob just walked in.

[BOB] Like I say in our Astoria Historical Society slide lecture: New Yorkers may not have found gold on the streets, but we can thank G. X. Mathews for putting diamonds on our walls. See those diamond-shaped patterns on the bricks? This guy used every design imaginable! [DEBBIE] Growing up, my entire world was this block. At Halloween you could cover a half block and get three full bags of trick-or-treat. There wasn't anything I longed for. I just have to round the corner and I get such a beautiful feeling. When I go down the block to the train, I see so many people I know, so I always have to leave a little early. If I ever needed anything, I'd never have to go further than my own backyard.

Doesn't anything bad ever happen here? Even your dish towel with the apples looks happy as it flutters in the afternoon air.
I have so much of a breeze, I have to keep relighting the pilot light on my stove.

September 1, 1998

GREG MILLER

L'CHAIM!

LOCATION
Lower East Side, Manhattan

RENT
$1,675 (sublet)

SQUARE FEET
1,200 (four-room apartment in 244-unit art deco co-op)

OCCUPANTS
Susan Enochs (marketing manager, Library of America), David Blankenship (graphic designer, Eric Baker Design Associates)

You just moved into an apartment house with a mezuzah on every door and four urologists downstairs. This six-building complex is so mysterious—large rooms, huge courtyard with a fountain, so pastoral and deathly quiet for Manhattan. And so far east. The Williamsburg Bridge just looms up. You might as well still be across the river in Brooklyn, where you lived for one and a half years near Metropolitan and Havemeyer and the chicken slaughterhouse.

[DAVID] We'd never been to New York until two years ago. We moved out here from San Diego with no return tickets. It doesn't matter what neighborhood we're living in. We're still surrounded by strangers.

Who are the strangers here?

[SUSAN] Ninety percent very old, ten percent young. The woman upstairs bought her apartment in 1931. The few young people we've met are living in the apartments of their grandparents. They were as excited to see us as we them.

How does it feel living with mostly one age group?

It's rather sweet. We'll see them holding hands walking to their apartments. One time I was going out. I was in a hurry. This old man told me not to run, as if I were a child. Another time I came home about 4 a.m. There was this lovely old couple standing in the courtyard. I wondered what they were doing up until 4 a.m.

That's probably when they _woke_ up. They want to be awake as much as possible while they're still alive. I heard you got this apartment through your jazz critic friend who moved into the building a few months ago, after he and his girlfriend were trapped for two years between Penn Station and the Big Cup in a four-hundred-square-foot studio. He looked for a new apartment for two years and sometimes he would be shaking from exhaustion, but then one sunny April afternoon, after looking at a place on Pitt Street where a dead pigeon was hanging upside down outside the window, he walked by a real-estate office, and there was an old Jewish man inside in a hat, and the jazz critic started to cry, and the man took him in his bronze Cadillac and brought him to this palace, and now he hops up and down when he tells all his friends he looks out on a courtyard with a fountain though the F train is seven blocks away but you can't have everything.

We owe our friend our life for telling us about this apartment. We want to go wash his dishes for him.

Your decor is minimal—Navajo white walls, cantaloupe trim—well, David's grandfather *was* a melon farmer—and Tibor Kalman's book on the coffee table. [DAVID] The apartment was baby blue and baby pink high-gloss when we moved in. [SUSAN] And two layers of linoleum from the sixties and eighties.

Are you sure you don't know more about this building? I just have a feeling about it. Well, somebody told me it was one of the first co-ops or something on the Lower East Side of minor historic significance.

[*Two days later. Telephone rings.*] Minor significance. You are living in one of the most *famous* co-op buildings in all of New York! Even your jazz critic friend, Mr. Social Conscience, didn't know that it was built by the Amalgamated Clothing Workers Union after they built the Amalgamated Homes in the Bronx. A state housing law was passed in 1926 that encouraged the building of low-cost housing through tax incentives. The union wanted to build happy, airy housing so people wouldn't have to live in tenements. In the beginning, the people—union and nonunion members, mostly Italian and Jewish—bought apartments for $500 per room and $12.50 monthly maintenance. In 1936, the *New York Times* reported that the WPA orchestra played every Friday night in the auditorium. *L'Chaim!* Originally, the bylaws stipulated that shareholders who left could realize only a modest profit on their apartments. Three months ago, the building became privatized. Now they can sell for full profit like any co-op. Uh oh.

January 12, 1999

NINA ROBERTS

THE WOMAN NEXT DOOR

LOCATION
Sunnyside, Queens

PRICE
$164,500 in 1997

SQUARE FEET
1,000 (two-story 1920s house)

OCCUPANTS
Irma Rodriguez (associate director,
Forest Hills Community House),
Angel Rodriguez (retired electrician),
Vivienne Michele Miranda (Irma's
goddaughter)

How did it begin?
[IRMA] I was walking home one night just after my father moved in. He was in his chair. I could see him through the window. I saw Sophie through the window in the same spot next door. I said, "Dad, you should ask Sophie to tea sometime." [ANGEL] I was alone here. She was alone there.

Do you see her every day?
Well, almost. [IRMA] When he first moved here, they used to go to Phipps Garden, the building down the street. They hold hands. Sophie moved to Sunnyside during World War II. Her husband died some years back. [ANGEL] She's got a piano.

How did you and your father end up roommates?
[IRMA] I'd been living in Forest Hills

for twenty-three years, two-bedroom apartment, $850. It was 1997. I said, "I could be paying a mortgage. This is nuts." My father had a condo in Parkchester that he had bought about sixteen years ago. He's ninety-two now. I know what happens with aging parents. I'm working in a senior center. A lot end up living with their children when they become ill. I thought it was important to do it before. Without the catastrophe. [ANGEL] Right off, it cost me about $30,000. With that, she closed.

Weren't you excited to move here?
Not really. Before, I was foot-free. I still went to play golf with the gang, Van Cortlandt Park. [IRMA] He says I'm bossy. I'm an only child, not by choice. My mother died when I was nineteen, during an operation. I'm fifty-three. I got raised around a lot of first cousins, West Side, 139th. Dad came to the States when he was sixteen from Puerto Rico. [ANGEL] The year that Lindbergh flew to Paris, 1927.

Why 1920s Sunnyside?
[IRMA] It had been a dream of mine for a long, long time. I didn't want a suburban-house house. I knew about Sunnyside because of my work. The house is now worth close to $300,000. Some people make a connection right away when they come here. Others don't get it. The houses are tiny, seventeen and a half feet wide.

It looks as if the architects were very sober when they designed it—"Oh, let's just use a simple pencil." Two-story houses, pale red brick. Though it's based on the idea of the nineteenth-

JAY MUHLIN

**century English garden community—
low density with the perfect balance
between personal and collective space—
there isn't the affectation of Anglo
architecture as in Forest Hills.**
It's sweet and peaceful.

**Sunnyside was designed by three of the
biggest names in utopian housing—
architects Clarence Stein and Henry
Wright and developer Alexander Bing.
Architecture critic Lewis Mumford
lived here.**
There are fights today between the
preservationists and the do-what-I-please
people. See, the houses aren't landmarked,
just the neighborhood. In the seventies,
when they got the national and city
designation, people had the option to take

back their garden. Some put up fences so
there were no more central courtyards.
My idea is to re-create the courtyards, give
owners a monetary incentive to take down
their fences.

Is your home life impacted by the war?
The only thing that really affects us is that
my dad's a Republican. [ANGEL] We got
different opinions. Once in a while if I say
something, she snaps at me.

How does Sophie feel?
Sophie's also very liberal, the whole slew
of them here, on down the block, with the
exception of those Hungarians. [IRMA]
Romanians.

April 15, 2003

TICKING CLOCK

LOCATION
Stuyvesant Town, Manhattan

RENT
$737 (rent stabilized)

SQUARE FEET
680 (one-bedroom apartment
in Stuyvesant Town)

OCCUPANT
Joseph Yranski (film librarian and
historian, Donnell Media Center,
The New York Public Library)

Before we discuss your Bohemian etched glass, your stuffed giraffe, and your bas-reliefs of Puccini, let's talk about Stuyvesant Town—it's so big and so red! Almost twenty thousand people, eighty-nine buildings, twelve playgrounds! How does a person get an apartment here?

You get on a list. I think you need to earn a certain amount of money in relation to the rent.

I understand turnover is less than one percent.

I've been here six and a half years—it took me eight years to get in. That was during the worst period. Now there's more turnover—some of the original tenants are moving to Florida.

What's it like having MetLife, a big insurance company, as your landlord?

I can't praise the administration enough. You can look out the kitchen window and see their tower blinking in the night.

Why did MetLife build Stuyvesant Town in the first place?

MetLife's president came up with a plan during World War II saying the rich were getting all the new apartments on Park Avenue, and the poor were getting housing projects, but nothing was being done for the middle class in service occupations.

Are all the apartments the same size, with L-shaped, midcentury foyers?

Not every apartment has a foyer. Most one and two bedrooms are the same square footage, though the configurations vary.

Your doorknobs look like the ones that talk in *Alice in Wonderland*. Do all the apartments have them?

I think so.

And all the bedrooms have flowered wallpaper?

No. The management allows you to indulge your eccentricities, as long as you restore it before you leave.

Everyone's bathroom has pale yellow tile?

Some have beige.

Will you live here forever?

I can see staying here for the rest of my life. It's clean—I only dust every three weeks. That doesn't sound like much, but it's what I love. I also love the fact that there's a Laundromat in the basement. Then, there's

GREG MILLER

the disposition of the other tenants. The sense of community. The floral beds are upgraded annually. At holiday time, they go all out with flying reindeers and menorahs on the oval. It has that forties look—George Bailey in *It's a Wonderful Life* running through town after he's discovered he's alive. I know many people love that film, but I happen not to be one of these people.

Well, it was a talkie, and your predilection is for silent films. Who do you think is prettier—Colleen Moore or Corinne Griffith?
Never mind.

Speaking of silence, it's so quiet in this apartment, though there was some Gershwin on the gramophone earlier. Now only clocks are ticking.
Those are just some of my clocks. The pocket watches are over there.

February 25, 1997

NEHEMIAH

LOCATION
East New York, Brooklyn

PRICE
$93,000 in 1998 ($457 maintenance)

SQUARE FEET
1,440 (three-bedroom row house)

OCCUPANTS
Victoria Heath (project manager, HUD), Natalie Octavia Credle (sophomore, East New York Academy)

We're sitting in your luxurious off-white living room with cocoa velveteen furniture and a crystal bowl full of pennies and you're saying you only had to put down $10,000 in cash for this three-bedroom house.

[VICTORIA] I heard about the Nehemiah housing program when my pastor, the Reverend Johnny Ray Youngblood, announced it from the pulpit, and I got on the waiting list. And the day I went to that closing, it was a *gorgeous* day. The night before, my pastor said in front of everybody, "Guess what this lady is going to be doing tomorrow here at the church? She's going to be closing on her Nehemiah home." There was thunderous clapping.

Nehemiah is the biblical prophet who rebuilt the walls of Jerusalem. These houses—for first-time homeowners only—are so affordable because they're city subsidized. No-interest construction financing is raised by the forty-five organizations in the East Brooklyn Congregations.

They told us how to do every step, how to get a mortgage with a low-interest rate. I've worked at HUD twenty-two years making sure apartment buildings are managed properly. I didn't know about *owning*. When I moved in, '98, I was on the couch waiting for the telephone man. I thought, "It's kind of airy in here. I'll get a blanket." Then I said, "Hey, put on the heat. You *own* this house." I was so used to others being in control. I was raised in East New York, then East Flatbush for sixteen years—that's when I was married—in public housing. You can't slam doors, can't have guests if the elevator isn't working. I just bought a new doorbell for my home, the kind that lights up at night, goes ding-dong. I love it.

Your steel-frame house was built in six days, like a magic act, by the Capsys Corporation, made right in a Brooklyn Navy Yard building where the ceilings are fifty feet high and they made gun turrets in World War II. It's funny how the 550 houses look alike, so Levittown, though they come in different colors. One man has twelve stone lions on all his gate posts.

I bought the stone balls. I don't like the lions. And those stone pineapples don't signify anything.

In the eighties, 1,100 red brick Nehemiahs went up in Brownsville; 600 more are supposed to go up in Spring Creek—that's where they dug up those

dead bodies last year, mob hits—but they say it's going to be a utopia now with a Home Depot.

Unfortunately, the Nehemiah waiting list is closed.

I was wondering if you're active in your community. I ask because EBC is part of the nationwide Industrial Areas Foundation, founded in 1940 by the late activist Saul Alinsky, who created the model for community organization, believing people should have the power to take control of their own lives.

I don't know about that stuff. I just *live* in the house. But EBC wants us to build a community, not just own a house. I'm on the transportation subcommittee. We got the city to put signs up to keep trucks from barreling through what is now a residential area. For years this was a torched wasteland.

Many Nehemiahs are owned by single women—on one block it's over half. Are you close with your neighbors?

It took me the better part of a year to know them. It's slow going. I don't know why. I'm *very* involved with my church, the worship choir. That's how I praise God, with song. And I don't clean the house unless I have music blasting. I've always got my barbecue going. I'm cooking franks, shish kebabs. My sister-friend Kim makes a mean macaroni salad. We play cards on the lawn. We're grooving to the DJ sounds from the projects on Williams and Dumont. This guy is bad. He's got to be my age, 'cause all the sounds are cool, R&B, "Ain't No Stopping Us Now." All day long he plays. He stops just when you've had enough. I don't know the guy, but I know he helps my summers.

August 14, 2001

RICHARD MEIER'S WESTBETH

LOCATION
Greenwich Village, Manhattan

RENT
$615.81 (variable)

SQUARE FEET
1,100 (duplex loft in former industrial building)

OCCUPANT
Barbara Prete (painter; arts administrator; voluntary president, Westbeth Artists Residents Council)

You are living in a building throbbing with historical significance! It is the first and only federally sponsored artists housing complex in the country, one of the earliest models of industrial loft conversion, and, before that, the site of the Western Electric and Bell Telephone laboratories, where the Orthophonic phonograph was invented! I saw the scientists smoking pipes in the newsreel. How did you get to Westbeth?

I got here in 1977, seven years after it opened. I had been living in East Fishkill with my IBM husband but then...

...one day you woke up, put your three kids, the German shepherd, and the IBM Selectric in the metallic-blue Volvo, said good-bye to the husband, and drove straight to Westbeth without ever looking back!

Well, first we visited a friend here. We arrived at 8:30 on a Saturday morning. She and her children didn't wake up until noon. It was so New York. She was dating someone from Lincoln Center and we went to the ballet that night. We left our seven kids together. They didn't come back until midnight. I thought they had been killed or something. Then my kids came in and they were so happy. They said, "Oh God, we went to a gay bowling alley and we have to move to Westbeth."

So you moved into one of the live-work spaces designed by the great modernist Richard Meier. There were no closets, no doors except to the bathroom, and complete respect for geometry and Le Corbusier. What was your rent in the beginning?

$400 something. Rents are set by HUD and determined by income on tax returns. $615.81 is my base rent. If I make more in a certain year, I have to pay a surcharge, just for that year.

It's such a good deal, nobody wants to leave. I heard there's an eight-year waiting list. About half the original tenants are still here. Yet when Roger Stevens, from the National Council on the Arts, joined with Jacob M. Kaplan, philanthropist and former head of Welch's Grape Juice, and put together the $2.5 million seed money to start Westbeth, they believed artists would stay for about five years, then move on to make room for new artists. Many did

GREG MILLER

not, or could not because of the city's soaring rents.

I do see new people in the building. 383 units are a lot of apartments.

I also heard Westbeth was never supposed to be just a piece of real estate but a real artists' community. There were puppet shows for the masses; the building manager walked through concerts wearing a velvet robe and dropping flower petals. Of course, back then people were reading *Open Marriage*. The space is so quiet and empty now.

Well, it was a different time. Regulations have tightened now. You can't have kids roller-skating down the hallways. But we can have events again. This used to be a rag pickers' neighborhood. Now it's gotten fancy. Westbeth is uniquely situated to come back as a showpiece. We'll do it by motivating the artists. I think Westbeth has always been a very hopeful place. I still hear music from the Merce Cunningham studio when I go to sleep at night.

July 22, 1997

THE FIRST LADY

LOCATION
Red Hook, Brooklyn

RENT
$315 (subsidized)

SQUARE FEET
500 (one-bedroom apartment in public housing project)

OCCUPANT
Emma Broughton (volunteer, Red Hook Senior Center; former school aide and counselor, HeartShare)

You're so happy the daffodils are up. Now, we first met at the Red Hook Senior Center down the street, with all the bright orange chairs, the pink and white crocheted dolls, the men playing dominoes.

I go there every day, help the ones who have canes. I carry their trays. I've been in the projects since 1958.

You have this soft Southern accent.

I was born in North Carolina, Durham. There were seven of us. My mother died giving birth to me. I think seven is a blessed number. I was raised by my grandmother. I moved to New York when I was twenty, in 1950, to live with my aunt, in Spanish Harlem. I married my husband a year later. He was in the garment business—bias and binding, making lapels for suits. I got in the projects on emergency. I had small kids. I was living in a very bad building up on Bergen.

I read that this red brick public housing project was the largest federally funded one of its time when the first part, six-story buildings, was finished in 1939. It has very nice landscaping. On sunny days, the trees lean toward each other over the walkways—well, on cloudy days, too. Architecture critic Lewis Mumford, usually so down-in-the-mouth, called it "Versailles for the millions." First lady Eleanor Roosevelt came to visit. Can't you just see her smiling, in her hat, happily looking upon a world well taken care of?

I met her, a very gracious lady. You should have *seen* the trees when I moved here. The center mall was nothing but green grasses, bushes with flowers on them—yellow bells. You didn't see one piece of paper in the project. They used to vacuum every morning. Not today. We had policemen who walked the development. If a child walked on the grass, he would yell, "Mother, get your child." When I moved in, it was really integrated—a lot of Italians, Jewish—a great community. It didn't matter what color you were. We had elderly people. My kids would go to the store for them. Then the piers started closing up in the late fifties; a lot of the Italians moved out. Newcomers have come, homeless, single parents. The mid eighties is when crack really hit. No, I was never afraid. When the drugs got bad, I started the anti-drug task force. My grandson got shot in

BRIAN KENNEDY

the back—but he's OK. I've never had a problem being afraid. Maybe I'm crazy. But I'm out a lot. I move around. If you become a prisoner in your house, you're finished. I can't stand to stay in this house all day. If I do, I feel sick. I have to be around people. I don't think I could live in a house where you don't have neighbors.

You have 10,000 or something.
I went to South Carolina to visit my sister-in-law. She said, "I feel so sorry for you." She could see I was miserable there. The houses are so far apart. At night, you just see the car lights on the highway.

So lonely. That sound of tires moving along, going away. How did you become so active politically? They call you the mayor of Red Hook.
Oh, council member Joan McCabe said that. I've been on Community Board 6 since 1984. I belong to a lot of organizations—American Legion Auxiliary, Red Hook Justice Center. After my husband died in '82, I decided to get active. I've always liked to do things, but in the background. People always come to me for information. I don't know why. All I did as a kid was run to the store for the neighbors. I think they picked me because they knew I'd come right back.

You're very excited about the Red Hook Public Library Reading Garden.
It was a garbage-strewn lot. I looked at it one day. I said, "It's an eyesore." I spoke to Howard Golden. That was four or five years ago. Angel Rodriguez put in for renovation money. Thank God, I'll live to see it completed. I'm talking to Felix Ortiz to get a mural for the wall. I want it to be beautiful.

April 2, 2002

A NORC

LOCATION

Chelsea, Manhattan

PRICE

$12,775.06 in 2000 ($558.12
maintenance)

SQUARE FEET

600 (one-bedroom apartment
in 2,820-unit not-for-profit
co-op building)

OCCUPANT

Tom Duane (state senator)

**You wanted to live in Penn South so
badly, you waited *sixteen* years!**

Let no one think I got special treatment.
When I joined the Democratic Club in '79,
people said, "Get on the list." I finally did
in '84, the smartest thing I've ever done.
But I wasn't called to see *any* apartment for
fifteen years. Last year I got a letter saying
there's an apartment but if you don't look at
it in ten days, we're taking you off the list.
Even though I wasn't crazy about it, I said
yes. If you refuse three times, you go to the
bottom of the list. But I didn't get that one.
Then there was one on the second floor. I'm
a little afraid about security, that someone
would get up on a ladder and shoot me,
though usually it's politicians who kill other
politicians rather than citizens. During AIDS
demonstrations, I get a lot of phone calls. So
I refused that apartment, but then I got this
one last November.

How did you feel? Elated?

First of all, I'm Irish, and I wouldn't be in
touch with my feelings anyway. But it was
like a dream come true. Especially because
I believe in the mission. It's just wonderful
to live in a co-op where, twice, the people
have voted to keep it affordable and not
take the profits and run.

**The last vote was just a few weeks
ago. Everything about the complex is
progressive. It was sponsored by the
International Ladies' Garment Workers'
Union.**

They have co-generation. When gas is
cheaper, they use gas. When oil is cheaper,
they use oil.

**A study in the early eighties identified
Penn South as a NORC, a Naturally
Occurring Retirement Community. Why
should anyone leave? The lobby was
pretty lively today. Some of the original
residents were lined up on a bench
talking about the matters of the day.
You've lived all over Chelsea since '76.**

First on 18th—then I gave up rent
stabilization for love. Later, I was in the
private sector and bought a co-op on 16th
and Sixth. But I always felt more like a
tenant than an owner. Co-op owners can
get very involved in discussions of what
the lobby should look like. That's not
exactly my thing. In this building, I'm a
cooperator, not an owner.

**You were raised in two center-hall
Dutch colonial houses—your father
worked on Wall Street—with three**

brothers. This was in Flushing, though you said in your world what was more important was the parish a person lived in.

If my grandmother was talking about someone, she'd say, "Oh, they live over in St. Kevin's." We lived in St. Andrew's. Whitestone is St. Luke's. Then they added St. Mel's. Jackson Heights is...

Enough! Your partner, Louis Webre, who works at Doyle, the auction house, said until this new apartment, your decor was mostly boxes, posters, and political buttons.

Ah, yes! CANDU, that's Chelsea Against Nuclear Destruction United, then, of course, Pass Intro One, Pass Intro Two, Pass Intro Seven, No Nukes...

You got all pink and animated when I brought up the buttons.

I had to send them to my mother's house,

because Louis made me. Louis lives in a rent-stabilized building on the Upper East Side. I've leaned very heavily on him to decorate. I want him to be happy when he visits.

Louis is very excited about feng shui. He explained how he had one wall in each white room here painted a color— aquamarine in the hall because it's the color of a pool and in feng shui, running water is good as it stirs up the chi with regard to movement. Then the yellow in the living room stimulates conversation, perfect for politics. I forgot what he said about the green in the kitchen. You've taken trips to Cuba, collecting Cuban paintings.

The two on the walls are my favorites—old cars. Here are two more, Cuban bulls. Louis said it's good feng shui to have a pair.

May 1, 2001

JAY MUHLIN

HOUSING WORKS

LOCATION
East New York, Brooklyn

RENT
$600 (sliding scale)

SQUARE FEET
350 (room in center for homeless people with AIDS/HIV)

OCCUPANT
Nathan Mosley (businessperson)

What is this painting of a cabin in the woods? The windows have yellow light, the way a house looks on a summer night, just before it gets dark.

That was my grandmother's house in Warrington, North Carolina. I spent every summer there. I painted it from my head. I have a great art therapist. She says, "You don't have to be Leonardo da Vinci." That painting with the bouquet of flowers, I made it for Shante. She's my girlfriend. She lives down the hall. Six of the thirty-two residents here are women.

You've lived at the Housing Works center for homeless people with AIDS/ HIV for two years. You were a drug user for twenty-seven out of the last thirty years, homeless for ten, living in boxes, the A train. And now you're in this bright room with a stuffed rabbit that says "Be Happy," crocheted curtains, perky green

plants, and an angel in a white satin dress hanging from the light bulb string. This 1997 beige brick building is so clean. It must be the most hygienic place in New York—creamy pale yellow walls, big television sets, weight room, dining area where we just saw the music teacher eating a sandwich. The first Housing Works opened in the East Village. How did you get here?

April 8, 1999—I'd just had my last pint of wine, same clothes on for months. I was sick every day—praying God would end my life. I checked in to the mid-Brooklyn sober up station. I'd been in and out for years. They referred me here. At first, it was more comfortable to sleep on the floor, in sneakers. When you live in a box, you have to get out quickly. My family moved from North Carolina to Brownsville when I was seven, 1961, then Bushwick. My friends and I were drinking wine, smoking pot. My father was a cook; my mother worked in a factory sewing vacuum cleaner bags. At fourteen, I got introduced to heroin. My parents had me arrested, put me in a Rockefeller program. I got out, overdosed, then acid, marijuana, alcohol. I met my kids' mother in '73. In between having kids—we have four—I started smoking crack. We lost our apartment. Three kids live in Red Hook now with their mother. I see them twice a month.

If your parents had stayed in the South, would you have gone in the direction you did?

Yes. My nephews down there went that way also. The seventies—that's what was

PAK FUNG

going on: peace, love, acid, 'ludes, black beauties. I'm definitely a product of the era.

What's your daily schedule?

I take twenty-four pills a day. When I first got here, my T-cell count was 164; my viral load was 68,000. Now my T-cell is 514, viral load undetectable. My custom-made medicine is working. I found out I was HIV-positive in '93. I was in rehab. They were paying people to take the test. Usually I get up at 7:30, see what's for breakfast. Sometimes it's too loud down there. Me, I stay out of the negativity. Not everyone here is drug free, but me and Shante are. I go to nine groups a week—nutritional, substance abuse. I used to make twenty-two. Now I do a lot of stuff on the outside. I sell porcelain dolls, colognes, and perfumes. I got my little shopping cart. I'm trying to get a vendor's license. For now, I'm like a specialty person—Mother's Day, Valentine's Day.

Can you stay here forever?

Until I go to that big Housing Works in the sky. Or I consider myself able to work. They don't rush you out. I'm anxious to let go. I want to live in Brooklyn.

With Shante? She mentioned it's kind of close quarters here.

We'll live separately, but in Brooklyn. Absence makes the heart grow fonder. Shante's barbecuing on the patio right now. She likes to cook. She's from Brownsville. When she came here, I saw her and I fell in love right away. I let her know. I said, "I got eyes for you." We go out a lot, movies, Central Park. We eat in the Village. I love gyros. Sometimes we go and bring sandwiches back here. I put on a little candle. Put on my Luther. Turn down the lights.

June 12, 2001

NO HOT PLATES

LOCATION
Lower East Side, Manhattan
RENT
$0 (exchange for work)
SQUARE FEET
100 (room in Bowery flophouse)
OCCUPANT
Nathan Smith (manager,
the Sunshine Hotel)

The Sunshine is one of the last of the Bowery hotels—a former pickle factory where the men live in four-by-six-foot wooden cubicles with chicken wire on top. I must say it's tidy and quiet. Some residents were chatting in the lobby. There's a nice breeze blowing from Stanton Street here in your room as you watch your twelve-inch Sharp TV.

I've got to get a new antenna. I like Koch. He comes on at four. I've lived here twelve years, been manager ten. I charge $70 a week for rooms, $49 for beds. We've got 83 rooms, 148 men in the dorm. Yeah, I've got a bigger room than the others. It's got wood paneling. The former manager put it in. He was Swedish. He shot himself right here in the bed. I used to live in another room. I really didn't want to leave. They said, "Nathan, you're the manager, take this room."

You have so many corduroy jackets— and books.

Mostly science. I love doing electrical experiments—you know, how circuits and throttles work. I didn't intend to be manager here. I came looking for a place to stay.

You came after you lost your job and your wife?

I was working in a bank, the executive office. They sent out for a folding wine rack made of metal and nobody knew how to open it. So we all linked arms and we were supposed to stomp on the rack. My left foot got turned around. The bank thought I'd sue. I just walked away. That's when everything started falling apart, no more pinstripes. My wife and I were living on Linden Boulevard. Well, one day, it was like a movie. My wife took all her stuff and moved out in the middle of the night. Then I went to Sterling Place. Mrs. Ford was the landlady. I used to take care of her boiler. She was always feeding me. I wired the bell from her apartment to mine. She was so fascinated with the button, she used to press it all day and night. I changed the buzzer to a light. It was driving me nuts. Then I applied for welfare. I needed Mrs. Ford to sign the letter, but when I went into the living room she was dead, sitting up straight in a chair.

You've also lived in the Palace Hotel on top of CBGB, but you didn't stay long because of the noise. Later you moved to the 63rd Street Y.

Alvin Ailey had his dance school in the neighborhood. It was lovely. Cost too much. So I work here five days a week at the desk, the rest of the time I spend in my room. I don't go anywhere. I'm not interested. I used to work in a Playboy Club years ago. I eat McDonald's. Not supposed to be any cooking here anyway. I used to go around kicking doors down, taking hot plates. Too many watts, blow a fuse....I had a maintenance man here, he shot a guy in the lobby. Live here forever? I wouldn't want to go west. My brother is a tax lawyer for the state of California. I can't go to my daughter. I don't know. I'll go to Wards Island, a nursing home. I'm a veteran. I'm still going to do what I'm going to do. I just want to do my electrical experiments. That's it.

September 15, 1998

GREG MILLER

ENTERTAINING THE RINGMASTER

LOCATION
Damrosh Park, Lincoln Center,
Manhattan

PRICE
$4,000 in 2000

SQUARE FEET
168 (1978 Argosy Airstream trailer)

OCCUPANT
Darby Smotherman (sound designer/
engineer, Big Apple Circus)

A hundred and fifty people live in a trailer camp next to the Opera House! I never knew! [We take a tour of the grounds behind a white picket fence. A man is talking in French on a cell phone.]
Some live in campers, a few in trailers. The riggers, concession workers, ushers stay in dorm-type trucks.

[We look inside.] Three bunks piled high in a sixty-square-foot space, only a cupboard each for their belongings, like submarines. Where do they go to the bathroom? Porta Potties! You have to wear a coat to go. It's freezing. The truck with the shower stalls has paper boxes opened up on the floors. This is, in essence, migrant worker housing. Oh, here's the cookhouse. [We go up the tiny metal stairs of another truck. Thin, yellow-flowered cloths are on four tables. Two men are playing a crystal chess set.] Look, jars of pickle slices and Wonder Bread.
[THE COOK, *knit hat on her head, slicing canned artichoke hearts*] You want to know what the circus is like—taste the coffee!
[DARBY] I bought my trailer three years ago when I joined. Then I got a truck, a Ford F350, to haul it.

[We go inside Darby's trailer.] This is like living inside a Polly Pocket. Do you entertain much—ballerinas, trained schnauzers?
Not really, because it's so small. I've crammed in five or six. The past few years, the acrobats and dog acts happen to be Russian and they kind of hang out together. I have the ringmasters over. There are two.

Here's one now. He just popped through the door with his waxed mustache.
[DINNY MCGUIRE] I just had sushi!

The Ringmaster is always seen as so cruel—Lola Montes—cracking his whip. But you don't seem to be. Then of course, there's Bergman's Sawdust and Tinsel with the rocking wagons, moving slow across the big gray sky, the ringmaster leaving his mistress in tears. She says to another, "I can't help my dress smelling of manure."
[DARBY] It's not like that at the Big Apple. It's very friendly. I didn't live in a trailer before I worked for the circus. I'm from Fort Worth. I went to college in Austin, University of Texas. I'd been a freelance sound designer for a while before I took this gig. Now I rent a storage space for my things.

BRIAN KENNEDY

How do you drive a truck *and* a trailer?
You get used to it. I'm fortunate in that I
have a big truck, a lot more power than
I actually need. If you get into a situation
where you have to back up—I got into
trouble once, pulling off, finding a hotel. For
Atlanta, I don't drive straight through. To
set up the trailer for a night—it's too much.
Things get bungeed and taped.

**I was reading this trailer "throw away
list." There were twenty-eight things
to do like "Put grate clips on stove.
Fold and secure lawn chairs." I always
love those photos of people sitting on
their lawn chairs in front of their trailer
doors. People go through so much to
be free from home, but they still have
to drag it behind them. Then, they
invariably recreate the humdrum. I
also read once that when utopias didn't**
**work, the world turned to mobile homes
for a better future. They reached their
height during the fifties, modernism and
all. Where else do you travel to?**
Our last show here is January 11. We're
in New Jersey in March, ten cities a year.
I travel full time. It was never really my
dream to run away and join the circus.
When I got here, I did. I like it. It's like a
small town. Everybody watches out for each
other.

**Oh the nets, the metaphors—that man
doing the cha-cha on tightrope, the
camels working their darndest to get
around the ring, another man trying to
reach a trapeze; when he finally does,
it falls.**

January 7, 2004

◇◇◇◇◇◇◇◇◇◇◇◇◇◇◇◇◇◇◇◇◇◇◇◇◇◇◇◇

THE FUTURE

LOCATION

Bushwick, Brooklyn

RENT

$1,450 (commercial)

SQUARE FEET

1,000 (loft in 1920s former knitting factory)

OCCUPANTS

David Button (senior, Pratt; bouncer, Northsix; art handler, Klotz/Sirmon Gallery), Aaron Ray-Crichton (senior, Pratt; computer graphics artist), Katie Stirman (dancer)

◇◇◇◇◇◇◇◇◇◇◇◇◇◇◇◇◇◇◇◇◇◇◇◇◇◇◇◇

Wait, I've been in this loft before. A man had just moved in. It looked like a big Kleenex box.

[DAVID] We don't know him.

Maybe it was another loft, the same building.

We built this 650-square-foot steel structure ourselves. Ninety percent is suspended from the ceiling. Nothing is supported by the floor, only about five percent. [AARON] Sit down at our guest workstation. Here's a computer model I created before we started working on the space because we wanted to agree.

We're flying down the stairs, too fast, like in a dream, sliding over the tops of the steps.

[DAVID] Some fruit punch?

Computer is better than real life because the apartment is animated instead of just sitting there—the walls and floors move.

[AARON] Here's just some lizard guy I made. And photos from the construction. That's me standing on a beam in the air. [DAVID] It's funny to look at that horrible time. [AARON] We were living underneath tarps. But it was exciting, exciting. [DAVID] Grueling and exciting. [AARON] I've never done anything like this before. [DAVID] There are great people in this building. You gotta see the roof.

I saw the roof the last time.

You've gotta see it now! It's different. Like about fifteen, seventeen of us got an order of wood. We lifted it on top by crane. We started at 2:30 in the afternoon and finished at 3:30 a.m. [AARON] There was a party the next day. [DAVID] A professional wooden deck. I made a 46-by-26-inch grill out of a trash can.

What do you call this second level?

[AARON] The mezzanine. It sounds better. Join us on the mezzanine. We have four computers up here. [DAVID] This network connects the entire building. [AARON] We have a business DSL line. [DAVID] Aaron is basically brokering out connections to seven apartments in the building.

Do you charge?

[AARON] It's barter. There's a massage therapist in the building. It's like a collaborative here. They used to call them communes.

Man and his plow.

It's all about the sharing of tools. Tools are not getting used by their owners to 100 percent efficiency. I have a giant hammer drill. [DAVID] Five or six friends in the building had to use it in the last few weeks. [AARON] Everybody in the building can share my printer. See this blue thing glowing?

What is it?

It just makes it look cool. It was only three bucks. [DAVID] Let's see, this cost us—$500 worth of steel. Total $800 to $1,000. [AARON] Welding takes up a lot of electricity. We had $400 electric bills for a while.

What about the robots?

[DAVID] Aaron is planning to fix the space so there will be sensors in each room. [AARON] You can control color and the amount of light through the computer. [DAVID] When somebody is in the bathroom, it will say "stop," and when they're out, it's "go." [AARON] Like in planes, you have a little "vacant/not vacant." In this case, when you bolt the door, the light will go on.

Will the master control be in your laboratory upstairs?

It will only be accessible on any of the computers that I allow. [*We go into the hallway.*] [DAVID] Look, the vending machine dispenses Busch beer. The landlord let somebody fill it. Here's Joshua's place— recording studio. Over here is the architect who inspired our space. [*We go inside.*] He hooked up a garage door to the ceiling. When he punches in a code, a stairway comes down. The bed is suspended from cable straps from the ceiling, six feet above ground.

Does he know we're here?

Sure. It's fine. [AARON] Look, the kitty litter box disappears into a drawer.

November 12, 2003

BRIAN KENNEDY

ACKNOWLEDGMENTS

I would like to thank the photographers for contributing their wonderful images to *Five Flights Up*, Kenneth Gross for his comments on the introductions, Don Forst who hired me to write the "Shelter" column, most recent "Shelter" editor Ed Park, and the following *Voice* colleagues and vast network of people who contributed their friends, intelligence, and expertise to the column, related stories, and the book: Danial Adkison, David Adler, Vince Aletti, Paul Anthony, Tom Bachtell, Robert Baker, Wayne Barrett, Grace Bastidas, LD Beghtol, Gina Bell, Jessica Bellucci, Lynn Bernstein, Carl Blumenthal, Larry Bowne, Lauren Braun, Kathy Brew, Francisco Caceres, David Callahan, Annie Chia, Laura Conaway, Kim Connell, Karen Cook, Cynthia Cotts, Carter Craft, Lisa Dabowski, Narayan Datt, Nathan Deuel, Jesus Diaz, Daniel D'Oca, Brian Drolet, Chuck Eddy, Linzy Emery, Kareem Fahim, Leslie Falk, Maria Elena Fanna, John Farley, Phyllis Fong, Eric Forman, Scott Forman, Matt Freedman, Andrew Friedman, Riva Froymovich, Janie Geiser, Howard Gladstone, Eric Miles Glover, Matthew Goldish, Bonnie Gordon, Margie Greve, Harvey Grossman, Roberto Guerra, Meg Handler, Mark Hansen, Ward Harkavy, Matthew Howard, Adamma Ince, David Isay, Joseph Jesselli, Joel Kaminsky, Andrea Kannapell, Dave Kehr, Ted Keller, Ben Kenigsberg, Janet Kim, Brent Kite, Lewis Klahr, Richard Knight Jr., Bhaskar Krag, Joshua Land, Kenneth Lang, Michael Lenehan, Dennis Lim, Katherine Linton, the late Julie Lobbia, Pete L'Official, James Magruder, Jay Mandel, Robert McCamant, Michael McKee, Patrick McMurray, Charles McNulty, Coco McPherson, Susan Meisel, Helaine Miller, Mary Miller, Michael Miller, Pauline Miller, Stephen Miller, John Milward, Judy Miszner, Jorge Morales, Dan Morrison, BJ Murray, Michael Musto, Alissa Neil, Alessandra Nichols, Chris O'Brien, Dian-Aziza Ooka, Andrew Patner, Eugene Patron, Nicholas Pavkovic, Gilberto Perez, Mort Persky, Anita Petraske, LJ Porter, Alex Press, Joy Press, Nita J. Rao, Darren Reidy, Kimberley Reinhardt, Stevie Remsberg, Tom Robbins, Mildred Robinson, Alex Roe, Don Rose, Jonathan Rosenbaum, Jody Rosenbloom, Jessica Rosner, Robert Roth, Shelly Salamensky, Michael Scasserra, Michael Schelp, David Schneiderman, Mark Schoofs, Staci Schwartz, Pearl Seligman, Ralph Seligman, Michael Shani, Ann Sheehan, Kelly Sheehan, Doug Simmons, Laura Sinagra, Dorothy Smith, Jennifer Snow, Linda Solomon, Diane Stevenson, Lynn Sweet, Basil Talbott, Patrick Trettenero, Maggie Triggs, Alison True, Minh Uong, Kara Walsh, Emily Weinstein, Laurie Wen, Cindy Whiteside, Lynn Yaeger, Thomas Yoder, Elizabeth Zimmer, and Jose Zuniga and to everyone at Princeton Architectural Press including Kevin Lippert, Katharine Myers, Nettie Aljian, Russell Fernandez, John King, Tiffany Wey, Dorothy Ball, Lauren Nelson, Joe Weston, Deb Wood, and my editor Clare Jacobson for a perfectly designed and realized book.

ROBIN HOLLAND

TONI SCHLESINGER

is a columnist at the *Village Voice*, a journalist, a fiction
writer, and a theater artist. She lives in **New York City.**